Principles and Techniques of Guidance

Chapter 14

Role of the Counsellor and the Teacher in Counselling

Since the development of systematic theories of counselling, numerous researches have been conducted on the personality characteristics and professional preparation of counsellors. All books on counselling invariably list the personality traits which have been considered essential for counsellors to perform their duties successfully. Traditionally, personality traits such as fairness, sincerity, intelligence, alertness and interest in other people were considered important to success in counselling, but very recently, the emphasis has shifted from personality attributes to the way the counsellor uses himself in his human communication.

Here we will describe the characteristics of the counsellor, role of the teacher and the administrator in the process of counselling.

Characteristics of a Good Counsellor

The personality characteristics of the counsellor are very important for him to carry on the counselling process efficiently and successfully. The characteristics that distinguish the counsellor have become the focus of much investigation in the last 30 years. National Vocational Guidance Association (NVGA) has emphasized the following characteristics — interest in people, patience, sensitivity to other attitudes and reactions, and emotional stability and objectivity and that they respect facts and are trustworthy.

Hamrin and Pulson conducted a study on the characteristics of counsellors and have listed the following in order of preference:

1. Understanding, 2. Sympathetic attitude, 3. Friendliness, 4. Sense of humour, 5. Stability 6. Patience, 7. Objectivity, 8. Sincerity 9. Tact, 10. Fairness, 11. Tolerance, 12. Neatness, 13. Calmness 14. Broadmindedness, 15. Kindliness, 16. Pleasantness, 17. Social intelligence 18. Poise.

Principles and Techniques of Guidance

Dr. S.S. Chauhan

Ex-Professor and Dean, Faculty of Education
University of Himachal Pradesh
Shimla

SECOND REVISED EDITION

VIKAS® PUBLISHING HOUSE PVT LTD

VIKAS® PUBLISHING HOUSE PRIVATE LIMITED
E-28, Sector-8, Noida-201301 (UP), India
Phone: +91-120-4078900 • Fax: +91-120-4078999
Registered Office: A-27, 2nd Floor, Mohan Co-operative Industrial Estate,
New Delhi-110044
E-mail: helpline@vikaspublishing.com • Website: www.vikaspublishing.com

SALES AND BRANCH OFFICES OF VIKAS® AND S CHAND AND COMPANY LIMITED

Chennai	:	Ph: 044-2363 2120, chennai@schandpublishing.com
Guwahati	:	Ph: 0361-2738 811, 2735 640, guwahati@schandpublishing.com
Hyderabad	:	Ph: 040-4018 6018, hyderabad@schandpublishing.com
Jalandhar	:	Ph: 0181-4645 630, jalandhar@schandpublishing.com
Kolkata	:	Ph: 033-2335 7458, 2335 3914, kolkata@schandpublishing.com
Lucknow	:	Ph: 0522-4003 633, lucknow@schandpublishing.com
Mumbai	:	Ph: 022-2500 0297, mumbai@schandpublishing.com
Patna	:	Ph: 0612-2260 011, patna@schandpublishing.com

Principles and Techniques of Guidance
ISBN: 978-81259-1153-1 Product Code: V7PTG69TEDU10ENAB01O

Second Edition 2001
Reprinted several times between 2001 and 2020, 2022
Reprint 2025

PRINTED IN INDIA
By Vikas Publishing House Private Limited, Plot 20/4, Site-IV, Industrial Area Sahibabad, Ghaziabad-201010 and Published by Vikas Publishing House Private Limited, E-28, Sector-8, Noida-201301

Preface

The present book is a product of my long experience and continuing effort to give proper place and importance to guidance over the last 40 years in the field of teacher education. I have been examining the possibilities of guidance as a primary means for helping each student to realize his potential to the maximum as a citizen for his own benefit and for the welfare of the society.

Before 1947, education in our country was largely confined to the elite. There was, therefore, no necessity for formalized guidance services. After independence, consequent upon the universalisation of education, all types of students entered schools with a wide range of individual differences in their intellectual abilities and socio-economic backgrounds. The need for guidance came to be felt in our educational system so that it could cater to the needs of individual differences among the students.

Our society is passing through a period of transition. There is conflict in social values and uneasiness in general about the future model of our society in the minds of people. For the last forty years a great revolution has been gradually taking place in medicine, education and industry due to technological developments. All types of industries have emerged and there is a growing need for more effectively trained workers for the proper performance of their duties.

The industrial development has brought revolutionary changes in our society and culture. Man has to modify his behaviour according to the emerging needs in order to face the challenges of a society heading towards rapid industrialization. The conditions in our country entail more and more education and even more obviously the kind of services in education that guidance is uniquely equipped to provide.

Since the last two decades due to automation, among other factors, our attitudes, values and beliefs have been undergoing profound changes. Automation is rapidly changing every area of human endeavour. We have, in fact, to learn and to prepare ourselves to adjust to new ways of life brought about by automation if we are to survive as a viable society. Besides, many other factors account for the emergence of the need for guidance, for instance, the high percentage of dropouts, the changing role of women, needs of exceptional children, increasing rate of delinquency and the mentally sick persons in our society. The great class consciousness and the endeavour of scheduled castes and tribes and other minority groups in Indian society, for their place in the schemes of things, have necessitated the introduction of guidance in our system of education. Moreover, Indian educationists are convinced that guidance is a prime means for promoting individual and social progress and that it can help us in establishing new social and moral values commensurate with our cultural heritage.

All agree that guidance is an integral part of education and education is an effective instrument of social change. Guidance must maintain the values of those who are challenging the existing system of society.

I as an educator believe that events of the coming decade will definitely be dominated in a large part by the challenges of the younger generation to our society. There is great need to understand the aspirations of this generation to adequately guide them to select proper educational and vocational courses so that their energies could be channelized in the best interest of the individual and the society as a whole.

Guidance is not only the responsibility of the school but is a huge task for the society which is interested in the welfare of its young people. Now, we believe more than ever that an awareness of the problems of guidance must not only come to Educators but to the family and the community. The turn of events has, in fact, made consummation of this last goal a necessity.

This book has been written with the following specific objectives:

1. To acquaint students of M.A., B.Ed., M. Phil., and M. Ed. classes of Indian universities with the basic principles and techniques of guidance.
2. To provide students with a framework of knowledge from which they may gain a perspective of guidance in a systematic way.
3. To give students an orientation to the services of guidance.
4. To help students understand the problems of guidance in India.
5. To familiarize students with emerging trends in guidance.
6. To encourage students to develop an appreciation of the field, its aspiration and problems. I hope that the students will find the book useful.

In the last I express my indebtedness to several authors, whose books I have consulted in the preparation of the book.

S.S. Chauhan

Contents

Appendices

PART - I

Chapter 1

Introduction to Guidance

It is a truism that a very minor percentage of our total population is capable of handling its problems independently without the cooperation and guidance of others. We find that majority of the people do not have either confidence or insight to solve their problems. They seek advice or guidance from others wherever there is a problem. There have always been people in the past who need occasional help from older or more experienced associates in meeting with their problems of daily life in the society.

Traditionally, in our Indian society, the leader of the family or the local community was supposed to provide the necessary guidance and advice whenever it was needed by any member of the family or the community. Needless to mention too often informal advice, given without a clear understanding of the problem involved, was likely to be not only ineffectful but harmful and misleading to the individual. With the passage of time, revolutionary changes have taken place in the fields of medicine, industry, business and agriculture etc. Changes in all walks of life coupled with extraordinary growth in our population have made the social structure very complex. The varieties of jobs, aspirations of multitudes for jobs, and minute vocational specialization have made the work of guidance very difficult. The head of the family or leader of the local community with his limited knowledge of the changed conditions is not capable of providing guidance to the youth of today.

In the last four decades, guidance movement has spread like a wildfire throughout the world and has generated a great amount of enthusiasm and zeal among parents, teachers and social workers who have devoted time to explore its feasibility and utility for the general population including school-going adolescents. All are convinced that proper provision of guidance services should be made for children at different age levels for the harmonious development of their personalities in the larger interest of the society and the individuals.

MEANING AND DEFINITION OF GUIDANCE

Guidance, in India, is comparatively a new field within the larger and more inclusive field of education. It covers the whole spectrum of education which starts from the birth of the child and continues till his death., This is a wide meaning of the term which includes all types of educaiton, formal, nonformal, vocational etc., which aims to adjust the individual in his environment in an effective way. Another meaning of the term is that guidance is a specialized service whose primary concern is with the individual. It may be said that guidance is given to individuals in making intelligent choice and adjustments. It is based on the democratic principle that it is the duty and right of every individual to choose his own way in life insofar as his choice does not interfere with the rights of others.

Guidance has been defined from different points of views. Some of the important definitions are given below which throw light on different aspects of guidance.

Crow and Crow in their book *Introduction to Guidance* have given a very comprehensive definition of the term guidance which runs as: "Guidance is assistance made available by professionally qualified and adequately trained men or women to an individual of any age to help him manage his own life activities, develop his own points of view, make his own decisions and carry his own burdens."

D.G. Mortensen: *et al*, in their book *Guidance in Today's Schools* have defined guidance as "That part of the total educational programme that helps provide the personal opportunities and specialized staff services by which each individual can develop to the fullest his abilities and capacities in terms of the democratic ideal."

According to the National Vocational Guidance Association (NVGA), "Guidance is the process of helping a person to develop and accept an integrated and adequate picture of himself and of his role in the world of work, to test this concept against reality and to convert it into reality with satisfaction to himself and benefit to society."

Welty, Turral and Weitzel say that "Guidance is that systematic, organized phase of the educational process which helps youth grow in his power to give point and direction to his own life, to the end that he may gain richer personal experiences while making his unique contribution to our democratic society."

Guidance, as defined by Jones, "is the help given by one person to another in making choices and adjustments and in solving problems."

Shertzer and Stone in their book *Fundamentals of Guidance* have given a very brief definition of the term guidance. "It is the process of helping individuals to understand themselves and their world."

NEED FOR GUIDANCE

The basic question which may be asked here is — What is the need for guidance? Why should it be given to an individual? Man when born is not capable of independent working. He is born with certain biological inheritance which does not render him capable of adjustment in his physical environment. The human child remains dependent for the longest period on his parents who are responsible for his development in early childhood.

Human beings by nature tend to seek advice and assistance from others whenever they are confronted with a problem. It is assumed that a person is bound to seek assistance from others, and the advice or assistance which other persons provide may not always be of great use or may some time prove harmful. Then why should guidance not be provided in a properly organized and systematic way? So there is a great need to provide necessary guidance at the appropriate time by well-qualified personnel.

India is a democratic country. Education which was confined to classes has now reached the masses with the declaration of univeralization of education and equal educational opportunities to all irrespective of caste, colour, region, economic and social difference. The success of democracy depends on educated and enlightened individuals who should share the responsibilities of running the administration smoothly and efficiently.

Guidance is an integral part of Education. Guidance is necessary for the following reasons:

(*a*) Guidance services if properly organized help to eliminate wastage and stagnation by developing the curriculum according to the needs and abilities of students.

(*b*) Students are helped to select courses according to their abilities, interests and aptitudes.

(*c*) Guidance services decrease the number of misfits by helping such cases to see things realistically and adjust themselves.

(*d*) Students are prepared for professional leadership in the changed socio-economic and industrial conditions in which different occupations have emerged which require specialized training.

(*e*) The child's healthy growth is encouraged.

(*f*) Problems of discipline and delinquency are solved.

(*g*) It helps to supply the right personnel for various jobs in private and public sectors.

(*h*) The population in our country is increasing at a tremendous rate and if it is not checked it will create chaotic conditions in the country. The individuals require guidance to plan their family.

(i) The increase in population, industrialization and westernization have created a number of problems for our adolescents who are facing frustration, conflicts and tensions and other strain and stress in the present decade. It is imperative to provide guidance to the young generation to save them from stress and strain of a developing society.

(j) Individuals differ in physical, mental, social and emotional characteristics. To provide for the maximum development of individuality, guidance is essentially needed, particularly for exceptional children.

(k) Problems of women are emerging as a new area where guidance is needed for proper adjustment in the family. The cases of divorce, separation and desertion are very rapidly increasing in our society which are posing a new threat to our traditional social system.

(l) There are other problems which are unique to our society as for instance problems of scheduled castes, problems of social conflicts, problems of retired persons and problems of industrial relations where guidance is needed.

FUNCTIONS OF GUIDANCE

Guidance as interpreted by workers in the field is applicable to all aspects of human life, i.e. physical, mental, social and emotional in all stages of development right from infancy to old age. The main objective of guidance is to help the individual to utilize his basic potentialities to the maximum for adequate adjustment in the environment. The following specific and interrelated functions are common to all types of guidance services.

1. The first function of guidance is to understand the individual and discover the real needs and problems of individuals and to explore the possibilities of personality development within the context of the education process.

2. The second function is to use information collected about students to adjust instruction to meet individual needs and to help to develop attitudes and patterns of behaviour that can help each individual to develop optimally.

3. The third function is to develop among teachers a greater understanding of child growth and development.

4. The fourth function is to provide such specialized services as orientation, individual inventory, counselling, occupational information, group guidance, placement and follow-up services.

5. The last and important function is to provide information and feedback conditioning research which evaluates the success of the programme of guidance of various types. The results of research, testing

and related studies about young people must be supplied on a continuing basis to administrators, curriculum planners and teachers as a means of ensuring the proper climate and conditions for learning.

SCOPE OF GUIDANCE SERVICES

Guidance is not a once-for-all activity but is a continuous process in the life of the individual. The following are the specific activities which fall within the purview of guidance.

(*a*) Personal — Social problems of the individual, their diagnosis and prescribing remedial measures to resolve them.

(*b*) Educational problems of the individual, and to suggest remedial measures for their resolution.

(*c*) Vocational problems — Helping the individual in the choice of an appropriate vocation and aiding him to acquire proficiency in the vocation.

(*d*) Appraisal of individuals — Students' appraisal is an important aspect of guidance personnel's work, which helps students to develop their potentialities to the maximum.

(*e*) Counselling — After making appraisal through various test and non-test techniques the guidance worker provides counselling to the counsellee keeping into consideration the strengths and weaknesses of his personality and other variables operating in the environment.

(*f*) Placement — In the placement services the counsellee is placed in an appropriate course vocation on the basis of guidance provided to him.

(*g*) Follow-up and Research — Follow-up is a process in which the guidance personnel follow up the incumbents after placing them in a course vocation and see whether they are progressing satisfactorily. Research is also one of the important activities in guidance through which curricular programmes are modified and improved.

GUIDANCE AND ITS RELATIONSHIPS

Guidance as a helping profession is closely related to all subjects and disciplines which are directly concerned with human beings and their welfare, for instance, education, humanities, sciences, discipline, administration and curriculum. Here we will discuss the relationship of guidance to education, curriculum and discipline only.

Guidance and Education

Guidance and education are closely related as both of them are concerned with the welfare of the individual and the society. Guidance may be defined as "a process of helping individuals to understand themselves and their world." This definition implies that guidance is a life-long continuous process which aims to help individuals to understand their personal characteristics, strengths and weaknesses of their personality and the social environment with which they interact. The main function of guidance as a helping profession lies is the preparation of youth to meet their problems satisfactorily in the present and the future. The second function of guidance is to help the individual to develop his unique personality characteristics. The students, the teacher and the parent must understand the developmental characteristics and their impact on adjustmentability and decision-making competency.

Guidance as a movement within the larger field of education has succeeded in focussing the attention of teachers, administrators and parents on the wide range of individual differences among pupils and on the respect for the individual. It has also made a valuable contribution in directing the attention to a careful study of the individual and initiating a cooperative relationship between the school and the community.

Now let us examine the meaning of education. Education does not have a single definition which is universally acceptable. A number of meanings and definitions has been suggested. Here we will select only four meanings for explanation which are relevant in the relationship between guidance and education.

1. *Education is a process of chance.* According to this meaning Education is a process of bringing desirable changes in the behaviour of human beings to enable them to adjust in their social environment in such a way that they may contribute to the maximum for the welfare of the society.

The human child at the time of his birth is helpless and absolutely dependent on others for his survival. He has the longest period of dependency, in which he acquires physical and social competencies which facilitate his adjustment in the society. All these changes are brought about by education in the repertoire of the growing child.

2. *Education is preparation for life.* According to this view education is preparation for successful and happy life. To live a successful and happy life an individual needs certain amount of knowledge skills, attitudes and personality characteristics which help him to solve the problems which he faces in realizing his goal. The children must be prepared to face the problems they are expected to face in adult life.

3. *Education as direction.* Education is the modification and refinement of unlearned responses, impulses, urges and drives with which infants are born. The process of modification implies control and

guidance. Control means the process by which an individual is made to subordinate his natural impulses to public or group interest, and guidance is the act of carrying children towards predetermined goals after their natural impulses are controlled.

4. *Education is instruction.* Traditionally our instructional process has been teacher-controlled. The teacher knows the aims and objectives of education decided by the society. He also knows the methods to be employed to reach the goal of education. The teacher plays an important role in the whole process of learning. The students in the present set-up of classroom teaching are the passive listeners. They have no place in the planning of experiences. They are to obey the commands of the teacher. Therefore it is not guidance.

But in the last 40 years,, some changes have been taking place in the traditional teacher-centred instructional methods. New instructional technology is fast emerging with its emphasis on individualization programmed instruction, personalized system of instruction discovery and inquiry methods in which the learner actively participates, are being tried out in some universities in our country. The role of the teacher is to assist the pupils to understand the ends and to accept them. Assistance so directed is guidance. Whenever in the learning process, the teacher assists the student to choose, the element of guidance is present but when the teacher selects the method, it is teaching. Thus we can say that teaching conceived of as assisting the learner to choose ends or methods is guidance.

Guidance and Curriculum

Curriculum is the accumulated experiences of the race which are transferred to the pupils in a planned way within the school or outside the school to shape their behaviour in such a way that they may prove useful citizens of the country. As a matter of fact, it is an instrument in the hands of the teacher with which he moulds the character of the pupils and advances the knowledge and competencies of his pupils to enable them to achieve the aims of education. Curriculum may be defined as the planned activities engaged in by pupils to induct them into society.

A curriculum has three components:

(*a*) Planned opportunities for learning.

(*b*) Using ways and means of making these planned opportunities for learning manifest to the students by means of textbooks, audio visual aids and study guides etc.

(*c*) The students' activities and resultant experiences are determined by the two components given above and the students' own varying aptitudes, abilities, interests and needs.

Guidance is the process of helping pupils to know and understand themselves and their world. This does not mean that guidance has no responsibility for the individual's intellectual development. Rather its primary concern is the emotional and social development of the individual. Guidance and curriculum are related in that both share the goal of helping individuals achieve their maximum potentiality and become capable of self-direction.

Curricular Contribution to Guidance

The new methods of instruction emphasize the use of inquiry method of study which relies more extensively upon independent study. It is anticipated in future that the present classroom methods of instruction will be replaced by individualized instructional methods.

Three major contributions of curriculum are as follows:

(*i*) Systematic curricular opportunities assist the pupil by offering experiences that contribute to a feeling of adequacy and belonging.

(*ii*) Curricular activities provide exploratory avenues through which pupils develop their interests and abilities. They develop self-concept.

(*iii*) Curricular experiences contribute to guidance by providing youth with the knowledge needed for educational and vocational planning.

Contribution of Guidance to Curriculum

Guidance makes the following important contributions to the curriculum:

1. Guidance workers can help in collecting facts essential to understand each pupil so that teachers can individualize instruction and provide satisfying experiences.
2. Counsellor can help teachers interpret and use these facts in contacts with parents and pupils.
3. Counsellors can help school administrators, teachers and parents with the application and implications of what is known about child growth.
4. Counsellors can help teachers use guidance tools more effectively in terms of interpreting tests, preferring pupils, pupil's planning and the like.

There are two major ways that guidance contributes to curriculum development. In the first instance the needs of individual and groups for curricular activities may become visible through counselling, testing, follow-up and other guidance activities. Counsellors can be instrumental in providing curriculum experts with data that describes the students' ability, range of achievements and strengths and weaknesses, interests, problems, educational objectives and other characteristics that are essential for curriculum development. In curriculum planning needs of students help to establish priorities.

In the second instance, counsellors help the students to understand and choose curricular offering best suited to develop social and vocational competencies necessary for effective living in a complex society.

Guidance and Discipline

Discipline has been used in different meanings by advocates of different philosophies of education. Naturalism views discipline as a consequence of wrong deeds. Students learn discipline through active participation in school activities not through imposition of restraints by external authority to bring conformity in the behaviour of children.

Idealism lays emphasis on self-discipline. It believes that human behaviour should bave internal control rather than external control of reward and punishment.

Pragmatism advocates that discipline is closely related to interests. If the teacher succeeds in arousing the interest of children in school activities then there is no problem of discipline. It means that according to pragmatists, discipline is preventive in nature. They provide conducive environment within the school for healthy, social and emotional development and encourage the formation of positive attitudes towards life. The school functions on democratic principles by enlisting active participation of students and teachers in planning and decision-making. Thus they prevent the emergence of misbehaviour in children.

From the point of view of guidance discipline is most often conceived as a means of correcting the faults in the personality of the individual caused by frustration and disappointment in achieving goals. Guidance provides assistance to such individuals by making them understand the reality of the situation in the right perspective.

A number of factors influence the school discipline in both negative and positive directions. The major factors which create disciplinary problems are authoritarianism, teacher's partial behaviour and negative attitude, lack of planning and minimum physical facilities, purposeless curriculum and the feelings of casteism among the students. There are certain factors which help to minimize the discipline problems: democratic administration which encourages the participation of students in decision-making; curriculum improvement schemes, provision of extra-curricular programmes, physical facilities and organization of counselling services.

Guidance and discipline are closely related because students who misbehave are most in need of counselling. Counsellors are needed to diagnose the problems of students and treat them. As a matter of fact the goal of discipline is self-direction or self-growth and the goal of guidance is also self-development and self-direction.

Counsellors can help the school authorities, and parents to reduce the problems in the following ways. The counsellor, on the basis of his data, can classify for teachers classroom activities that will help in minimizing problems of misbehaviour. He can also help teachers to identify as early as possible students who may need help in future. He can also help students, teachers, parents and administrators to establish codes of student conduct that are workable and acceptable.

In conclusion, it may be said that guidance services in school have a direct impact on the problem of discipline.

Brief History of Guidance

It is very difficult to trace back the history of the origin of the guidance movement as it exists today because it has been the result of continuous efforts of individuals and institutions who from time to time have contributed to the growth of the guidance movement. Here, it is not possible to mention the names of all individuals and institutions which have contributed in the development of guidance. Only those important individuals and institutions will be referred to whose contribution has been most relevant to the movement in the present form.

As a part of the educational system in ancient India, seats of learning flourished in different regions of the country. Taxila and Nalanda Universities were supposed to be the highest seats of learning where scholars came not only from India but also other countries i.e. China, Japan, Cambodia, Ceylon etc. to receive education at the hands of distinguished scholars. The admission to these universities was processed through a very strict admission test conducted by Dwarpandita who worked as a counsellor for the new entrants to the campus. This process of admission worked in more or less the same way as our present-day educational guidance.

In ancient India, the whole of the society was divided into four "Varnas" — Kshatriya, Brahmin, Vaish and Sudras. Sudras were not entitled to education. The three high castes were educated in accordance with their assigned duties. Education, in a strict sense, was only confined to Brahmins. Therefore there was hardly any question of providing guidance.

In the Muslim period, education was given in mosques and temples and was mostly of a religious nature. The mass of people remained without educational facilities. Hardly any kind of guidance was provided to the students as regards the selection of courses for study.

In British India, there was no guidance upto the end of nineteenth century except sporadic efforts by some individuals. The guidance movement gained impetus in the twentieth century. The development of the movement may be conveniently divided into the following two broad phases — 1. 1900 to 1947, and 2. 1947 to the present day.

Guidance from 1900 to 1947

As a matter of fact, the actual guidance movement was introduced in the second decade of the present century, in the year 1915. By this time psychological testing had acquired popularity in the west. In India the beginning was made by Dr G.S. Bose of Calcutta University who for the first time opened the applied psychological laboratory in the Department of Psychology of the university. The Department of Applied Psychology did pioneer work by using mental testing tools in India. They expenimented in providing vocational guidance on the basis of testing. No doubt, the work done in Calcutta University was not of great importance but it initiated the use of tests in guidance and has historical importance as being the first effort which generated curiosity and enthusiasm among psychologists to use tests in guidance.

The next landmark in the development of the guidance movement is the establishment of Batliboi Vocational Guidance Bureau by Mr. S.R. Batliboi in Bombay in the year 1941. The Bureau developed and standardized some aptitude tests for use in guidance. No doubt, the Bureau worked for a short period of six years but it rendered valuable service to the community and to the guidance movement since it introduced the concept of scientific guidance and aptitude testing in that city of Bombay.

The next important development was the establishment of an institution of psychological research and service in 1945 in the University of Patna. The department not only provided educational and vocational guidance to college students but also offered assistance to persons in meeting their social and personal problems. All are convinced that to tackle the personal, educational and vocational problems of our youth, guidance is necessary. State governments, universities and private agencies are doing their best to provide guidance services. The guidance services as they exist today do not cater to the needs of the masses who really need assistance in selecting educational and vocational courses. There is a great need to strengthen our guidance services to meet the demands of students.

Being encouraged by the success of the work at Patna and Calcutta, the Central Government established an employment selection bureau in the Ministry of Home Affairs and employed specialist staff.

Parsi Panchayat started a vocational guidance bureau (1947) in Bombay with the psychological tests, books and other testing materials bequeathed by Mr. Batliboi. This bureau performed excellent service to the locality of all communities by providing vocational guidance services. The bureau laid specific emphasis on counselling and individual work. Dr. H.P. Mehta, its director, started the publication of a journal *Vocational and Educational Guidance*. The bureau continued for more than a decade and then had to be closed due to paucity of funds.

The greatest landmark in the development of the guidance movement was made by the U.P. Government by establishing Bureau of Psychology at Allahabad in 1947. The bureau spread its network throughout the state by creating district psychological centres at district headquarters. It started providing educational and vocational guidance to the students of high schools and intermediate colleges in the state. The bureau also started a diploma for graduates of psychology in Educational Vocational Guidance.

From 1947 to Present Day

Maharashtra and Gujarat, formerly part of the state of Bombay, started a guidance bureau in 1950 to cater to the needs of school-going children. The bureau emphasized the importance of collecting and disseminating occupational information and to train the guidance personnel to effectively manage the guidance services in schools and the community. The bureau has been making consistent efforts to create an awareness about the utility of guidance among principals, teachers and parents in the state.

The Secondary Education Commission was appointed in the year 1952 to study the conditions of secondary education and to make recommendations for its improvement. The Commission emphasized the importance of guidance in schools. The Government of India established a Central Bureau of Educational and Vocational Guidance in 1954. The main objective of the central bureau was to coordinate the activities of state bureaus which were afterwards opened in almost all the states and to provide leadership in the field of guidance.

Keeping into consideration the importance of guidance, the All India Educational and Vocational Association was formed in 1956 to coordinate the work being done in different states. The guidance movement is gaining ground in our country. Needless to mention, there is great wastage and stagnation in our educational system right from primary to university level. The guidance services will certainly reduce the amount of wastage and stagnation.

Limitations of Guidance Services

Though organization of guidance services is considered essential to channelize the energy of modern youth in the proper direction for the welfare of the individual and the society, in our country guidance services are at an initial stage and have to be geared properly to meet the challenges of a developing society. There are certain specific problems which are unique to our country. Some of the problems are given below:

1. Guidance services whether personal, educational and vocational have been and still are limited in our country by lack of properly trained personnel in the profession. In our country the facilities as well as time to provide guidance services at different levels of education are too meagre.

2. It is wrong and unrealistic to assume that guidance is a panacea for all educational problems. It is simply one of the means of education for personalizing its services and goals.

3. Guidance in school is limited in what it can do in terms of career and occupational choices but how most effectively to combine student abilities with career and occupational choices is the greatest problem which the guidance workers face in our country. There is no central coordinating agency which may coordinate the work of different organizations working in the country.

4. Guidance workers use tests to assess the potentialities of individuals but the realiability of testing instrument is open to question. Moreover the testing material employed by untrained persons may be unreliable. In our country, there is a lack of reliable and valid testing materials which may be used for heterogeneous groups of pupils.

5. The conditions of living in our society are too complex. It is very difficult for any one person to resolve quickly the problems of another person in any simple setting. No doubt guidance is able to furnish much to the insight needed for resolving the individual's problems, but such insight needs to be used in terms of all our efforts.

ASSIGNMENTS

1. Define guidance and describe in brief its need for adolescent.
2. What are the functions of guidance?
3. Trace the history of the guidance movement in India.

REFERENCES

Shertzer and Stone Shelly C.: *Fundamentals of Guidance* (3rd ed). (Boston, Houghton Mifflin Co., 1976)

Miller, Carroll H.: *Foundations of Guidance* (2nd ed) (New York, Harper and Row Publisher, 1971)

Mortensen Donal G. and Schmuller, Allan M.: *Guidance In Today's School* (93rd ed). (New York, John Wiley and Sons, 1976).

(A list of guidance bureaus is appended in the appendix)

Hansen James C.: *Group Guidance and Counselling in the Schools*.

Crammer Stanley H.: (Appleton — Century Crafts, New York, 1971).

Chapter 2

Basic Principles of Guidance

It is an essential pre-condition for an individual to understand the basic principles of a discipline before he attempts to acquire and use the knowledge of the various operations involved in the application of the knowledge to human life.

The basic principles of guidance have been described in all books of guidance but most of the books available on guidance have either vaguely and ambiguously described the basic principles or have included the statement of assumptions, aims and practices under the principles. The students are consequently confused as regards the basic principles of guidance. The basic principles of guidance as accepted by most authorities in the field of guidance are described as follows:

1. *Individualization*. The present guidance movement all over the world emerged as an effort to implement the principle of democracy which has full faith in the supremacy and dignity of the individual. The individual should be given complete freedom to shape his personality and guidance should be provided whenever the individual needs it. The very success of democracy as a form of government is based on the premise that individuals should be given opportunities for their harmonious development so that they can contribute the maximum for the welfare of the society. This is possible only when each individual develops his mental abilities, interests and aptitudes in unique ways. For individualizing education at different levels, proper organization of guidance services is very essential. Briefly we can say that the first basic principle of guidance is primarily concerned with the personal development of the individual. Kehas states: "This concept of personal development assumes that it is desirable for individuals to have opportunity both to think about the kind of self they are building and have built and to confront themselves with the meanings they attribute to their experiencing and the consequences such attributions will have on their future self." Therefore guidance could be conceptualized as the school's provision for enabling students to create meaning in their lives.

2. *Respect to individual differences.* Individuals differ to a great extent in their physical, mental, social and emotional development. No two individuals are alike. Guidance recognizes these differences among students and is concerned with their personal development by understanding the unique developmental characteristics, needs and problems of the individuals. Miller points out that guidance operates in the zone in which the individual's own unique world of perceptions interact with the external order of events in his life context. Therefore, the processes and practices employed by guidance are designed to assist individuals to understand the world.

3. *Guidance is a life-long process.* Guidance is not a once-for-all activity but it is a continuous life-long process which starts from early childhood and continues till the death of the individual.

4. *Emphasis on self-direction.* The individual gains confidence, insight and understanding of his problems and makes his own decisions. Guidance makes the individual better adjusted to his environment and leads him to self-reliance and self-direction.

5. *Guidance for all.* Guidance should not be confined only to the maladjusted but should be provided to all types of children. It will be of great use to devote attention to normal and superior children also in an attempt to stimulate their intellectual growth.

6. *Guidance is oriented towards cooperation, not compulsion.* No individual can be compelled to submit to guidance. It is a process which depends wholly on the mutual cooperation of the individuals. The consent of the individual is the prior requisite condition for providing guidance. Unwillingness creates resentment and resistance.

7. *Guidance deals with the whole individual.* Brouwer stressed that the "Individual is not a disembodied mind, nor is he a body without mind. He is psychological organization in constant interaction with a complex array of environmental forces. As an organism he necessarily responds to his environment as a whole being."

8. *Guidance is an interrelated activity.* It is very difficult to see a problem clearly in isolation. It is correlated with the total programme. It demands a comprehensive study of the individual in his social and cultural setting by the use of scientific techniques. For example, educational, vocational and personal-social guidance is interrelated but could be distinguished as different aspects of the total guidance programme.

Guidance to be effective needs complete information about the individual. Great harm may be done to the individual, if decisions are made on the basis of incomplete and unreliable data. Complete information from different sources should be collected about the individual to give final decision on any problem.

9. *Guidance is a systematic and well-organized activity.* Guidance is not an incidental and isolated activity. In spite of its being a broad-based programme, it has a definite purpose to achieve. It, therefore, requires the cooperation of all workers working in the school complex.

In recent years, the concept of guidance has become broad-based. The concept of education and guidance is related. Education aims to bring changes and improvements in the personality of the students through instructional and co-curricular activities. Guidance also is one of the tools of education. It is an integral part of education. It is very essential that guidance services should supplement and complement all instructional work to enable the child to develop into a wholesome personality.

The guidance programme should be evaluated in terms of its effectiveness and improvement. Evaluation is essential in the never-ending cycle of formulating goals, meaningful progress towards them, and determining the new goals which emerge as the result of new conditions.

CRITICISM OF GUIDANCE

The following criticism of guidance has been mostly taken from the experiences of guidance workers in the west. All these criticisms are also applicable to Indian conditions.

1. In the west the view is gaining ground that guidance and counselling have lost their identity to psychology. As Hoppock stated:

> Massive as this programme has been, and still is, the foundations upon which it rests are beginning to crumble. Client-centred counselling now challenges the basic assumptions underlying the whole concept of testing and diagnosis as the indispensable preliminary to clinical counselling.

2. Another criticism is that guidance personnel are inadequately trained to perform the functions that originally served as the basis of their employment. In India, guidance work is being done mostly by teachers. There are very few schools which have established fulfledged guidance cell.

3. Another criticism is that ".... counsellors spend all their time with college-bound students and neglect the large number of youth who enter the labour market.

Walton has stated that a real danger lies in a tendency on the part of school guidance workers to stress that with which they are most familiar, curricular and college guidance areas, and to neglect that which is not their natural interest, the vocational area".

In our country, guidance services have not been organized and if at all they exist on some institutions, they are only meant for adolescents seeking jobs. Educational and personal guidance services hardly exist in our higher secondary schools.

4. Another criticism is that guidance is atheoretical that is, that present-day guidance practice is not and cannot be based upon any theory. The contention is that attention has been directed to providing a service to students to the detriment of building theories that explain the behaviour of individuals involved in the guidance process.

5. Another criticism is that counsellors have confined their activities to those which take place in their office. Mostly counsellors remain in their offices passive and withdrawn from the life, interests and concerns of students.

6. A final criticism is that counsellors' responses to female clients are based on outdated stereotypes of women. The charge is that counsellors from such a frame of reference are unable to serve females in contemporary society in such crucial areas as education, marriage, employment and family etc.

All the above objections raised against the guidance services may be resolved to a great extent if concerted efforts are made by all persons to improve the existing guidance services in our country.

ASSIGNMENTS

1. What are the basic principles of guidance?
2. What are the main criticisms against guidance services?

REFERENCES

Shertzer/Stone: *Fundamentals of Guidance*, Houghton Mifflin Co., Beston, 1976.

Gones, A.J.: *Principles of Guidance*, McGraw Hill Book Co., New York, 1963.

Smith: *Principles and Practices of Guidance Programme.*

Chapter 3

Foundations and Kinds of Guidance

Every child is born in a social environment where he acquires a number of learning experiences which help him in the process of adjustment. Before entering the school, a child gains many significant experiences which shape his future personality patterns. The main objective of the teacher is that he should begin with the child as he is at entrance in formal schooling. The school should organize learning and educational experiences in such a way that every individual child develops his inherent potentialities to the fullest, maximum limit in his own and social interest.

Education as a formal process is conducted by those persons who are recognized by pupils and public alike; the responsibility of the teacher as an agent of society is to assist students in learning and systematize facts and learning experiences in all subjects. Curriculum-makers are charged with the creation of curricular learning experiences.

Guidance is based on sound principles of various disciplines. Here we will describe the philosophical, psychological, and socio-cultural foundation of guidance services.

1. Philosophical Foundation

Before we attempt to see the bases of guidance in philosophy, let us see the stand of major philosophies of education on the aims of Education. Naturalism lays emphasis on the development of the individual in such a way that he may lead a complete life by achieving the five specific objectives: (a) self-preservation, (b) economic efficiency, (c) upbringing children, (d) maintenance of social and political relations, (e) use of leisure.

According to idealism, the aims are two-fold; one for the welfare of the individual and the other for the good of the society. The first aim emphasizes self-realization which means the actualization of the highest potentialities of the self. The social aim of Education for the idealists is to have a democratic society in which values of equality, fraternity, justice and liberty are respected.

Pragmatism does not believe in setting general aims of education. It emphasizes the importance of effective experiences which help the individual to adjust to their environment. Pragmatism stresses human purposes and satisfaction of human wants rather than one grand purpose towards which the universe is to move.

Realism does not believe in general or common aims of education. Dr. Broudy, an exponent of realism, presents the aim of education as "the preparation for good life". Broudy defines it in the context of the school, "The task of the school is to transcribe the good life, the good individual and the good society into learnings that presumably will contribute to their production."

Realism suggests four basic principles which lead to a good life. They are self-preservation, self-determination, self-realization and self-integration. The aim of education can be achieved by knowledge, development to character and vocational efficiency.

Lastly, the philosophy of existentialism believes that every individual is unique and his uniqueness must be developed by education. In other words, individual differences among the pupils should be respected. In brief, "an uncompromising affirmation of authentic freedom and individual uniqueness is the message of existentialism for the philosophy of education today."

Man is endowed with higher mental abilities which enable him to systematize sensory work as an instrument of decision-making, problems-solving and integrating knowledge. Problem-solving cannot be viewed as exclusively intellectual, emotional or one-dimensional regardless of the aspect of the personality that is isolated. The quality of problem-solving depends upon the integrated functioning of the total personality.

Briefly, we can say that the quality of man as a human being arises out of his ability to solve problems in an effective fashion, to operate an integrated personality and to make proper adjustment to the world.

A guidance worker's main job is to understand persons as problem-solving organism for performing this job. A guidance worker must know the inherent potentialities of the individual and environmental variables influencing the personality development of the individual. Following are the philosophical bases of guidance service

(a) *Respect for individuality*. Democracy is the government of the people, for the people, by the people. The success of democracy depends on the premise that individuality should be respected and opportunities should be provided to the individual for the development of his capacities to the maximum for the welfare of the individual and the society as a whole.

Guidance helps to aid the development of individuality by giving educational, vocational and personal assistance so that every individual develops in his own way. The individual is the centre of all guidance activities. The individual through guidance activities is helped to develop his individuality. The aim is an individual who is capable of meeting his needs satisfactorily and of solving his problems efficiently. All disciplines are directly or indirectly connected with the welfare of the individual and the society.

(b) *Value system*. Philosophy is concerned mainly with the aim of life and out of the aims a value system gradually emerges. It is according to this an individual moulds his personality. The value system of an individual influences his personality, his choice of profession and all his other life activities. The aims of major philosophies have been given in the beginning of this chapter.

Guidance is based on the philosophical concepts which respect the individuality and emphasize the development of an integrated personality.

2. Psychological Foundation

Psychology provides the key concept of man as a developing human organism. Psychology is the study of behaviour. It is mostly concerned with phases of development and the characteristics emerging in physical, intellectual, social and emotional dimensions of development at different age levels. Psychology contributes not only to the total nature of guidance but also to the details of its everyday practice. The tools to measure the human characteristics developed by psychology are used by guidance workers.

(a) *Individual development*. Man is the product of constant interaction of hereditary and environmental forces. His development is a complex product of many variables which produce in each person a unique combination of characteristics and patterns of behaviour that separates him from all other persons and yet at the same time unites him with all human beings. The maturational process within each person takes place in a definite cultural and physical environment. The motivational factors create separate values, goals and life objectives. The development of an individual takes place through the complex process of learning and problem solving. Psychology attempts to understand human behaviour and guidance workers use the concepts and principles that emerge about man as a complex being.

(b) *Dimensions of individuality*. Early psychology used to assess the individual differences through psychological methods. Gradually more improved and sophisticated methods were developed to collect data about the characteristics that separated man from man. Interests, intelligence, values, personality, adjustment patterns etc. came to be the first concerns of the research psychologists who attempted to delineate the ways in which man differed from man.

(c) *Human potentialities*. Every person in the process of growing and developing as an individual creates personal goals and objectives, persons at all stages create plans and hopes for themselves. The potential for success in any venture depends on the capability, opportunity and aspiration level of the individual. Guidance becomes a type of human investment as it helps individuals to understand themselves through psychology and to profit from education.

(d) *Adjustment and development*. If we minutely examine the process of human development and adjustment we find that human life is a continuous process of development and adjustment in different situations. Thus we see that in order to provide proper guidance it is very essential to know the process of human development and the characteristics which emerge at different age levels.

(e) *Self-realization*. Self-realization means to achieve the maximum development of one's aspirations, potentialities etc. for the welfare of the society. It is the highest achievement in mental satisfaction, development and equilibrium in an individual's life.

3. Socio-Cultural Foundation

Sociology is concerned with the origins and patterns of society. Man is the unit of sociological studies. Man as a social animal is affected by the society of which he is a member and at the same time is creative within, and contributory to, the society in which he lives. Society can be viewed as a part of the total culture that man creates for himself. Man has bound himself to others through the creation of society as a conceptual design of life. Life within each society is circumscribed by customs, beliefs, value patterns and by the institutions that have been developed within the society. The individual must be born, must grow, must explore and develop as a person in a society. The conceptual designs that can help guidance workers appreciate life as it is lived in different societies for practical data that enter into problem solving issues of all types.

Every child is born in a social environment where he acquires a number of learning experiences which shape his personality and aid in the process of social adjustment.

(a) *Social change*. In our country after independence, several social changes have taken place due to industrialization and universalization of education. These social changes have opened new avenues of employment which necessitate the organization of guidance services.

(b) *Industrial revolution*. Industrial revolution in the last decades in our country has brought revolutionary changes in all walks of life. This revolution has created a number of vocations which need specialized training for which guidance is needed.

(c) *Role of women*. Traditionally women in our society were confined within the four walls of home; their area of work was to rear up children, cooking food and to run the family but due to education after independence, women have become conscious of their rights also. Their activities are not only confined to home but now they are entering into all types of professions to supplement the income of the family.

Thus we see that guidance as a movement has emerged on sound foundations of several disciplines.

TYPES OF GUIDANCE

Guidance is the oldest subject in the world. Human beings and animals have been providing guidance to their young ones to adjust in the environment in order to live effectively. With the passage of time guidance has acquired importance in various walks of human life. It has become a specialized subject of study and has been divided into different branches. Here we will discuss the various types of guidance services.

W.M. Proctor has given the following list of guidance services:

1. Educational guidance
2. Vocational guidance
3. Guidance in social and civic activities
4. Guidance in health and physical activities
5. Guidance in the worthy use of leisure time
6. Guidance in character building.

Jones, in his book *Principles of Guidance*, has given the following list:

1. Vocational guidance
2. Courses, curriculum and school guidance
3. Civic and moral guidance
4. Leisure time, vocational and cultural guidance
5. Social guidance
6. Leadership guidance.

Koos and Kefauver classify the different kinds of guidance as follows:

1. Educational guidance
2. Vocational guidance
3. Recreational guidance
4. Health guidance
5. Civic-social-moral guidance.

Brewer expands the number of items in the list to nine:

1. Educational guidance
2. Vocational guidance
3. Religious guidance
4. Guidance for home relationship
5. Guidance for citizenship
6. Guidance for personal well-being
7. Guidance in right doing
8. Guidance in thoughtfulness and cooperation
9. Guidance in wholesome cultural action.

Paterson, *et al*, have the following list:

1. Educational guidance
2. Vocational guidance
3. Personal guidance
4. Health guidance
5. Economic guidance.

The above classifications of guidance may be grouped into the following three broad categories:

1. Educational guidance
2. Vocational guidance
3. Personal-social guidance.

1. EDUCATIONAL GUIDANCE

Educational guidance is aimed to aid students to solve their problems related to education at different levels of education — from primary to university. Students differ as regards their intellectual abilities and interests. They are guided to select courses in accordance with their intellectual abilities so that after completing formal education they may effectively adjust in their environment.

Educational guidance has been defined in different ways. Let us examine here two important definitions. According to Myers, "It is a process concerned with bringing about, between an individual pupil with his distinctive characteristics on the one hand, and differing groups of opportunities and requirements on the other, a favourable setting for the individual's development or education."

According to C.C. Dunsmoor: "Educational guidance is primarily concerned with the student's success in his educational career. It relates to the student's adjustment to school and to the preparation and carrying out of suitable educational plans in keeping with his educational needs, abilities and career interests."

Need for Educational Guidance

Had there been no individual differences among the students, the need of guidance services would have never arisen. Guidance is needed because individuals differ in intellectual abilities, interests, motivation and in their levels of aspiration. To cater to the needs of individual students, educational guidance is needed in schools. The following are the specific areas where educational guidance is essential.

(a) *Choice of courses.* In our schools students are provided with hardly any type of educational guidance. The students after passing their junior High School Examination enter the High School where no planned assistance is offered to them as regards the choice of courses. Mostly students choose course on the advice of their friends or insistence of their parents or entirely on their own initiative. Sometimes students are forced to offer courses because of non-availability of particular group of subjects in the school. At least no student from rural areas offers particular course with long-range planning of his future career in mind.

In our country it is very unfortunate that many inappropriate choices are made because of ignorance and illiteracy of parents. They have fixed idea of the vocation their child should follow irrespective of the intellectual and other competencies of their wards.

Innumerable instances can be cited of poor choice of courses in relation to the students' low ability combined with high ambition. Sometimes high ability coupled with a low level of aspiration creates equally serious problems. Many able students choose courses below their real capacity.

In short we can say that a great harm is being done to the individual and the nation because of lack of educational guidance to the students in choosing subjects of study. The new pattern of education recently introduced in the country will provide educational guidance which will definitely improve the existing conditions.

(b) *Decision as to further education*. Students in the present system of education rush to colleges or universities for higher education irrespective of their aptitude for higher studies. Majority of our students go to higher study because they do not have the knowledge of other professional courses or training. There is a great need to provide proper guidance as regards the suitability of the individual to pursue higher education.

(c) *Making the grade*. Another important area where educational guidance is needed is the area of giving students help to progress satisfactorily in the course chosen. In our country, a large percentage of students fails because of lack of educational guidance. This results in wastage and stagnation of national talents. Choice of unsuitable courses and poor classroom teaching account for the high percentage of failure in high school and intermediate examinations all over the country. Educational guidance will help students markedly to make satisfactory progress.

(d) *Education of exceptional children*. Generally in our schools, the teacher proceeds with the average student in mind with the result that gifted, slow learner, deaf and mentally and physically handicapped are not benefited by classroom teaching. Educational guidance is most essential for different categories of exceptional children if we are interested in the welfare of the individual and the society.

The Nature of Educational Guidance

Educational guidance is important to help students to choose appropriate courses and to make the maximum progress in them. It is a positive developmental programme meant for exploring the educational needs of students and helping them to develop their potentialities by providing suitable opportunities.

The process of educational guidance involves knowledge of students' abilities, interests, awareness of educational opportunities and counselling.

Objectives of Educational Guidance

1. The main objective of educational guidance in schools is to help students understand their strengths and weaknesses and to aid in the process of adjustment.

2. To aid students in the positive development of attitudes, value system, adjustment skill and decision-making competencies, in short, to help them to develop into free and responsible citizens.

3. To develop individual potentialities, it is dedicated to aiding students to individualize and make personally meaningful the academic, social and ethical aspirations of the institution.

4. To increase the accuracy of the individual's self-perception.

5. To screen individuals who have some difficulties in learning and to suggest means and measures to rehabilitate them.

6. To suggest courses of study to individual students.

7. To encourage the harmonious development of the students.

2. VOCATIONAL GUIDANCE

Vocational guidance has been defined in different ways. National Vocational Guidance Association in USA has adopted the following definition after careful study and discussion on the subject. "Vocational Guidance is a process of assisting the individual to choose an occupation, prepare for it, enter upon and progress in it. It is concerned primarily with helping individuals make decisions and choices involved in planning a future and building a career — decisions and choices necessary in effecting satisfactory vocational adjustment."

The concept of guidance as evolved by NVGA stresses the fact that vocational guidance is a process that continues in the life of the individual over a long period of life. It is not a once-for-all activity.

The problem of vocational guidance is that of assisting an individual who possesses certain assets, liabilities and possibilities, to select from many occupations one that is suited to himself and then to aid him in preparing for it, entering upon, and progressing in it.

Need for Vocational Guidance

The reader may ask why we need vocational guidance. The answer to this question is — vocational guidance is needed because of two sets of differences; differences among individuals and differences among occupations open to them. We need vocational guidance to find out suitable vocations for the individual to minimize the percentage of misfits and to increase the national rate of productivity. Vocational guidance is further needed to eliminate frustration, tension and failure from the life of the workers. Specific aims of vocational guidance are as follows:

1. To assist the student to acquire such knowledge of the characteristics, functions and duties regarding the group of occupations within which his choice will probably lie as he may need for making an intelligent choice.

2. To enable students find general and specific abilities and skills required for the group of occupations under consideration in terms of qualifications, age, sex and preparation.

3. To give opportunities for experiences in school and out of school which will give such information about condition of work as will assist

the individual to discover his own abilities and help him in the development of his interests.

4. To help the individual develop a definite point of view regarding the choice of an occupation.

5. To assist the individual to acquire the technique of analysis of occupational information and to develop the habit of analysing such information before making a final choice.

6. To assist individual secure such information about himself, his abilities, general and specific, his interests and his powers as he may need for a wise choice.

7. To assist economically handicapped adolescents to pursue their occupational choice.

8. To assist the students to secure knowledge of the facilities offered by various educational institutions for vocational training and the requirements for admission to them, the cost of attendance etc.

9. To help the worker to adjust himself to the occupation in which he is engaged; to assist him to understand his relationship to workers in his own and related occupation and to society as a whole.

10. To enable the students to secure reliable information about the danger of alluring short cuts to fortune through short training courses and selling propositions and of such unscientific methods.

3. PERSONAL-SOCIAL GUIDANCE

Personal-social guidance is meant to provide assistance in all problems which do not come within the purview of educational and vocational guidance. This type of guidance starts from early childhood and continues throughout the life of the individual. In the opinion of the author, the personal-social guidance has acquired a great importance in our existing conditions because of the following reasons.

(a) *Emotional problems*. Our population is increasing at a very high speed. The job opportunities for educated people are not available to all. This results in frustration and tension and creates a number of emotional problems.

(b) *Mental illhealth*. Increasing percentage of mentally disturbed and unhealthy people necessitates the organization of personal-social guidance services in the school and the community.

(c) *High percentage of delinquency*. In our society the percentage of crimes and delinquent acts of all categories (sex crimes, murder, theft, fraud) is increasing day by day causing great anxiety in the minds of those who are actively associated with the well-being of the individual and the community. Therefore, it becomes necessary to provide personal-social guidance to adolescents for proper adjustment.

(*d*) *Attitudes.* Social prejudices against the minority group and scheduled castes are inherent in our society. If we want to eradicate these social evils we have to organize group guidance for the community.

(*e*) In our country, we need guidance for family welfare to check the increase in population and family tensions caused by industrialization.

(*f*) Change in attitude toward life values, social system and superstition also necessitates guidance.

Aims of Personal-Social Guidance

1. To increase the accuracy of the individual's self-perception.
2. To help the individual to solve his adjustment problems at home and in school and society.
3. To increase the accuracy of his environmental perceptions.
4. To integrate his self-perception with perceived environmental realities.
5. To present relevant information when needed.
6. To improve the individual's ability to make and execute plans.

ASSIGNMENTS

1 What are the psychological foundations of guidance? Illustrate with examples.
2. What are the various types of guidance services? Describe them in brief.
3. What is the nature of educational guidance? What needs can it meet in a Higher Secondary School?
4. Define Vocational Guidance. Why do we need it?
5. Why is personal-social guidance needed for adolescents? Illustrate your answer with examples.

REFERENCES

Brewer, J.M.: *Education As Guidance.* (Ny, The Macmillan Co.).

Crow and Crow: *An Introduction to Guidance* (New Delhi, Eurasia Publishing House, 1962).

Jone, A.J.: *Principles of Guidance* (Ny, McGraw Hill Books).

Myer, G.E.: *Principles and Techniques of Vocational Guidance* (Ny McGraw Hill Book Co., 1941).

Taber, Hidla: *School Culture* (American Council of Education, Washington D.C., 1955).

Chapter 4

Factors and Theories of Career Development

Factors Affecting Career Development

There are many factors which influence the career development of individuals. Often career planning has been ineffectual because it is based upon an effort to match intellectual ability and interests with an occupation, without considering other important variables. Here, in this chapter we will discuss briefly some of the important factors which influence career development.

Career development has been defined as "the total constellation of psychological, sociological, educational, physical, economic and chance factors that combine to shape the career of any given individual." The following are some of the important factors which affect the career development of an individual:

1. *Intellectual ability.* Intellectual ability is an important consideration for career development. Every profession needs a certain level of intellectual abilities without which an individual cannot function efficiently on his job. College training is universally required by the professions demanded by the bulk of occupations classed as semi-professional and considered highly desirable for managerial positions. Thus we see that intellectual ability remains a significant factor in the educational and vocational choice of an individual. It has been reported by guidance personnel that children with high intellectual abilities aspire to high-level occupations and duller children are more interested in lower-level occupations.

2. *Aptitudes.* Various combinations of aptitudes or special abilities influence performance in a given field of endeavour. Occupations differ quantitatively from each other in specific aptitudes demanded. Any one occupation usually draws upon several identified abilities as a prerequisite to entrance.

An individual's aptitudes exert influence on the vocational level he is likely to attain, the training he is likely to be admitted to or succeed in, and the quality of work he is able to perform. It should be kept in mind that special aptitudes, typically, correlate more highly with success in training than with success in work performance.

3. *Influence of schooling*. Schooling exerts a powerful influence upon an individual's choice of a career by clarifying and modifying some of the forces which are set in motion by the family and by providing a stimulating environment. The school environment and the facilities provided influence the career development of students to a great extent. The influence of faculty members, the policies and philosophy of an institution, its resources and facilities, the faculty attitudes and behaviour — all these contribute to students' perceptions of the relationship among their educational preparation, their personal development and their career potential. It will not be out of context to say that in India, the highest percentage of IAS, and military officers come from public schools where the environment is conducive to the harmonious development of an individual's personality. The influence of school is shown in the saying, "The battle of Waterloo was won on the playfields of Eton."

4. *Family*. Family influences, including child rearing practices and socio-economic level, appear to affect vocational development. According to Werts certain group of occupations are inherited. Though it is not known why an association exists between a father's occupation and his son's career choice, this relationship is present and influences the career development of some students.

The nature may be more important than nurture in individual's ultimate choice of a career. Particular patterns of personality organization foster particular types of ability. A particular occupation may demand from its workers personality traits quite different from those demanded by another occupation. Empirical studies of occupational demands testify to the primary importance of personality traits, over all other types of occupational information. A study by Teevan was concerned with whether a correlation between personality and vocation could be demonstrated before the individual became actively engaged in the vocation or it was the vocation itself which tended to fit its members into a common mould. Teevan concluded that a correlation between personality and vocation could also be demonstrated during the period preceding entrance into a profession. Behind the idea that vocational choice results from motivational or personality factors is the assumption that differences in personality structure cause individuals to develop certain needs which they seek to satisfy through occupational choices.

Holland is of the opinion that choice of an occupation is an expression of personality and that members of an occupation share similar characteristics.

There are many researches which report correspondence among personality, vocational interests and personality manifestations.

Baird concludes that the undecided student was more intellectually, and less vocationally oriented than students who made a choice.

Kessarjian *et al* reported that inner-directed and other-directed differ to a great extent as regards their professional preferences, occupational interests and their social values. It has been reported that inner-directed value scales are lower on economic, social and political scales than other-directed. Super has reported that personality traits seem to have no practical significant differential relationship to vocational preference, entry, success or satisfaction.

5. *Self-concept*. The reason for entering an occupation may be related to the protection and improvement of one's self-concept. It is possible to view career development as the attempt on the part of individuals to enhance or defend their self-concept.

Persons choose an occupation that they perceive as congruent with their self-concept. Self-esteem would, therefore, influence individual's perceptions of their ability to perform different tasks and occupational roles. According to Karman, only persons with high esteem choose occupations that are congruent with self-concept.

6. *Values*. What individuals value in work itself as well as the rewards it offers is presumably internalized in their vocational development and influences their choices of occupations. The values held by an individual are the products of a host of variables including rearing, education and environment.

According to Underhill (1966) values influence those who seek careers in humanities, education and law while career choice in medicine, engineering, physical sciences and business influences the persons' values.

Occupational values held by individuals constitute an essential and important element of their motivational structure and, if understood, can provide invaluable insights into the decision-making process.

7. *Stereotypes and expectations*. Stereotypes and expectations appear to be associated with and influence students' vocational choices.

The information that students have regarding occupations may well be based upon stereotypes of what workers in an occupation do. Holland and Parker suggest that stereotypes of occupations held by students form part of the foundations for vocational choice.

Similarly, it has been reported that high school students express preference for high status occupations even though they realistically do not expect to enter these occupations. Students eventually realize that their own abilities, interests, and skills are limiting factors and that their choice must be changed.

8. *Interests*. Bordins (1943) has presented a theory of the nature of vocational interests based on the individual's responses to the Strong Vocational Interest Blank (SVIB). It is his contention that theories of vocational interest have taken one of three directions. (a) The static point of view, in which vocational interests are believed to be fixed after the individual has reached maturity, (b) the dynamic view, in which the vocational interest is seen as a product of psychological influences and as such subject to change with shifts in the psychological equilibrium, and (c) the empirical view, in which there are merely sets of preferences that distinguish successful persons various occupations from people in general. He has offered a well-defined theory of vocational interests. Interests are strictly inventoried. They are considered to be a by-product of personality and are subject to change whenever the self-concept changes or when there is a change in knowledge of the occupational stereotype.

9. *Realism as a factor in occupational choice*. There is vast array of data that show that the obvious approach of using answers to direct questions about interest is often unreliable, superficial, and unrealistic. Research seems to indicate that the expressed interests of children and adolescents are unstable and do not provide useful data for diagnosis and prognosis. There are several factors which partially explain this situation. First, most persons have insufficient information about different jobs and courses of study. Second, a related factor is the prevalence of glamorized stereotypes regarding certain vocations. A third factor might be that expressed interests are frequently the outcome of an awareness of social pressures. Expressed interests are stated because they are often demanded or approved by the society or environment in which the individual is reared.

Stephenson draws the following generalizations regarding the realism of vocational choice from a review of the literature on this topic.

(*a*) A large percentage of every prework age group has made no occupational choice whatsoever.

(*b*) For making a choice, there is a strong tendency to select from a narrow range of occupations.

(*c*) Occupational choices are largely in the upper range of occupational hierarchy with a higher percentage in the profession.

(*d*) The distribution of occupational choices has very little correspondence either to the national or local distribution of job opportunities or to the father's occupation. Most studies have shown that as children progress from childhood through adolescence their vocational choices become more realistic — realistic in the sense of being more in line with the individual's capacity, interests or opportunities for placement or with the occupational distribution found in the community, state or nation.

Super and Overstreet conducted a study of vocational choice of ninth graders. They suggest that the ninth grade is the most crucial point for individuals in planning their occupations, that taking students' occupational aspiration at face value is often a mistake and that seeking to help them formulate a specific occupational objective at the ninth grade level may be strategic error.

10. *Sex differences.* There are wide sex differences in attitudes, interests and intellectual patterning of males and females which are of considerable importance in career development.

Differences in relative masculinity and femininity were related in many ways to occupational interests and occupational choices.

In our country, cultural and social aspects of sex differences tend to become as important as the physical aspect. Though a much larger percentage of women is working today in big cities than ever before independence and the trend is steadily increasing, there is still resistance to the entrance of women into the labour force. Such resistance is expressed subtly but effectively by encouraging women to enter only certain occupational fields, such as clerical, teaching, nursing, medicine, stenography etc., while discouraging them from entering occupations in which men traditionally dominate such as military, police, administration and engineering etc.

Certain fields have tended to develop as men's fields and certain others as women's fields. Perhaps in no case is one sex completely excluded but in a few fields the ratio of males to females runs higher than ninety-nine to one.

Cegelka *et al* investigated the extent to which the vocational interest of ninth grade students differed as a function of sex and aptitude. Significant differences were found between males and females on 19 of the 24 on Ohio Vocational Interest Survey (OVIS). Males scored higher on manual work, machine work, inspection, crafts, numerical and appraisal work. Females scored higher on personal services, caring for people or animals, clerical work, nursing, teaching and counselling etc. These researchers note that sex bias may contribute to labour power under-utilization and that it has direct implications for counselling.

11. *Environmental influences.* A child's particular socio-economic inheritance may have a direct and important effect on the occupations open or attractive to him more than does his physical inheritance. The economic and occupational level of the home affects the vocational goals of youth by influencing their aspirations to be similar to those held by their parents and by discouraging aspirations to levels much above or below the parental occupational status.

One of the most important general cultural factors influencing occupational choice is the degree of conformity required by the society, either in the degree of rigidity of particular patterns of behaviour or in the number of different acceptable stereotypes.

Lyman reviewed several studies concerned with differences among socio-economic groups with respect to the value attached to various aspects of work. She reported that a larger proportion of respondents in the higher income groups mentioned congeniality and a smaller proportion mentioned economic benefits. It is further reported that middle class persons desired a job offering self-expression, while working class individuals preferred a job offering security.

Although socio-economic studies vary in the validity of their methodological approaches, they all agree that persons at the lower end of the socio-economic scale are more likely to emphasize the economic aspects of the work than are persons at the upper end of the scale who tend more typically to stress the satisfaction intrinsic to the work.

Theories of Career Development

Before we write about the value of a theory let us define as to what we mean by a theory. A theory is a way of organizing and systematizing what is known about a phenomenon. It serves as a model which is used to know what to look for, what to expect and where to go. The model leads to a statement of relationships believed to prevail in a comprehensive body of facts. The theory of career development is of great value for teachers and for the counsellors because they need to seek constantly for insight into the reasons students are motivated to make certain career choices. Only by doing so will they be able to understand and help them.

The ultimate goal of education and also one of the goals of the guidance movement is to prepare individuals who find satisfaction and zest in life and who may contribute to the welfare of the society. A major intermediate guidance goal is developing students who have acquired the behaviour needed to be successful in an occupational career. Researches have been conducted in an attempt to develop systematic theory of career development so that students can be properly guided. In the following pages we will describe some of the major theories of career development.

1. Super's Vocational Development Theory

Donald E. Super and his associates have made an attempt to develop a theory of vocational development which is referred to as a self-concept theory. The vocational development, according to them, takes the form of ten propositions which are as follows:

(*a*) Vocational development is on-going, continuous and generally irreversible process.

(*b*) Vocational development is an orderly, patterned process and thus predictable.

(*c*) Vocational development is a dynamic process of compromise or synthesis.

(*d*) Self-concepts begin to form before adolescence.

(*e*) Reality factors play an increasingly important part in occupational choice with increasing age.

(*f*) Identification with a parent or parent substitute is related to the development of adequate roles.

(*g*) The direction and rate of the vertical mobility of an individual from one occupational level to another are related to his intelligence, parental socio-economic level, status needs, values, interest and skill in interpersonal relationship and supply and demand conditions in the economy.

(*h*) The occupational field is related to the interests, values and needs of the individual.

(*i*) Although each occupation requires a characteristic pattern of abilities, interests and personality traits, the tolerance is wide enough to allow both some variety of individuals in each occupation and some diversity of occupation for each individual.

(*j*) Work satisfaction depends on the extent to which the individual can find adequate outlets in his job for his abilities, interest, values and personality traits.

The degree of satisfaction the individual attains from his work is related to the degree to which he has been able to implement his self-concept in his work.

Work and occupation provide a focus for personality organization for most people, although for some persons, this focus is peripheral, incidental or even non-existent and other factors such as social and the home are central. According to Super, then, vocational development is an on-going, continuous, and generally irreversible process. It is a process of compromise within which his key construct, the development and implementation of the self-concept operates. The individual chooses occupations whose characteristics will allow him to function in a role that is consistent with his self-concept which, in turn, is a function of his own developmental history.

2. Anne Roe's Theory of Career Development: Childhood Determinants

Anne Roe's theory puts primary emphasis on childhood determinants of future vocational choice. The family environment and the training given to the child in early years set the patterns of personality which will play a decisive role in the choice of future career.

Rejection, acceptance, domination and democratic attitudes of parents towards their children lay foundation for certain personality characteristics and these characteristics are ımportant for certain types of occupations. Anne Roe has advanced a scheme of classifying occupations and explanation for vocational decisions. Occupations have been divided into the following eight groups as shown in the following diagram.

Diagram

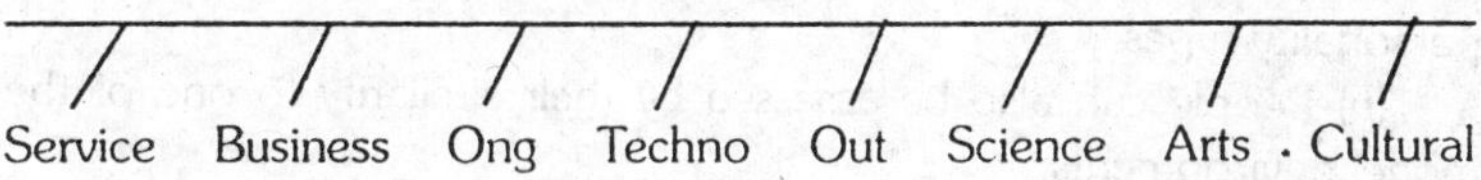

And then each of the above occupations has been divided into six levels from highest to lowest.

Now let us understand by example how she illustrates her scheme of classification. For instance, under the service group, she mentions: (*a*) School work supervisor, (*h*) Social workers, (*c*) Policemen, (*d*) Taxi drivers, (*e*) Elevator operators.

All these workers have in common the fact that they serve others, but the training needed for each job is quite different and the gap in ability between high and low is great.

3. Holland's Theory of Career Development

Gohn L. Holland approached the theory of career development from a different angle. He categorized all persons into six personality types, namely, realistic, intellectual, social, conventional, enterprising and artistic and six environments with similar names were proposed.

According to him, individuals who are in the process of making a vocational choice search for situations that satisfy their "adjustive orientation".

Vocational preferences are correlated with individual ways of coping with stress and frustration and their ways of utilizing outstanding abilities. Thus preferences are associated with self-conceptions. Stability in vocational choice is greater when the individual's choice is appropriate to the sex role. The individual selects vocations in which he or she may engage in attractive roles and activities and avoids those viewed as distasteful. Holland has summarized his theory as·

(*a*) There are six kinds of occupational environment.

(*b*) Everyone has a developmental hierarchy estimated by his coded interest inventory scores which impel him toward one of the six occupational environments. This hierarchy is a product of a number of variables interacting with the developing personality of an individual.

(c) Everyone has a level of hierarchy which impels him to a particular level of vocational choice. The formula for this is anaıogous to intelligence plus self-evaluation.

(d) The hierarchies are mediated by self and occupational knowledge.

Holland has consistently tested his formulations and made modifications.

(*a*) All individuals can be assessed by their similarity to one of the personality types.

(*b*) People can also be assessed by their similarity to one of the model environments.

(*c*) Individuals' interaction with their environment determines their behaviour.

(*d*) If personality types are consistent with environment models, there is greater possibility in predicting interaction and congruency.

(*e*) The inter-relationship between individuals and environments can be predicted.

4. Tideman and O'Hara's Theory

According to Tideman and Hara, career development is "Those aspects of the continuous, unbroken flow of a person's experiences that are of relevance to his fashioning an identity of work." They view career development as affording an opportunity for the expression of hope and desire as well as limitations upon life. In their study they have attempted to find out the relationship between personality and career development. As, they said, "career development is a process of fashioning a vocational identity through differentiation and integration of the personality as one confronts the problem of work in living."

The processes of differentiation and integration are as follows:

5. Stefflare's Theory of Career Development

Stefflare has set ten propositions that explore various psychological factors capable of influencing vocational development.

(*a*) An occupation permits an expression of the individual's public personality which is a special instance of differentiation of function.

(*b*) The occupational persona (work role) represents the individual's choice among those masks he would like to wear and those that society will permit him to wear.

(*c*) An occupational role may represent avoidance reaction as well as, or instead of, approach reaction.

(*d*) The importance of the work aspect of the public personality: the occupational persona varies from being psychologically peripheral to being central.

(*e*) The societally determined forces that determine the occupational persona of any individual vary from the accidental to the essential.

(*f*) The expression of the public personality through an occupation — the selection of an occupation must be made on complete information.

(*g*) The stability of the choice of an occupation after additional information about the work role becomes available varies directly with the psychological commitment to the occupation on the part of the counsellor.

(*h*) As further information about the self comes to light it is more apt to lead to change within the occupation for those who are psychologically committed to the occupation as opposed to change to a different occupation for others.

(*i*) The occupational persona and the self-concept have a symbolic relationship that moves toward congruence.

(*j*) The selection of an occupational persona may express any of four relationships between the self and society. The four relationships are fitting, permitting, transforming and binding.

6. Bording and his Associates' Theory

Bording and his associates present an analytical scheme of vocational choice based upon identifying the gratifications that varieties of work offer to individuals. They emphasize the importance of early experiences to educational pursuits. They made the following assumptions:

1. There is a continuity in the development process which links the earliest work of the organism in food getting and mastery of the body and coping with the stimulations of the environment to the most highly abstract and complex of intellectual activities.
2. The complex adult activities retain the same intellectual source of gratification as the simple infantile ones.
3. According to them, the pattern of needs is established by the age of six but continual modification continues through the lifespan.

The seeking out of occupational outlets of increasingly precise appropriateness is the work of the school years but the needs which will be the driving forces are largely before that time.

ASSIGNMENTS

1. What are the various factors which influence the career development of the individuals?
2. Critically examine the career development theory of Super or Anne Roe.

REFERENCES

Mortensen, Dpmaid G.: *Guidance in Today's Schools* (John Wiley and Sons, New York, 1972).

Shertzer Stone: *Fundamentals of Guidance* (Houghton Mifflin Co., Boston, 1976).

Myers, George E.: *Principles and Techniques of Guidance*, (McGraw Hill Book Co., New York, 1976).

PART - II

Chapter 5

Appraisal of Students: Test Techniques—I

(MEASURING INTELLIGENCE AND ACHIEVEMENT)

In this chapter and the next two chapters we will examine the methods of collecting relevant information in terms of quantitative and qualitative characteristics which help to understand the individual and provide him proper guidance.

The basic premise of the individual pupil appraisal is that individuals are alike as well as different. Appraisal is concerned with providing data that will highlight the individuality of each student. It seeks to establish a distinctive picture of the individual by comparing him with others in terms of quantities of general human characteristics. Appraisal data indicate how one is similar to, and different from, others.

An important purpose of appraisal service is to gather information about students that will aid them in understanding themselves and make meaningful decisions about their future career.

Appraisal service is also used by the school staff and parents to understand and help the students.

According to Cronbach, there are two philosophies of testing: psychometric and impressionistic which have influenced contemporary interpretations of human behaviour. The psychometric interpretation of human behaviour obtains numerical estimates of single aspects of performance. It rests on the dictum, "If a thing exists, it exists in some amount and if it exists in some amount, it can be measured." On the other hand, the impressionistic approach leads to a comprehensive descriptive picture of the individual. This approach was developed by Gestalt psychologists who look for significant cause to understanding an individual's dynamic characteristics by all available means and integrate them into a total picture.

PRINCIPLES OF APPRAISAL

The following specific principles should be followed in the appraisal of students:

1. *Collection of useful data.* Only such data should be collected as are justified, (a) for immediate use for a student's benefit or (b) for

planned research purposes that will improve school programmes, thus having a longer range benefit for the students.

Implicit in the principle is the corollary that all data sought will be around scientific principles of behaviour, thus prohibiting collection of data on pre-scientific accountings of behaviour. The school will collect and maintain data possible about each student.

2. *Retention of data*. Data will be recorded and retained for only as long as there is a demonstrable need, that is, beyond its immediate use (a) such data will have a future use or benefit to the student or (b) such data are needed for planned researches into school programmes.

3. *No violation of privacy*. No datum will be sought that is a demonstrable invasion of privacy unless the purpose of that datum is made known to the student; and if such a datum is given, it may not be recorded in a central file. It will be recorded on temporary records maintained by the guidance practitioner or other professional employee and destroyed promptly when the need for which the datum was collected no longer is present. Public attention has been focussed on the danger to privacy now practised both in educational institutions and by other community agencies. A student's complete cumulative record may be examined by him and, if the student is a minor, by his parents.

4. *Confidentiality*. No person other than a member of a school may examine or be told any portion of information from a student cumulative record without the explicit permission of the student or his parents.

5. *Accuracy*. Student cumulative records are a major supervisory responsibility of school administrators. They are monitored and maintained by trained personnel, and are systematically examined to ascertain that they accord with all principles, and that the data in them are accurate and current.

Criticism of Testing

Mental testing has no doubt made tremendous progress in the last seventy years all over the world but in the recent past both psychologists and the general public have started criticizing the results obtained by mental testing, Some of the criticism are given below:

1. *Classification by ability measures*. The criticism is that classification labels of bright, average, inferior are applied to individuals based on their measured intelligence and that these labels go through their school career. It is assumed that these labels establish expectancies in the minds of teachers and become self-fulfilling prophecies for the individual. Murphy states: "The straggling and starvation go on in schools, hospitals,

clinics, families wherever we freeze our expectation of a child in terms of the belief that tests are the truth, the whole truth and final permanent truth about a child's potentialities. Judgements are too often weighted on the negative side."

2. *Lack of validity and reliability.* Validity refers to the degree of accuracy with which the test measures what it is designed to measure; reliability refers to the consistency of the test. People have criticized both the validity and reliability of tests.

3. *Tests reflect race social class and cultural background.* Many psychologists have asserted that standardized tests of ability and achievement are based upon middle class experience, achievement and school success. As a consequence, children born and bred in impoverished environments or environments which are culturally different are penalized because their experiences limit their effectiveness in test situation.

4. *Partial view.* Testing fosters limited conception of ability, achievement and personality. Critics assert that tests used in schools are based heavily upon verbal and quantitative skills that do not encompass all types of achievement needed in our society. They point out that the prominence given to these skills by testing throughout the schooling period tends to discourage the development of other qualities such as social ability, creativity and honesty etc.

5. *Testing is an invasion of privacy.* Critics often level the charge that testing is an invasion of an individual's privacy. Many individuals feel not only that administering a test violates a person's right to privacy but that these test results are posted on a cumulative record that follows an individual through school and on into a work position.

6. *Test data are not reported to the person tested.* Another criticism against testing is that feedback about test results is not given to the person.

7. *Testing encourages test-taking skills.* Another criticism is that testing encourages students to develop test-taking skills rather than skills that facilitate true learning. According to this charge, students learn for the sake of passing tests rather than understanding and mastering the content.

8. *Testing leads to mechanistic decision making.* Traditionally, educational testing has been designed to measure the progress and attainments of students. It is charged that these data are too often mechanically used without regard to other factors to make evaluation of the individual.

9. *Testing over-emphasizes individual competition.* A final criticism of testing is that it stresses competition and success rather than co-operation. Too much emphasis is placed upon doing better than

fellow students when what should be encouraged is co-operation and team work.

PURPOSES OF TESTS

Cronbach has given the following purposes of tests:

1. *Prediction*. Tests of various types are given to individuals to obtain solid basis upon which decisions can be made. Decisions involve predictions of how well individuals will do at a later time. It is assumed that predictions based on quantitative data are more accurate and reliable and provide a balance against wishful thinking.

2. *Selection*. Tests are also used in selection of candidates for admission, jobs or some training.

3. *Classification*. Classification means to divide invidual s into classes or groups on the basis of some criteria, for example, classifying students on the basis of aptitude, interest and mental abilities.

4. *Evaluation*. Tests are used to assess and to evaluate programmes, methods, treatments and the like.

Counsellor's Use of Tests

1. The counsellors may use tests to secure accurate and reliable information about each student's abilities, interests, adjustment problems in order to give proper guidance to the individual. By understanding each pupil's strengths and weaknesses, the counsellor can provide better assistance to the individual.

2. Counsellors may make use of test results for further performance. Tests can provide an improved basis for prediction regarding the likelihood of success in those activities in which prospective performance can be measured.

3. Counsellors may use tests to help students arrive at decisions basic to planning their educational and vocational future.

4. Counsellors use tests to diagnose students' problems. For example, problems of social adjustment, growth and development or academic deficiencies may be identified and plans for their amelioration may be mutually determined.

5. Counsellors use tests to help them evaluate the outcomes of guidance or counselling.

Types of Tests

Tests have been classified in different ways on the basis of purpose, content, form, procedure and function. The following classification gives an idea of various categories of tests.

TESTS

1	2	3	4	5	6	7
Standardized	Individual	Speed	Performance	Objective	Maximum	Norm
vs	*vs*	*vs*	*vs*	*vs*	*vs*	*vs*
Teacher made	Group	Power	Paper-Pencil	Subjective	Typical performance	Criterion referenced tests

Here, we will discuss the appraisal of mental abilities and achievement of an individual. The guidance worker should very cautiously use test scores in combination with other reliable information.

1. MENTAL ABILITY TESTS

It is universally acknowledged by all teachers that one of the single variables which affects schooling is the quality of behaviour called intelligence. The term 'intelligence' has been interpreted in different ways by psychologists. Some representative concepts of intelligence are given below:

1. According to L.M. Terman, "Intelligence is the ability to think in terms of abstract ideas."
2. According to D. Wechsler, "Intelligence is the aggregate or global capacity of the individual to act purposefully, to think rationally and to deal effectively with his environment."
3. H.H. Goddard, "The degree of availability of one's experiences for the solution of immediate problems and the anticipation of future ones."
4. G.D. Goddard, "Intelligence is the ability to undertake activities that are characterized by difficulty, complexity, abstractness, economy, adaptiveness to a goal, social values, emergence of originals, and to maintain such activities under conditions that demand concentration of energy and a resistance to emotional forces."

Brief History of Ability Testing

History of testing intelligence is as old as human race on earth. Prehistoric human beings used crude methods of measuring human abilities. Systematic effort of measuring intelligence can be attributed to Max Wundt who established an experimental psychology laboratory in Leipzig (Germany) to study individual differences in human beings. His methods were largely based on physical reaction time. He believed that intellectual functions can best be measured through tests of reaction time and sensory discrimination.

James McKeen Cattell, an American psychologist, after obtaining his Ph.D. at Wundt's laboratory returned to America and began measuring reaction time, colour discrimination, strength of grip and sensitivity to pain of college students in America.

The mental tests which Cattell and other experimental psychologists used were basically tests of sensory discrimination, speed of motor responses and similar types of motor activities. Intellectually ability was identified as sensory activity of an individual, but these mental activities bore little relationship to academic ability or to what most people view today as intellectual ability.

The early attempts to measure intellectual ability proved relatively useless as predictors of accomplishment in school work and other tasks that are supposed to require intelligence.

The first systematic effort to measure intelligence was made in the beginning of present century in France, where a high percentage of students failed in the examination. The Superintendent of Public Instruction appointed a committee under the chairmanship of Binet to devise some measures to screen and select slow learners in Paris schools. Binet and Simon, another member of the committee, developed (1905) paper-pencil test items to test complex mental functions including judgement, reasoning, memory and arithmetic reasoning etc. The 1905 scale had 30 items arranged in order of increasing difficulty. The weaknesses of 1905 scale were identified and removed in the revised scale of 1908. The revised scale created interest among the psychologists of the UK and the USA who gave valuable suggestions for the improvement of the scale. The revised scale was developed in 1911.

Sample of Bluet's 1911 Mental Age Scale

Age—3
1. Points to nose, eyes and mouth.
2. Repeats two digits.
3. Enumerates objects in a picture.
4. Gives family name.
5. Repeats a sentence of six syllables.

Age—4
1. Gives own sex.
2. Names key, knife and penny.
3. Repeats three digits.
4. Compares two lines.

Age—5
1. Compares two weights.
2. Copies a square.

3. Repeats a sentence of ten syllables.
4. Counts four pennies.
5. Unites the halves of a divided rectangle.

Age—6
1. Distinguishes between morning and afternoon.
2. Defines names of familiar objects in terms of use.
3. Copies a diamond.
4. Counts thirteen.
5. Distinguishes between pictures of pretty and ugly faces.

Age—7
1. Show right hand and left ear.
2. Describes a picture.
3. Executes three commands given simultaneously.
4. Counts the value of six sons, three of which are double.
5. Names four cardinal colours.

Age—8
1. Compares two objects from memory.
2. Counts from twenty to zero.
3. Notes omissions from unfinished pictures.
4. Knows date.
5. Repeats five digits.

Age—9
1. Gives changes from twenty sons.
2. Defines familiar words in terms superior to use.
3. Recognizes all of the pieces (9) of money.
4. Names the month of the year in order.
5. Answers or comprehends 'every question'.

Age—10
1. Arranges five blocks in order of weight.
2. Copies two drawings from memory.
3. Criticizes absurd statements.
4. Answers or comprehends difficult questions.
5. Uses three given words in not more than two sentences.

Age—12
1. Resists suggestions as to length of lines.
2. Composes one sentence containing three given words.
3. Names sixty words in three minutes.
4. Define three obstract words.
5. Discovers the sense of a disarranged sentence.

Age—15
1. Repeats seven digits.
2. Finds three rhymes for a given in one minute.
3. Repeats a sentence of twenty six syllables.
4. Interprets pictures.
5. Interprets given facts.

Adult
1. Solves the paper cutting test.
2. Rearranges a triangle in imagination.
3. Gives differences between pairs of abstract terms.
4. Gives three differences between a president and a king.
5. Gives a main thought of a selection which he has heard read.

The Standford-Binet Scale 1916

The Binet-Simon scale created great enthusiasm among the psychologists all the world over. There have been several English translations and adaptations of the 1911 scale. The most popular and widely used scale was prepared by Lewis Terman of Stanford University in the year 1916. He tried to select items from the Binet-Simon Scale as well as completely sample the tasks that required intelligence but that were not so dependent on school experiences. The ratio 1.2 was determined from the formula.

$$1.2 = \frac{\text{M. A.}}{\text{C.A.}} \times 100$$

For many years the Standford-Binet intelligence scale was a kind of standard against which other intelligence tests were validated.

Two inadequacies were noted by the workers in the field: the weakness of the scale in testing adults and very young children, and the lack of a second form to permit re-testing. Therefore, in 1937, Terman and his associate Merrill published a revised and undated version of the test having more floor and ceiling and two parallel forms (L and M).

Standford Binet-Simon Revised Scale 1937

Certain changes were introduced in the scale which are as follows:

(i) Number of items raised to 129 in each form (L and M).
(ii) The revision provides contact with wider range of testing for bright children.
(iii) The examiner must first establish his basal age, year level at which he can pass all sub-tests. Then testing continues until the child's ceiling age — the lowest year by adding to his basal age the number of months credit received for passing each sub-test upto his ceiling age.

Standford Scales — 1960

The latest revision of the Standford-Binet scale was published by Houghton Mifflin in 1960 consisting of an updating of the best items from the 1937 (L and M forms). Like its predecessors, this scale is used to measure intelligence from age 2 years to adulthood. The test materials include various toy objects for the lower age levels, one large and one small spiral bound booklet, a test booklet, a test manual and a record booklet for indicating the examinee's responses.

In case a particular sub-test is not administered correctly, there is an alternate sub-test at each age level. It is also possible to shorten the administration time by giving only four selected sub-tests instead of sex provision of division 1-2.

The Wechsler Test 1939

The Standford-Binet scale in spite of its merits was not a very satisfactory measure of the intelligence of adults. Therefore, there was great necessity to develop a test of intelligence for adults. Daird Wechsler, a psychologist in Bellevue Hospital in New York, developed an intelligence test strictly for adults in 1939. He added form-II to the early form-I in 1947. Form-I was completely revised and restandardized and published in 1955 as Wechsler Adult Intelligence Scale (WAIS). This test was designed to test the intelligence of adults from 16 to 75 years, a correction for deterioration being applied to the scores of examinees at the upper end of the age range.

Diagnostic Significance of WAIS Scores

The test scores on WAIS can give very important information to the counsellors because verbal and performance I.Q. and the pattern of scores on the 11 sub-tests were thought to be characteristic of certain types of mental disorders.

Large differences between sub-test scaled scores and between verbal and performance I.Qs. are, however, of some use in the diagnosis of organic brain damage and certain mental disorders, and in differentiating between intelligence and opportunity.

The scores on WAIS also help to diagnose depression, psychoneurosis and personality disorders. The test is highly reliable to measure the intelligence of adults. Its test-retest coefficient is .90.

Group Test of Intelligence

A group test is one that can be given to a number of subjects at the same time by a single examiner. Group tests and their use were made later than individual tests. The history of the emergence of group tests can be traced back to First World War when the USA was compelled to join the war. It was felt necessary to construct and devise such measures of intelligence testing that could be given to a large number of prospective soldiers and officers for their classification for various jobs, consistent with their mental ability. The army asked the American psychologists to develop tests for classifying recruits.

One of Terman's students, Arthur O. Otis, and his colleagues began to experiment with methods by which tests of mental ability could be given to a group of subjects. The Army Alpha and Army Beta were developed in a short period. Army Alpha is verbal group test of intelligence and is meant for literate persons. Army Beta is a non-verbal group test of intelligence and is meant for illiterate persons. These two group tests proved remarkably successful in screening recruits. After the World War I, several psychologists devoted themselves to develop group tests of intelligence.

Characteristics of Group Tests

All group tests have been developed on the assumption that intelligence is general capacity and can be measured by sampling a variety of mental activities.

In almost all group tests, the items are placed together in separate sub-tests or parts, beginning with the easier and progressing by intervals to the most difficult.

Every group test is standardized for a special ranye of ages or school grades.

Group tests are scored more ripidly and more objectively than those individually administered.

Most group tests impose time limits for each of the several sub-tests or parts. Some group tests are entirely non-verbal in content and others are entirely verbal.

Representative Non-verbal Group Tests

(1) *Pintner-Cunnigham primary mental test*. This is one of earliest and well-known group scales. It is meant for children of kindergarten and first and second grades.

(2) *The Chicago non-verbal examination*. This is another early and well-known scale. It was designed for use from 6 years through adulthood. The types of items in the scale are similar in most respects to those in other scales.

(3) *The Pressey-Primer scale*. This scale consists of four tests, requiring in all four the same type of response, namely, the crossing.

(4) *Large-Thorndike grade*. This scale is meant for grades 2 and 3. The items consist of identification of animal and human figures, classification of pictured objects shown to the child and association of similar objects shown in the pictures.

(5) *The Haggerty delta 1*. This test is meant for grade 1 to 3. It consists of 12 exercises, out of which six are meant to give orientation to the infants and six are the tests.

The Haggerty delta 2. This is designed for grades 3 to 9. It is an adaptation of the army intelligence test.

(6) *Dearborn intelligence scale*. This scale has been designed specially for grades IV to XII. It consists of seven sub-tests.

(7) *The Raven progressive matrices*. This test was developed in England. It is a widely used test. It consists of geometric figures and designs. The subject apprehends relationships between figures and selects appropriate part for completion of each pattern or system of relations.

The Cattell Culture Free Tests

Some psychologists attempted to develop group scales which may not be influenced by verbal material and form or acquired skills and experiences in the environment of different cultures. These scales have been developed for use in all cultures.

IPAT. This test is available for three levels: Scale 1 for ages 4 to 8 and mentally deficient scale 2 from 8 to 12 years and for selected adults, and scale 3 from the range of high school through superior adults.

COMPARISON OF INDIVIDUAL TESTS AND GROUP TESTS OF INTELLIGENCE*

Individual test	Group test
1. It is administered to an individual at a time.	1. It is administered to many individuals at the same time.
2. It is costly in terms of administration and time.	2. Group tests are not costly in terms of administration and time.
3. It requires a trained tester to administer it.	3. No trained testers are required to administer the test.
4. The tester can study the behaviour of the individual thoroughly as there is face-to-face interaction.	4. There is no face-to-face interaction and behaviour of individuals cannot be studied.
5. Individual tests are more reliable. We can provide guidance to the individual on the basis of his scores on the individual test.	5. Group tests may be influenced by reading ability and speed of the individual.
6. Individual tests are most suitable for children who cannot read or write.	6. Temporary poor health, lack of motivation and poor vision may affect test score.
7. Individual tests provide qualitative performance of the individual.	7. They are suitable for other children and adults who can read, write and co-operate.

* They are influenced by cultural environment, by schooling and to some extent by the subject.

Individual test	Group test
8. The tester can adapt to the needs of the individual child, finding the level at which he can succeed. The examiner can motivate by means of praise and encouragement.	8. The tester cannot adapt to the needs of the individual students. Cheating is possible.
9. There is an absence of competition in individual testing.	9. There is competition in group testing situation. Speed and reading ability influence the test scores.
10. There is greater informality in administration.	10. There is formality in administration.
11. It is possible to eliminate a lot of errors committed through inattention and cheating.	11. A child may become bored and spend time gazing outside.
12. Instructions are made clear before starting.	12. Instructions may not be understood by the entire group of students.

CONSTANCY OF IQ

The constancy of IQ has received a great deal of attention from educational psychologists because of its usefulness in modern education. There are two opinions, one group of psychologists holds the opinion that IQ remains relatively constant over the years changing only very slowly. Another assumption which is generally sustained by a majority of psychologists is that if a determined effort is made, a change in IQ can be effected. There is considerable empirical as well as theoretical evidence to indicate that such constancy is far from absolute. They put forth empirical evidences to prove their point of view.

Honzike (1948) conducted studies to see the change in IQ over a period of years. He reported that between 6 to 18 years of age considerable change occurs in IQ, 60% of the group changed upto 15 points of IQ (1938) also reports lack of constancy of IQ over the years in the study conducted at Harvard University.

The IQ does not remain constant over the years. Fluctuation can be expected to occur for a number of reasons, ranging from the unreliability of the tests, the effects of practice or other factors operating from one test to another, differences in the content of the tests in relation to the various abilities of the testee. The latter is of particular importance when the results of the childhood tests with their emphasis on sensori-motor tasks are compared with the results of those tests where the emphasis is on abstract reasoning.

Jones (1954) pointed out that correlation between the IQ of infants and their IQ a few years later is typically negative. It is not until the age of 12 months that this correlation reaches Q and then begins to become positive. It is not until the fourth year that any degree of stability in the IQ is attained.

Bayley (1955) points out, eventually, that investigators can come across the hard reality that infants exhibit a very limited range of behaviour beyond sensori-motor functioning upon which to base an estimate of intellectual ability. She suggests that instead of continuing to think of intelligence as an integrated or simple capacity which grows through childhood by steady accumulation, it is better seen as a dynamic succession of developing functions with the more advanced and complex functions in the hierarchy based on the prior maturing of the earlier and simpler one.

A good part of the fluctuation occurring in the IQ stems from the fact that no test is completely reliable. Thus we would expect one-third of the testees on the average to gain upon retest up to 5 IQ points and another third to lose up to 5 IQ points, another 14 per cent would lose from 5 to 10 points and other 2 per cent at each end would gain or lose more than 10 IQ points. These fluctuations can be expected on the basis of chance alone and have nothing whatsoever to do with any change, occurring as a result of an increased or decreased rate of intellectual growth. They simply reflect fluctuations to be expected as a result of the limitations of the measuring instruments, the carelessness of the psychometrist, and fluctuations within the testee arising from fatigue, loss of motivation, distractibility and other personal factors. It is also possible that mental growth, like physical growth, goes by spurts and stops.

In addition, directional shifts in IQ may result from exposure to special environmental influences. Thus since most IQ tests include vocabulary questions, one might raise his IQ if he were to be subjected to intensive vocabulary drill. Whatever such directional shifts in IQ actually represent a shift in intelligence or just an invalidation of the norms of the test is the crucial question around which the whole controversy of the constancy of IQ revolves. To use an extreme example, coaching on the items of the test would certainly result in increased IQ but would not imply a corresponding increase in intelligence. But we could hardly assume its applicability to a wide variety of situations calling for intelligent behaviour.

A significant study of Sontag (1958) on concomitant factors in IQ from infancy to 10 years indicates that twice as many girls were in the group of greatest decline in mental growth rate. Emotional dependence upon the parents during the age from 3 to 6 was found to be detrimental to intellectual growth. Many of the girls revealed what Sontag called "slide into femininity", an adoption of the adult female role in which achievement is important only in the area of being more feminine and charming. In contrast, the child who learns to meet some of his needs through aggressive competitive problem solving is apparently laying the groundwork for a high need for achievement which, in turn, relates to an accelerated mental growth rate. The traits associated with gain in IQ included aggressiveness, self-initiation, competitiveness and interest in problem solving, all of which are masculine traits. Of special significance is the growing belief that intellectual development can be promoted through early stimulation. The curve showed a sharp straight line increase in score from 10 to 16 years, then an abrupt inflection and a slow steady decline involving a recession by the age of 55.

These findings have been confirmed in later cross-sectional studies by Raven, 1948 and Wechsler in 1958. Psychologists are still busy in conducting studies to know the definite nature of the curve of the growth of intelligence.

The intelligence quotient (IQ) is one of the most common expressions used in mental testing which has been picked up and passed by all. The constancy of IQ is an important conception which must be used with caution. Some conclusions have been drawn by psychologists which are listed as follows:

1. A given IQ indicates the same relative ability at different ages.
2. A subject's IQ score, ignoring errors of measurements, remains the same from one age to all others unless there is a change in ability level.
3. A given change in IQ indicates the same amount of change in relative standing regardless of the ability level of the subject.

PERFORMANCE TESTS OF INTELLIGENCE

A performance test is one in which the subject has to perform some thing or to manipulate some concrete material without much use of the language ability. There are some categories of people and children who cannot be tested with the help of verbal tests of intelligence. Performance tests are useful for the following categories of children and people.

(1) *Deaf and dumb.* Those children or people who cannot hear or speak can be tested with the help of performance tests. The directions can be given in pantomime with a minimum of language.

(2) *Illiterates.* Illiterate adults and children who cannot write or whose language development is deficient may be tested with the help of performance tests of intelligence.

(3) *Shy and withdrawn children.* Children who are shy or fear face to face interaction with the tester may be tested.

(4) *Educationally deficient children*. Children who are educationally deficient and who take interest in concrete material and its manipulation can also be tested.

(5) *Foreign children*. Children of foreign countries who do not understand the language may be tested with performance tests.

Generally performance tests are used to supplement other tests of intelligence. Performance tests provide more reliable data for an individual's capabilities. They are more useful in clinical work. These tests provide an opportunity for close observation of the behaviour of the testee in test situation and his method of solving problems.

Some Performance Tests

(1) The Healy-Fernald group of tests was the first measuring tool to test intelligence by performance.

(2) *The Pintner-Paterson scale*. This performance scale is the first organized scale. The scale was standardized in 1917. It consists of Healy-Fernald performance tests and several other tests, developed by earlier psychologists. The scale includes fifteen sub-tests. The tests are administered without the use of language either by the examiner or the examinee. The tests are useful for deaf and dumb and those who lack language ability. They have been found a very valuable supplement to verbal tests of intelligence.

(3) *Form boards*. There are several performance tests in which form boards are used. The Ferguson form board was developed in 1920 and revised 1939. It consists of six form boards which increase in difficulty. These tests were standardized on children and college seniors who had some educational problems. They are currently used for children who come for clinical-guidance.

(4) *The Kent-Shaknow form board series*. This performance case was developed in 1928. It is a widely used and known scale. It has two forms, one for clinical use and the other for industrial use. Basically, the scale provides an insight into the analytic-synthetic and manipulative skills of the subject. It also provides close observation of the behaviour of the subject and his mode of tackling a problem.

(5) *The Goodenough drawing test*. This test was developed by Florence Goodenough in 1926. It is the most widely used test to measure the intelligence of children from 3½ to 13½ years. The child is asked to draw a picture of a man as best as he can, without any time limit. Draw-a-man test is a very popular test of intelligence. It requires no training and no specific material for administration. It has been adopted in Indian conditions by several research workers. This test is a useful device as an adjunct to verbal tests when mental retardation in children is suspected.

Advantages of Performance Tests

Performance scales are most useful with older children and adults who are mentally retarded. They have clinical significance in the case of older children.

Since the performance tests do not require use of language, individuals do not 'block' as a result of feeling of inadequacy resulting from lack of schooling.

Children proceed on performance tests with confidence, since the material is visually present in concrete form. Performance tests provide an opportunity to observe the qualitative aspect of behaviour of the individual under standardized condition in a variety of test situations.

Performance scales are useful and provide valuable information when supplemented with verbal tests of intelligence.

They are useful for those who have a language handicap.

Weaknesses of Performance Tests

(1) Performance scales are more susceptible to practice effect and chance success is more frequent than in verbal tests. Hence their reliability co-efficient is low.

(2) They are limited in the range of mental functioning tested. They fail to differentiate among above average children.

(3) The conventional performance scales fail to test fine mental abilities such as the ability to make abstraction or concept formation.

Some Misconceptions Regarding the Use of Intelligence Tests in Education

The following are the misconceptions regarding the use of intelligence tests in education.

(1) The first misconception is that intelligence tests measure something called "native ability", something fixed and immutable within the individual that determines his level of expectation for all time. No doubt, genetic studies of identical twins reared separately under different conditions have proved that the individual intellectual abilities, but intelligence tests do not measure such an entity, at least not directly. Intelligence tests measure individual's performance on certain type of mental tasks. The type of mental tasks included in intelligence tests are influenced by experiences in school and home. The experiences depend on many factors as the education of parents, availability of books in home, socio-economic condition and a variety of experiences the child gets in his surroundings. Thus the notion that intelligence tests measure inherent ability is absurd.

(2) The second misconception about intelligence tests is the notion that prediction made from test scores is or should be perfectly accurate.

(3) The third misconception is that standardized test scores are perfectly reliable.

(4) The fourth misconception regarding intelligence tests is that a battery of tests can tell all one needs to know in making a judgement about a student's competence, present and potential, and about his effectiveness as a human being. The fact is that no test or battery of tests can give a total picture of a child. No doubt, tests can illuminate many areas of child's development. They can suggest something about his strengths and weaknesses. They can show in certain respects how he stands among his peers. But there are many areas of learning where we must still rely upon the observation and judgement of teachers if we want to get a complete description of a child as functioning individual. Any evaluation of a child that depends solely on mental tests scores is bound to be misleading and incomplete. There are subtle and supremely important human elements in the teaching-learning situation that no combination of tests yet devised is able to capture.

It is therefore advisable for guidance personnel that they should very cautiously use the scores of intelligence tests in giving educational and vocational guidance to the individuals.

II. MEASURING ACHIEVEMENT

Of the total amount of time which the teacher spends in the construction and use of testing instruments, by far the greatest portion is devoted to the measurement of academic achievement. In this category are several kinds of instruments with which every teacher is at some time more or less directly involved. Achievement tests may be divided into two broad categories (*a*) Teacher-made tests and (*b*) Standardized achievement tests.

(*a*) Teacher-made Tests

These tests are constructed to measure the achievement of specific instructional objectives relating to particular units of work. Such tests are usually of the paper and pencil variety and are composed of one or two kinds of test items, essay and objective. Essay items get their name from the manner in which the student responds. He is required to produce a written response ranging in length from a few sentences to several pages. Essay items are particularly useful for measuring the ability to organize information and communication clearly and effectively. Objective items are of several different varieties such as short answer, completion, true-false, multiple-choice and matching. They require the student to either supply a word or phrase in answer to a question or choose the correct response from among the alternatives provided. These items get their name from the objective manner in which they are useful for determining whether the student has knowledge of certain facts and principles, whether he understands the significance, or importance of these facts or principles, and whether he can apply them to the solution of unique problems. The construction of classroom achievement tests is the responsibility of the teacher.

Values of Teacher-made Achievement Tests

1. Teacher-made objective tests may be better adapted to the needs of students and goals of the individual school.
2. They are easy to construct and score.
3. Sampling of more behavioural characteristics is possible.

Limitations of Teacher-made Achievement Tests

1 . Teacher-made objective tests lack reliability.
2. The scores of teacher-made tests cannot be compared with the results of tests given by other teacher.
3. Such tests may also lack validity, in this context, it refers to the extent to which tests measure what they purport to measure.
4. They test the memorization of facts. Higher mental abilities are not tested by them.

(*b*) **Standardized Tests of Achievement**

While these tests are composed of the same kinds of items as those in teacher-made tests, their purpose is essentially different. They are not designed to measure the achievement of immediate and specific instructional objectives, their purpose instead is to assess overall achievement in one or more subject areas of skills at various points during the child's schooling. The term 'standardized' refers to the fact that these tests are designed to be administered, scored and interpreted under standard conditions. Because of this feature they are useful for making comparisons between pupils and between groups even when the tests have been administered at different times and in different places.

Standardized tests have norms based upon a very large group called a norming sample. Although the composition of the norming sample depends to some extent upon the purpose of the test, it generally includes representatives from various cultural, religious and ethnic groups, from rural, urban and suburban communities and from a wide range of geographic regions of the country. The norms indicate the average performance of children at various ages and grade levels. In a sense they represent a kind of "national" average with which individuals or groups within a given school or class may be compared. Since the results of standardized tests form an important basis for the evaluation of student's progress and achievement, their use is appreciated everywhere in the field of educational measurement.

Values and Limitations of Standardized Tests

1. Standardized tests of achievement are more reliable because of the uniformity of scoring and time allotted to complete the test. Directions and instructions are always the same.
2. Such tests are the result of much experimentation. Every test is revised after many trials. The language and concepts are selected after careful formulations have been tried out in actual examinations.
3. Norms are available for each grade.
4. The achievements of pupils in different schools can be compared with the help of these tests.

It seems obvious (and yet it is not always realized in practice) that achievement tests should correspond closely in content and emphasis to the objectives, content and emphasis in the instructional sequence itself.

Thus, paper and pencil teacher-made tests should be so constructed that they measure accurately the achievement of the kinds of objectives for which they are appropriate. The achievement of some instructional objectives cannot however be measured accurately by the paper and pencil test, either teacher-made or standardized. Ability to perform laboratory operations in chemistry, typing speed and accuracy in a typing course, creation of a water colour in art, and performance on musical instrument all represent abilities that can be evaluated only on the basis of observing the individual as he performs the tasks involved. Although performance tests are of major importance in certain specialized subject areas, techniques for conducting them differ markedly from one area to another.

In addition to an interest in what the child knows and in what skills he has developed as a result of participation in school learning experiences, there is often interest in how he performs certain tasks. The processes by which a pupil obtains a correct answer must often be determined on the basis of direct observation. In the elementary grades, for example, a great deal of emphasis is put upon the development of good work habits and study skills. Furthermore, the teacher is often interested in assessing attitudes, interests, and motivation for school tasks. Since observation of the pupil in the actual learning situation may form an important parth of the total body of evidence upon which the pupil is evaluated, the use of informal observational procedures cannot be excluded from the field of educational measurement.

Achievement Tests in Specific Areas

When a guidance worker wants more information on pupil achievement in a particular area, it is desirable to administer specific achievement tests because an achievement test has more test items which represent the instructional objectives of a particular school or teacher. Achievement tests are available in almost all subjects. Here we will describe a few of them.

1. Reading Test

Reading tests are a more common and widely used tool in guidance and counselling to assess the strength and weakness of a student or group of students.

(a) *Survey reading tests*. Survey reading tests are used to determine a student's overall reading ability. These tests generally include vocabulary items and sections of paragraphs or passages about which questions are asked. The students' knowledge of vocabulary and comprehension and speed are tested.

(b) *Nelson reading test*. This test has been designed to measure reading skills in grades 3 to 9. It contains two sections : a vocabulary test of 100 words and a paragraph test of 75 items measuring reading comprehension. There are two parallel forms and the test takes 30 minutes to complete. The norms of the test are available which are expressed as percentile ranks grade equivalents and age equivalents.

(c) *Nelson-Denny reading test. Forms C and D*. This test was developed in the year 1973 to measure the reading ability of grades 9-16. Two parallel forms of the test are available, each form consists of 100 vocabulary and 36 comprehension items. Testing time is 30 minutes percentile and grade equivalent norms are available.

Diagnostic Reading Test

Diagnostic reading tests are administered to diagnose the reading disability of an individual. These tests are very comprehensive and contain a long list of items divided into word recognition; reading passages, phonetics and pronunciation, silent and oral reading, spelling and sound discrimination. These sub-tests are highly correlated to each other.

(a) *Diagnostic reading scales*. The diagnostic reading scales were developed by Spache in 1972. The test is meant to diagnose the reading disability of grades 1-8 and high school students with reading disability. There are three word recognition lists, 22 reading passages and 8 supplementary phonics tests on this graduated series. The test is very comprehensive and assesses all aspects of reading skills.

2. Mathematics Test

Diagnostic test in mathematics. The tests of Mathematics are of three types, survey, diagnostic and prognostic.

(a) *Survey mathematics test*. This type of tests, generally, contain items requiring the examinee to demonstrate his understanding of tests and operations, and his ability to apply this knowledge in solving problems.

(b) *Cooperative mathematics test*. This test was developed in 1962. It contains a series of nine tests which cover all areas of Mathematics as for example Arithmetic, Algebra, Geometry, Trignometry, and Calculus. The test takes 6 hours to complete and each sub-test takes 40 minutes to complete.

The Arithmetic test is meant for grades 7-9 and the structure system test is for grades 7-8. The remaining tests are meant for students who have completed a course in the particular area. Norms in percentile are given for all tests.

(c) *Standford modern mathematics test*. This test was developed by T.L. Kelley and others in 1965 to measure the acquisition of concepts, vocabulary and operations included in modern Arithmetic courses at the elementary level. The test takes 50 minutes to complete. Pencentile and Stanine-score norms are available.

Prognostic tests in mathematics. Prognostic tests in Mathematics have been designed to predict success in Algebra and Geometry, but compared to prognostic tests in reading such tests in Mathematics are not widely administered.

Two prognostic tests in Mathematics are very important. Orleans-Hanna tests and the Algebraic Aptitude Test. The algebraic aptitude test emphasizes mathematical reasoning ability, knowledge of terminology, recognition of relationship, flexibility in analysing and the ability to call on elements of Arithmetic.

3. Social Studies Tests

(a) *Cooperative social studies tests*. The cooperative Social Studies test was developed in the year 1964. Social studies test contains items from civics, history, geography and economics. This test measures seven areas of social studies. This test is meant for grades 7-12. There are two parallel forms. Completion time for each test is 40 minutes. The norms are available.

4. Science Achievement Tests

Instruction in science has changed so much during the last ten years that many of the older tests in science are no longer appropriate. A cooperative science test published by Educational Testing Service is a comprehensive battery of tests for secondary school science.

In addition to the tests in all school subjects, there are tests which are meant for professions like law, medicine, nursing and business and skilled trades.

Iowa Tests of Educational Development

These tests are meant to measure the general educational and intellectual development of students from nine through thirteen. They were developed in the University of Iowa for national use. There are four different types of Tests: (a) Background test, (b) Reading Test, (c) Vocabulary Test, (d) Sources of Information Test. These tests measure a wide range of abilities: The test takes 459 minutes to complete.

Use of Achievement Tests in Guidance

Achievement tests play an important role in measuring the academic achievement of students in various subjects in order to provide guidance. The following are the specific uses of achievement tests in guidance.

1. Achievement tests can help in the diagnosis of students' weaknesses and strengths in various subjects of study.

2. Achievement tests can help in designing remedial measures in a specific subject or in the total programme of the school.

3. Achievement tests, if properly used, can help in securing objective and definite data by which improvements can be made in school programmes.

ASSIGNMENTS

1. Define intelligence and describe in brief the uses of intelligence tests.
2. Compare individual and group tests of intelligence.
3. What are the advantages and limitations of achievement tests?

REFERENCES

Freeman, F.S.: *Theory and Practice of Psychological Testing.* (Holt Richart, NY. 1962).

Leona, E. Tyler: *Tests and Measurements* (Prentice Hall, NY. 1973).

Buros, D.K. (ed): *The Fifth Mental Measurements Year Book.* (Highland Park, NY. 1959).

Cronback, Lee. J.: *Essentials of Psychologlcal Testing* (Harper and Brothers, NY. 1960).

Chauhan, S.S.: *Advance Educational Psychology* (Vikas. New Delhi, 1978).

Note

A list of important tests is appended at the end of the book. For detailed information on tests, please see, Bulletin No. 3, October 1979 issued by NCERT.

Chapter 6

Appraisal of Students: Test Techniques—II (Contd.)

(INTEREST, APTITUDE AND PERSONALITY)

III. MEASURING INTEREST

Tests of interest do not contribute as much as cognitive tests (intelligence and special abilities tests) to the prediction of scholastic or occupational criteria of success. They have been more successfully used in counselling and guidance. They often add important information to that obtained from interviews and ability tests in academic and counselling situations.

Information on a person's interests or preferences can be obtained in various ways. The most direct method is to ask the person what he is interested in, but this method has its own pitfalls. For example, the person may have little knowledge of his interests or he may give fake information about his interest due to ignorance. These expressed interests are sometimes more useful than less directly obtained information, and should not be overlooked in counselling situations. There are four methods of determining interests; observing a person's behaviour in various situations, inferring interests from the person's knowledge of special terminology or his scores on other ability tests, and administering an interest inventory to him. There are four types—expressed interests, manifested interests, tested interests, and inventoried interests. Of the four methods, the interest inventory has been the most widely used. An interest inventory permits a broader sampling of behaviours and preferences and also provides objective scores of individual and group comparisons. The tests of interests serve two important purposes in guidance and counselling.

Undoubtedly, one's knowledge of what is involved in a particular occupation and one's pattern of interests affect the occupational choice. The counsellor can improve vocational selection in various jobs by measuring the interests of persons. No doubt, interest inventories although not very good as predictors of school grades or occupational success, do predict the tendency to persist in a certain kind of occupations and stimulate the individuals to think about their vocational goals and provide vocational guidance for selecting appropriate vocation keeping into consideration their chances of future success.

The counsellor, while interpreting the results of an interest inventory should make clear to the examinee the distinction between interests and abilities, indicating that people often do not possess the abilities for activities in which they are interested or that they are uninterested in activities for which they have satisfactory abilities. Scores on interest inventories should be used in counselling only in the light of other information about the examinee, for instance, his scores on ability tests, grades and personal history.

The guidance personnel should keep the following facts in his mind while employing the test scores obtained in interest inventories.

Stability. Individual patterns of likes and dislikes usually begin to develop long before adult experiences with particular occupations. Children's interests are relatively unstable. By the time a person has reached the ninth grade and certainly by the eleventh grade, his preferences for particular types of activities are fairly constant. Though interests become stable after the late teens, some people do change their interests even in adulthood and caution must be used in interpreting the results of inventories administered below the tenth grade.

Fakability. Interest inventories and all self-report measures can be faked to a great extent but it does not mean they do not serve any purpose. No doubt fakability in inventory limits its usefulness as a selection device but it can still be valuable in counselling.

Response sets. The scores of inventories are susceptible to response sets, especially on ambiguous questions. Of particular concern are the response sets of acquiescence (tendency to agree rather than disagree) and social desirability. One technique designed to minimize these response sets is the forced choice format.

Socio-economic level. Inventories such as Strong Vocational Interest Blank (SVIB) have been designed primarily for counselling persons who plan to enter the professions. Until recently there were simply no interest inventories constructed specifically for people planning to enter skilled, semi-skilled or unskilled occupations. A reason for this state of affairs was the research finding that interest in one's work appears to be more important to people in higher socio-economic positions. Security and money were reported to be more important in lower level occupations. Therefore, it seemed futile to try to construct an interest inventory for skilled occupations and below, where interest was supposedly not a factor in determining whether or not a job was liked. In the past few years, Indian psychologists have been attempting developing interest inventories suited to Indian socio-economic conditions. In the following pages we will describe some of the important and widely used interest inventories.

1. Strong Vocational Interest Blanks (SVIB)

The Strong Vocational Interest Blank (SVIB) was developed by E.K. Strong Jr during his research following World War I. In his researches, he discovered consistent differences in what people reported liking and disliking. He, therefore, decided to construct an inventory to assess these individual differences in interests. His inventory introduced two major procedures:

(*i*) The items dealt with the subject's like or dislike for a wider variety of objects, activities or types of individuals and commonly encountered events in daily living.

(*ii*) The responses were empirically keyed for different occupations on the premise that persons engaged in different occupations were characterized by common interests that differentiated them from persons in other occupations.

The SVIB consists of 399 items, most of which are responded to on a 'like', 'indifferent to', or 'dislike' basis. The items are broken down into groups made up of professional occupations, school subjects, measurement activities, types and peculiarities of people.

Initially, the SVIB came in two forms, one for women and one for men. Strong recommended that SVIB should not be used with individuals below the age of seventeen.

The men's blank was published in 1927 and the women's blank in 1933. The revision of men and women blanks were published in 1938 and 1946 respectively. The most recent revisions were published in 1966 and 1969 respectively.

The SVIB for men has 399 items divided into the following eight parts:

Part-I	Occupation.
Part-II	School Subjects.
Part-III	Amusements.
Part-IV	Activities.
Part-V	Types of people.
Part-VI	Order of Preference of activities.
Part-VII	Preference between two items.
Part-VIII	Your abilities and characteristics.

The SVIB for women contains 389 items divided into eight parts, but the format and the number of items in each part are different from those on the men's blank.

Socio-economic scale. Since the SVIB is oriented toward the types of careers that the college educated enter, it is not ordinarily appropriate in vocational planning of skilled, semi-skilled and unskilled occupations.

Time limit. Though the SVIB has no time limit, it has been observed that most of the examinees finish it in 45 minutes or less.

Reliability. Extensive studies to establish reliability of SVIB occupational scales have been conducted by researches. The test-retest reliability comes to .90 over 30 days, .75 over 20 years and .55 over 35 years. These figures indicate that interests, as measured by the SVIB, are sufficiently stable for use in the vocational counselling.

Validity. The studies on the validity of SVIB had been conducted upto 1962 till the death of Strong. The follow-up study of 663 was conducted for 18 years. The study indicates that scores on the SVIB, administered 18 years earlier were highly successful in predicting occupational satisfaction. However, the results of this study and others have failed to demonstrate that scores on interest inventories can predict occupational success. Scores on interest inventories can be used to predict satisfaction with an occupation as well as persistence in it but they cannot forecast how successful a person will be in that occupation.

2. Kuder Preference Records and Interest Surveys

Another important inventory which is generally used in educational and vocational counselling is Kuder Preference records and Interest Surveys developed by G. Frederic Kuder. There are in all four inventories which are briefly described below:

A. Kuder Preference Records and Interest Survey

Use	...	This is used for the purpose of counselling and placement of high school students and adults.
Format	...	168 triads of items to be marked 'most liked' and 'least liked.'
Range and Time	...	High School; no time limit.
Scales	...	Ten interest scales.
Reliability	...	.70 and .80.
Validity	...	Several studies of the relationship KPR-Vocational job satisfaction support its validity.

B. Kuder Preference Record Personal

Use	...	It is used for counselling and placing beginning workers.
Format	...	168 triads of statements describing various personal and social activities. One activity in each triad to be marked 'most liked' and 'least liked'.
Range and Time	...	High School and adult; no time limit.
Scoring	...	By hand.
Scales	...	Five personal interest scales.
Reliability	...	The reliability of the five scales range from .76 to .89.
Validity	...	The validity is found satisfactory.

C. Kuder General Interest Survey

Use	...	It is used in vocational counselling.
Format	...	168 triads of items. One activity in each triad is to be marked 'most preferred' and 'least preferred.'
Range and Time-Grades	...	6 to 12, no time limit.
Scoring	...	By hand.
Scales	...	Ten interest scale.
Reliability	...	Test-retest reliability after six weeks by sex and grade, .70 to .80.
Validity	...	No long-term evidence is available.

D. Kuder Vocational Interest Survey

Use	...	Selection, placement and counselling.
Format	...	100 triads of statements. In each triad one activity is marked most preferred and one least preferred.
Range and Time	...	Grades 9-12, college students and adults. No time limit.
Scoring	...	By hand speed computer.
Scales	...	77 occupational scales.
Reliability	...	Test-retest reliability .90.
Validity	...	Validity is found satisfactory.

3. Minnesota Vocational Interest Inventory

The Minnesota Vocational Interest Inventory was developed during and after World War II by K.E. Clark using the format of Kuder Preference records and Interest Survey. The inventory was developed by conducting research on navy enlisted men and non-professional civilians. It consists of 158 forced choice triads of statements concerning occupational activities. The examinee has to mark 'most liked' and 'least liked' activities. The MVII is employed for males of 15 years and older and takes 45 minutes to complete. It can be scored by hand for 21 occupational scales.

The reliability of the inventory over a 30-day interval ranges from .62 to .88.

Other Interest Inventories

The SVIB and Kuder inventories are certainly very popular instruments but they have by no means entirely captured the market. Many other empirically and rationally constructed interest inventories are available. Following are the important interest inventories.

1. *General Interest surveys*. Two inventories have been published by California Test Bureau.

Occupational interest Inventory (OII) developed by E.A. Lee and L.P. Thorpe has two parts. Part I consists of 100 paired statements based on description of the duties in a particular occupational field. The examinee indicates which number of each pair he prefers. Part II of the inventory contains 30 triads of statements pertaining to activities; the examinee marks the one activity out of three that he most prefers.

2. *Picture interest inventory*. The inventory was developed by K.P. Weingarten. It has two parts. The first part of the inventory consists of 53 triads of pictures that he would most like to perform and the one he would least like to perform. The second part consists of 30 pictures. He indicates whether he likes or dislikes each of the activities illustrated in pictures.

These two inventories are meant for grade 7 through adult and take 30-40 minutes. The test-retest reliability of the 01 is .80-.93 and that of PII is .76-.92.

3. *California occupational preference survey*. The inventory was developed by R.R. Knapp *et al*. It requires the examinee to indicate his degree of preference L (Like very much), I (like moderately), d (dislike moderately) and D (dislike very much). It consists of 168 occupational activities in phrase form. The survey takes 30-40 minutes to complete and is appropriate for secondary school students. Reliability is .90, but no validity data are reported in the manual.

4. *Ohio vocational interest survey*. It is the most recent survey developed by A.G.D'Costa *et al* in 1969. It has 280 statements of

activities. It is designed for students of 8-12 grades. It takes 60-90 minutes to complete it. The inventory was standardized on 45,000 students in grades 8-12.

Limitations of Interest Inventories

(*a*) It is very difficult to ascertain the accuracy of the statements made by the individual reporting his interests.

(b) The interest of the adult worker in the activities may have been attained after he secured the job, he may not have had this interest when he was in school.

(c) It has been reported that interests of adolescents are not permanent and hence cannot be used as indicator of future occupational selection.

(d) The families or patterns of interests as found by Strong are not necessarily related to success in the occupation.

IV. MEASURING APTITUDES

Aptitude means a person's capacity to profit from further training. According to Bingham, aptitude "is a condition symptomatic of a person's fitness, of which one essential aspect is his readiness to acquire proficiency, his potential ability and another is his readiness to develop an interest in exercising his ability." The development of aptitude tests has been made with a specific purpose to measure potential achievement or to predict level of further performance of an individual.

Aptitude tests play an important role in providing educational and vocational guidance. The guidance worker or the counsellor, on the basis of the aptitude test's score, can do a better job of advising persons or placing them in appropriate training programme or occupation.

Implications of Aptitude for Guidance

1. Aptitudes are not inborn and unchangeable characteristics but are the complex result of the constant interaction of hereditary and environmental factors.

2. Learning in any area is conditioned by the learner's readiness to learn.

3. A specific aptitude in the form of talent may show itself early and respond readily to training in future.

1. Test of Aptitude

Scientific management acquired importance in the field of industry and business in the early part of this century. It emphasized the importance of selecting appropriate workers for industry. To select suitable persons, tests were devised to help match individuals to jobs. Several tests of special abilities were developed for use in educational and vocational counselling, job selection and placement.

An aptitude test may be defined as a test which measures a person's potential ability in an activity of a specialized kind and within a restricted range.

Most of the tests of psychomotor abilities were developed in 1920s and 1930s to predict performance in certain skilled jobs and trades. The experience of the workers in the field of guidance has shown that tests of psychomotor abilities have not proved very useful in vocational counselling. They have been more helpful in predicting performance on repetitive jobs such as routine assembly and machine operation than on complex jobs involving cognitive and perceptual abilities of a higher order.

The guidance worker should keep in mind that whenever he uses a psychomotor test as a selection device, it is wise to determine its validity in that particular situation. Some of the aptitude tests are described below:

(a) *Strong-Berg dexterity test*. In the Strong-Berg dexterity test, the examinee is required to place 54 biscuit-size, coloured discs (red, yellow, blue) in a prescribed sequence as rapidly as possible. It takes an average adolescent or adult from 5 to 10 minutes to complete the practice trials and two test trials. The manual gives distributions of scores obtained by groups of foundry moulders, assemblers and welders, punch press applicants, general factory workers and others.

(b) *Large and small manual movements*. There are two commonly used tests which involve a combination of finger dexterity and gross movements of the arms and hands. The tests are:

(i) *Pennsylvania bimanual work sample*. This test was developed by J.R. Roberts.

(ii) *The bennet hand tool dexterity test*. This test was constructed by G.K. Bennet. Both of these tests use nuts and bolts. The subject has to place them into the holes of an 8" by 24" board. These two tests are supposed to predict manual dexterity for various groups of industrial applicants.

(c) *The perdue pegboard test*. This test was developed by J. Tiffin. The test consists of five tasks for measuring manual dexterity and fine finger dexterity. The examinee puts into holes, first with right hand, then with his left hand, and finally with both hands. On the second part of the test, the examinee puts a pin into a hole, places a washer and collar over the pin, puts another pin in a hole etc. The entire test takes 5 to 10 minutes to complete. The test is used for machine operators, production workers, industrial and general factory applicants and packers.

2. Mechanical Ability

Intensive study of mechanical ability has been made to develop suitable tools to measure the mechanical abilities needed for various types of jobs at the University of Minnesota during the 1920s and 1930s. Three tests were constructed:

(a) Minnesota Mechanical Assembly Test.
(b) Minnesota Spatial Relations Test.
(c) Minnesota Paper Form Board Test.

A brief description of the tests is given below:

(a) Minnesota mechanical assembly test. It involves reassembling a set of mechanical objects. The task requires manual dexterity and space perception in addition to mechanical comprehension.

(b) Minnesota spatial relations test. The test consists of four boards A, B, C and D. Each contains 58 metal blocks in recesses having different geometric shapes. The examinee's task is to pick-up the blocks and return them to their proper recesses in the board as quickly as possible. Performance is scored both for time and errors and can be compared to norms for junior and senior high school boys and girls as well as adults. The reliability of the test is .80.

(c) Revised Minnesota paper form board test. This is a paper and pencil adaption of the Minnesota Spatial Relations Test. It consists of 64 multiple choice items, each containing a frame showing a geometric figure divided into several parts and five answer frames containing an assembled form.

The reliability of the test is .80. It has proved useful in predicting grades in shop and engineering courses as well as supervisor's ratings and production records in inspection, packing, machine operation and other industrial occupations.

3. Clerical Ability

Clerical ability is not a unitary factor distinct from general intelligence. In clerical ability, manual dexterity and speed of perceiving differences and similarities are necessary. Verbal and mathematical abilities are also important. Many tests of clerical ability contain items similar to those found on general intelligence tests and items to measure perceptual speed and accuracy. Several tests of clerical and stenographic ability have been designed. One test is described below.

Minnesota clerical test. This test was developed by D.M. Andrew and D.G. Paterson. The test is widely used in the selection of clerks, inspectors, and other occupational specialists where speed of perceiving and manipulating symbols is important. The test consists of two parts; one in which the examinee checks identical pairs in a list of 200 pairs of numbers and 200 pairs of names respectively.

The test is applicable to grade 7-12 and to groups of clerical workers and applicants. The reliability of the test by test-retest method is .70 to .80. The scores are moderately correlated with teacher's and supervisor's ratings on clerical work.

4. Aptitude in Music

Psychologists in order to measure aptitude in music developed tests to measure it. The earliest of these tests was designed by Seashore to measure Musical Talents. This test was meant for grade 4 through college level. The test cosists of the following aspects of hearing:

1. Pitch discrimination.
2. Intensity of loudness discrimination.
3. Time discrimination.
4. Discrimination of timber.
5. Judgement of rhythm.
6. Tonal memory.

Total scores, for the six parts of the test, are used to develop a profile of the individuals.

The Drake musical aptitude test. This test measures two aspects of musical aptitude — musical memory and rhythm. This test is used with subjects of 8 years and olders.

The Meier art judgement test. This test measures aesthetic judgement of the individual in a global manner. The material of the test consists of one hundred pairs of representational pictures in black and white. One member of each pair is a reproduction of a recognised masterpiece, while the second member has been altered from the original in an important aspect so as to make it inferior to the original. Subjects are informed as regards the alteration made (shape, angles) but they are not told which is the original. Subject is required to indicate his preference in the pair. Meier believes that aesthetic judgement is the most significant index to talent in art and success in a career in art.

Aptitude tests have been developed almost in all areas of life as law, medicine, teaching, engineering and military services in recent years.

Uses of Aptitude Tests in Guidance

(a) Aptitude tests can be used for the purpose of guidance in selecting subjects for studying in schools and colleges. They can be used for helping the individual to select the profession of his choice. The psychologist and the counsellor must supplement the results of aptitude test with intelligence tests, school records, interviews and interest tests.

(b) The employer can use aptitude tests in selecting persons for different jobs.

(c) Aptitude tests can be used in admitting candidates for various types of professional training as teaching, medicine and engineering etc. Aptitude tests should be used only as one source of information in a total picture.

5. Measuring Personality

Personality has been defined in many ways on the basis of the approaches with the help of which the psychologists have tried to understand and explain it. A basic assumption is that the personality relates to what people do or what they experience. A second assumption is that personality is fixed and enduring so that score remains relatively immutable of which more surface features are modifiable.

Personality, according to the most general definition, is a composite of mental abilities, interests, attitudes, temperaments and other variables characterizing thoughts, feelings and behaviour.

Wright *et. al.* 1970 defined personality; "These relatively stable and enduring aspects of the individual which distinguish him from other people at the same time from the basis of our predictions concerning his future behaviour." According to Allport, "Personality is a dynamic organization within the individual of those psychological systems that determine his characteristic behaviour and thought."

Personality Assessment

The history of personality assessment is as old as man on the earth. In primitive age people informally attempted to test the personality of their fellow beings with the help of crude methods mostly involving the use of physical strength. There were no formalized techniques of personality assessment in those days. With the development of civilization, new methods were evolved. There are numerous instances of personality assessment with the help of different puzzles, physical feats and other means in literature. In this chapter we will describe only personality inventory, situation tests and projective techniques to acquaint the readers with the procedures followed in measuring personality.

Objectives of Measuring Personality

The first main objective of personality assessment is to understand the individual behaviour in all its aspects, characteristics that one possesses in order to predict his future behaviour and to devise measures of controlling socially unacceptable behaviour. The first objective aims to describe, predict and control an individual's behaviour. The guidance can properly channelize the energies for efficient adjustment in the environment.

The second objective is to describe, predict and control group behaviour. Every group has some common characteristics which are different from members of other groups as high and low, urban-rural, Indian-English. The guidance worker must know the predominant characteristics of the group to effect desirable changes.

The third objective is to describe the influences which the group exercises on members and vice versa. To understand the personality characteristics of adolescents, it is necessary to understand the characteristics of the group to which they belong. Here we will describe only the test techniques of measuring personality.

1. Situational Tests or Behavioural Tests

Situational tests are a very recent development in personality testing. In situational tests, the behaviour of the individual is evaluated in action. Sometimes the counsellor confronts him with situations of his life. The individual's behaviour is assessed by judges or rated by his peers. Situational tests can use the following techniques:

(*a*) *Sociometric methods.* This method of assessing personality was developed by J.L. Moreno in 1946. He defined this method as a technique for revealing and evaluating the social structure of a group through the measurement of the frequency of acceptance rejection among the individuals who constitute the group. This method permits the analysis of each person's position and status within a group in respect to particular trait of personality. It also reveals the structure of a group. This is a simple method. It will be made clear by an illustration from the classroom situation. The following questions may be asked to assess the structure of the class as a group:

(i) With whom do you want to sit in the class?
(ii) Name two students, with whom you would like to go on picnic?
(iii) Name two persons, with whom you would like to live in the hostel?

Sociometric tests can be devised for a number of purposes and social situations.

(*b*) *Psychodrama*. Psychodrama is a very useful technique used in assessing personality. As the word psychodrama implies, the individual has to play a role spontaneously in a specified situation. His behaviour is observed by trained observers. The psychodrama is generally played with two or more persons depending upon the nature of their problems. It is assumed that individuals project their inner feelings and conflict in the role they play. The central principle of psychodrama is spontaneity of the role of the individual. This technique is used to assess the personality of maladjusted persons. The director or the therapist plays an important role in organizing the situation in which the participants may express the maximum of their emotional pent-up feelings. He selects the appropriate situations, assigns roles to individual participants, observes and interprets the action of the individuals. The psychodrama is an important technique to release the emotional conflict and re-educate the individual for better adjustment in life. It is a learning procedure.

The director in psychodrama may use a wide variety of themes depending upon the problems of individuals.

Slightly deviating in purpose and emphasis is sociodrama. Sociodrama deals with the problems of the group, its structure and thinking, Sociodrama portrays social problems with which the audience is concerned. Situational tests are generally used in selection for military services, to assess the potential personality characteristics of officers in army, navy and air force. Various types of tasks are given to a small group of candidates. The instructor observes the personality characteristics of individual participants as cooperation, leadership, initiative, far-sightedness. Let us illustrate the situational test with the help of an example.

Task	Crossing a brook and taking an instrument on the other bank of the brook.
Material	Few boards, a log, ropes, a pulley and a barrel with both ends knocked out. All members of a small group are on equal footing, no one is designated as leader. It is the test of leadership, emotional stability and trust and tolerance. The behaviour of each participant is minutely observed

and assessed by the instructor. A number of situations can be created to assess the personality characteristics of the individual.

Evaluation of Situational Tests

Sociometric methods can play an important role and provide valuable information as regards the structure of the group and status of the individual member of the group but it does not provide information regarding the causes of the structure or status.

Psychodrama and sociodrama are based on the theory of psychological catharsis through activity. Psychodrama as a therapeutic technique provides an individual insight into his problems. The situation technique provides an individual insight into his problems. The situational tests used in military are psychologically sound. They are a miniature form of actual activities. They provide holistic view of the personality of the recruits and give reliable information.

The use of situational test techniques is difficult in practice because it requires staff of trained and experienced psychologists to observe and interpret behaviour along with elaborate facilities to create task situations.

2. Personality Inventory

The first objective tests to be developed were adjustment inventories in the early attempts to measure personality in the USA as part of the effort to save time in selecting recruits for First World War. R.S. Woodworth was the first psychologist who invented the first inventory which he called the personal data sheet. The inventory consists of 116 questions about common physical and mental systems to be answered with check marks by the appropriate answers (yes or no). The total number of yes was taken as a measure of general maladjustment. The approach is perfectly straightforward, obvious and direct.

After the First World War, there was a su.ge of personality testing. The authors of many other adjustment inventories followed in Woodworth's footsteps usually revising and extending his items. The number of self-reporting tests of various traits mushroomed in the 1920s and 1930s.

Bernreuter developed a personality inventory which includes a measure of adjustment, among other traits, which were scored on a logical or a theoretical basis. The author thought about a trait like introversion, drawing on what the concept originator wrote about it and made up a set of items describing various aspects of introverted behaviour.

Minnesota Multiphasic Personality Inventory. MMPI is an indirect type of objective inventory published in 1943. The inventory realises that early inventories relied on the face value of the items and on the subjects' ability to report his own feelings and behaviour accurately. It uses instead the method of empirical keying. It comes in a group form with printed answer sheet, and in an individual form in which the 550 items are printed on separate cards, which the subject sorts into three slots in a box marked "true/false" and "cannot say".

A typical item is a statement that might have been taken from a psychiatric interview, indeed many of them were. Some are rather extreme, psychotic symptoms as 'My soul sometimes leaves my body'. Some items represent milder psychological and physical symptoms as 'I have a great deal of stomach trouble'. The items of MMPI cover the total personality. The original aim of the authors of the inventory was to create an aid to psychiatric diagnosis. The inventory was developed to detect pathological cases. The examiner scores the answer on the empirical scale and then draws inference from the resulting profile.

Hathaway and his collaborators made a determined effort to enhance the usefulness of the MMPI by providing several correction keys to alert the user that 'S's' answer may not be taken at face value. Anyone who does not want to commit himself on an item does not understand it or feels that neither 'T' nor 'F' is the right answer for him, can omit the item in the group form or sort it 'cannot say' in the individual form, because some subjects will use this escape hatch. The simplest control score is just a count of these. If as many as one-fifth of the items are answered this way the test is considered invalid.

The A-S Reaction Study

The A-S (Ascendance-Submission) reaction study by G.W. Allport and F.H. Allport (1928) was one of the first trait measures. It has only moderate retest reliability (.74) and the evidence for its validity is even weaker. The criteria were ratings by self and others. It can hardly be regarded as a precise or trustworthy measuring stick for A.S. Yet most of its content seems meaningfully relevant to that trait. The subject merely checks the answers he considers most self-descriptive.

The sixteen personality factors questionnaire (16 P.F.) was developed by R. B. Cattell on the basis of factor analytic studies of personality. The questionnaire gives complete information in shortest time about the personality traits of the individual. It is a comprehensive questionnaire that covers all the main dimensions along which individuals can differ. The 16 P.F. test has two forms containing 187 items in each form. Each item represents a statement as follows:

Item	Response
I like to watch team games	Yes/Occasionally/No.

The subject is asked to respond to all the items of the test and is instructed to express his choice most honestly. The 16 P.F. test is called by some psychologists as standardized and systematic impersonal interview. The test gives reliable information on 16 personality factors. It was developed on the basis of wide research for the most significant characteristics of personality.

The Eysenck Personality Inventory (EPI)

The inventory was recently developed by H.J. Eysenck and Sybil B.G. Eysenck for assessing neurotic tendencies. The inventory has been developed on the assumption that there are only two dimensions of personality, the stable, the stable-unstable and introverted extroverted. The inventory is brief consisting of 57 questions, reasonably reliable and statistically independent measure of extroversion and of neuroticism. The test itself is a recent, only slightly modified version of the Maudsley personality inventory which has had high reliability ranging from .70 to .90. The interval consistency coefficients range between .75 to .90. The test incorporated a brief 'L' scale adapted from the MMPI which is intended to detect invalid records.

Evaluation of Personality Inventory

The reliability of personality inventories ranges from very low to satisfactory coefficient .8, depending on the traits being measured. The following table shows the reliability of two personality inventories.

S. No.	Inventory	Reliability	Method
1.	MMPI	.90	Odd even
2.	Security-insecurity inventory	.52 to .89	retest
		.84	retest
		.86	Odd even

The validity index of personality inventories is open to criticism because determination of validity is difficult. Validity coefficients vary from low to satisfactory. The MMPI when validated on individuals gives coefficient .4 to .7. Personality testing is still in the process of development and traits of personality have not yet been defined precisely. The use of personality inventories encourages analysis of traits into constituent elements and provides a better understanding of each trait.

Personality inventories are particularly useful in group trends i.e. in differentiating between groups of adjusted and maladjusted rather than among individuals.

Development is a continuous process and personality traits and attitudes may also undergo change. So it is said that inventories will be less reliable in terms of test-retest. Use of inventories should be made by professionals who can make insightful analysis of human behaviour. Traits to be measured should be included in the inventory. The criteria for validating personality inventory should be made more reliable. The meanings of items should be made as nearly uniform as possible for all persons. The serious limitations of inventories are that the subjects may distort their answers for specific purposes. The information collected sometimes fails to give any relevant diagnostic information regarding the problems of the individual.

3. Projective Techniques

Interview and other self-reporting techniques have some inherent limitations to assess the unconscious structure of personality. Psychologists who study the unconscious motivation of personality attempted to devise a new kind of instrument generally called projective techniques. Projection, according to Freud, means externalizing of conflicts or other internal conditions that had given rise to conscious pain or anxiety. Projective tests of personality assessment are those which evoke responses from the unconscious and provide an opportunity to delve into the depth of the unconscious build of an individual's personality. The meaning of projection here is to encourage the subject to use his imagination freely.

Projective techniques have a long history in psychology. Binet (1895) was the first psychologist who had suggested the use of ink-blots as measures of visual perception in his tests. Dearborn of Harvard University reported the use of inkblots as early as 1897. Since then a number of projective tests have been developed and used successfully in assessing personality. Projective tests are standardized sample of behaviour which is not stimulus bound. The essence of projective technique can be briefly described as "it is to examine the personal production of a subject and to interpret it for the light it may throw on his personality". According to Lindzey (1961) a "projective technique is an instrument that is considered especially sensitive to convert an unconscious aspect of behaviour. It permits or encourages a wide variety of subject responses; it is highly multidimensional and it evokes usually rich response data with a minimum of subject awareness concerning the purpose of the test."

Characteristics of Projective Techniques

Projective techniques of assessing personality were developed as a protest by psycho-analysis and Gestalt-oriented psychologists against the behaviouristic and statistical emphasis in the testing of personality in 1920s. The basic assumption of all projective tests is that the subject structures or reacts to the materials of the test by expressing his unconscious strivings and mechanisms. It gives a global picture of the personality of the subject. It is more up-to-date or fully evolved psychological approach, which attempts to explore central and more enduring make-up of the personality. The following are the main common characteristics of projective techniques in general.

1. *Ambiguous material.* Projective tests often use ambiguous material to which the subject must respond freely, often, in a descriptive form. Ambiguous material means that every subject can interpret the test stimuli in his own way. It is assumed that because the stimuli are ambiguous subjects will project their own needs, feelings and conflicts into the test situation.

2. *Evoke responses from unconscious.* Projective tests are based on the implicit assumption that the test stimuli evoke responses from the unconscious of the subject. The subject projects his inner feelings in the test situations.

3. *Multi-dimensionality of responses.* The dimensions in which the subject can respond are various as physical, intellectual, social and emotional. It is possible for the subject to make a great variety of responses to the test task.

4. *Freedom to respond.* The projective test provide full freedom to the subject to respond to the test stimuli. He is not restricted as regards the nature of responses. Perhaps the essence of projective tests is that the end product consists something produced by the subject.

5. *Holistic approach.* It means that projective tests attempt to study the totality of behaviour. They do not explore the molecular behaviour of the individual. They emphasize the moral approach to understand personality.

6. *Answers are not right or wrong.* In projective test the responses of the subject are not scored or evaluated as right or wrong. They are evaluated qualitatively.

7. *Purpose of the test is disguised.* The purpose of projective test is not disclosed to the subject otherwise he becomes test conscious and may hide his real feelings.

L. Frank, 1948 classified all projective technique tests into the following categories.

1. *Constitutive tests*. Under this method come all those projective tests which require imposition of structure upon relatively unstructured material as Rorschach.

2. *Constructive tests*. These types of tests require arrangement of material into pattern as in mosaic's test.

3. *Interpretive tests*. In these tests the testee has to interpret the test situation presented to him as in TAT and CAT.

4. *Cathartic tests*. Cathartic tests are those tests which help to release pent-up emotional feelings as doll play.

5. *Refractive test*. Those tests in which conventional modes of communications are altered as handwriting or altered as handwriting or speech and draw-a-man test etc. These tests are intended to apply particularly to detailed analysis of peculiarities of style in habitual activities.

Important Projective Tests

1. Rorschach Ink Blot Test.
2. Thematic Appreception Test (TAT)
3. Children's Appreception Test (CAT)
4. BG Test
5. Szondi Test.
6. Mosaic Test.
7. Blacky Picture Test.
8. Clous Picture Test.
9. The Word Association Test (free and controlled).
10. Sentence Completion Test.
11. Psychodrama.
12. Sociodrama.
13. Draw-a-Man Test.
14. Toy and Doll Playing Test (World Game).
15. Clay Modelling.
16. Graphology.

It is not possible to describe all the projective tests here. We will select only two most important tests for detailed discussion.

1. Rorschach Inkblot Test

Rorschach inkblot test of personality is one of the most popular and widely used tests. The use of ink blots for purpose of analysing personality was pioneered by the Swiss psychiatriast Harmann Rorschach in 1921. The test material consists of ten 5½ by 9½ inches cards. Each card contains one bilaterally, symmetrical, black and white (5 cards) red and grey (2 cards) or multicoloured (3 cards) ink blot similar to the one given below.

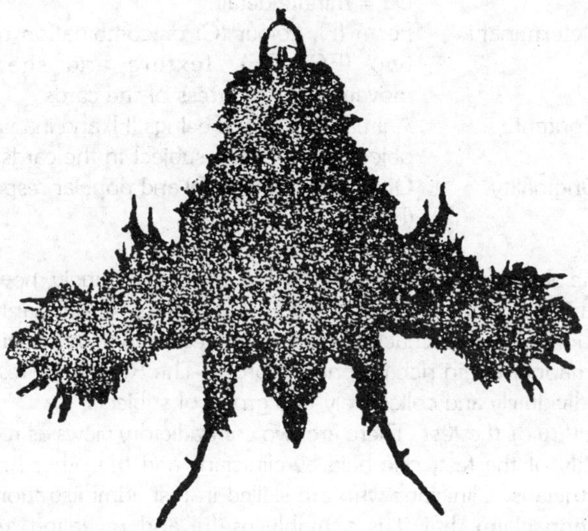

Fig.

Administration. Before administration of the test, the tester should establish complete rapport with the examinee. The purpose of the test is not disclosed to the examinee. The subject is asked to sit comfortably in a chair free from external distractions. The cards are presented individually and viewed at no greater than arms length, but the examinee may turn the card if he desires. The examinee is also present with a blank on which he locates his responses. He is asked to look at the inkblot and to tell what he sees there or what might be represented by the inkblot.

After all the cards have been presented, the examiner generally conducts an inquiry into the details of the subjects' responses on individual cards. The behaviour of the examinee during the test session is observed and recorded.

Interpretation of the responses. To score and interpret Rorschach test records is an exceedingly complicated task which cannot be accomplished without special training. The experimenter first analyses a Rorschach test record by scoring each response in terms of four features as follows:

1.	Location.	The responses of the subject may be W = whole blot. D = major detail. Dd = minute detail.
2.	Determinant.	Form (F), colour (C) or combination of the two (FC, CE), texture and shading, movement in progress of the cards.
3.	Content.	Animal (A), human beings (H) and inanimate, objects seen by the subject in the cards.
4.	Originality.	Original responses (O) and popular responses (P).

None of the above four categories should be interpreted singly, however. Each much be considered in relation to the others. Customarily the interpretation of a Rorschach record is expressed not in concise or statistical manner but in rich descriptive prose. The Rorschach test can be used individually and collectively to a group of subjects.

Reliability of the test. There are two contradictory views as regards the reliability of the test, one held by clinicians and the other held by psychometricians. Clinicians who are skilled in test administration and interpretation claim that it is a highly useful and revealing test of personality of mental patients. According to them, the index of reliability is sufficiently high, .75. Psychometricians, on the other hand, claim that the test is not highly reliable because different testers, confronted with the same set of responses, often arrive at different description of personality. Thus the interpretation is dependent on the personal opinions of the testers.

Validity of the test. According to clinical psychologists, the validity of the test ranges from .5 to .8, i.e., vary high but according to psychometricians, the validity is very low. Rorschach test has furnished many bits of evidence corroborating points inferred from the TAT, most of what it rather directly suggests is confirmed by the case history and other tests but it adds little that is new, at least, on the issues of major interest. The validity of Rorschach test has been attacked by Eysenck on the following points.

(1) If Rorschach protocols are scored blind, even trained and experienced testers produce very different personality descriptions.

(2) The second objection of Eysenck regarding validity of Rorschach test is that if the same tester rescores the protocols his agreement with the original interpretation can be far from perfect.

(3) The attitude and personality of the tester may influence the responses of the subject.

(4) The fact that there is more than one scoring system does not inspire confidence in the test.

(5) There is considerable evidence that what the subject thinks affects the results. In real life situations we cannot control feelings and thinking of an individual and this quite extraneous factor does affect the test results.

Clinicians tried to answer the objection raised by Eysenck that Rorschach test is generally used on those individuals whom the tester knows very well. Rorschach gives insight into the problems of an individual and the way he interprets his world but this is only usable in the light of a person's experiences.

A Scandinavian psychologist, Holley has conducted research on Rorschach test and attempted to quantify the responses of the subjects. At present this work by Holly is in its early stages. If further research supports his findings he will confirm that the clinical intuition of the Rorschach users were correct.

2. Thematic Appreception Test (TAT)

Thematic appreception test, more commonly known as (TAT), was devised by Morgan and Murray in 1935 in the course of a research programme at the Harvard psychological clinic. The test material consists of 31 cards, 30 depicting various scenes and one blank card. The pictures are marked in such a way as to indicate four overlapping sets of twenty each, one for boys, one for girls, one for males over 14 years of age and one for females over 14. The TAT pictures depict various situations in which the individual normally moves. It is called a test of imagination.

The experimenter first establishes perfect rapport with the subject and does not disclose the purpose of the test. The subject is asked to sit comfortably in a chair free from external distractions of any kind. Then the subject is presented one card and the following instructions are given.

"This is a story telling test. I am going to show you some pictures, one at a time and your task will be to make up as dramatic a story as you can for each. Tell, what has led up to the event shown in the pictures, describe what is happening at the moment, what characters are feeling and thinking and then give the outcome. Speak your thoughts as they come to your mind. Do you understand?"

Generally the pictures are given in two sessions. The number of pictures depends on age, sex, and type of problem. TAT pictures are administered individually as well as collectively to a group of subjects.

The behaviour of the subject as regards his emotional expression, time and turning of test cards is recorded. After the administration of test cards, an enquiry is made from the subject to determine the sources of the stories. The total time for each card is recorded.

Interpretation of the TAT. There are many techniques to interpret the TAT stories. None of the techniques is perfectly correct.

The general practice is to approach the stories with the background of general knowledge about the person which helps orient the investigator to what is relevant and helps him to rule out various obviously inappropriate hypotheses that otherwise cause him to waste time.

Second, as the skilled interpreter makes himself more and more throughly familiar with the stories, he begins to notice divergences which are unusual, rare or repetition or very intensely stated or accompanied by signs of strong emotions.

Whatever the procedures the investigator follows, he uses the account to generalize from particulars. He translates the test responses as raw data into statements about aspects of personality. The two rational assumptions that guided Murray's initial work with TAT were that the attributes of the hero or main character in the story represent tendencies in the respondent's own personality and second, the characteristics of the hero's environment represent significant aspects of the respondent's own environment.

The stories of TAT are scored in the following manner:

(*i*) Hero of the story.
(*ii*) Needs and conflicts of the hero.
(*iii*) Unusual responses.
(*iv*) Deletion and addition in the pictures.
(*v*) Emotional expression.

Validity of TAT. How useful or valid is TAT as personality assessment procedure? There are two different views one held by clinical psychologists who are of the opinion that it has a high index of validity and it is a very useful instrument to diagnose mental abnormalities but psychometricians hold the view that validity of TAT is very low because there is a lack of standardized procedure and final normative data, low reliabilities, over-enthusiastic and under-critical acceptance of intuitive hunches about the supposed meanings of certain responses.

One problem with TAT is the difficulty of determining whether a need, or personality characteristic will be present in the subject's overt behaviour in real life situation as opposed to existing only on the fantasy or unconscious level.

Murstein (1963) summarized the research pertaining to the relationship between the judged aggressiveness of the heroes in TAT stories and over-aggressive behaviour of the subject. He concluded that generally the relationship was positive.

Evaluation of projective tests. 1. Projective tests can yield very useful data in the hands of trained and experienced workers. Guidance personnel should have special training to score projective tests.

2. The quantitative scores derived from projective tests often have low reliabilities when assessed by psychometric method. It is blamed by some psychologists that the usual methods of assessing personality are not applicable to projective instruments, for examples, split-half method is said to divide the cards in such a way as to obtain comparable halves.

3. Another problem with projective tests is of test construction. In general the stimulus materials used in projective tests have not been chosen with any thought toward ensuring that the various scoring categories would be adequately represented by the stimuli. It is often true as with TAT the scoring system was not developed until some years later the stimulus materials were selected.

4. Another problem involves standardization of instructions. Directions for the administration of the projective instruments are not standardized and thus the examiner can significantly influence the subject's responses. Even more vexing is the problem that subjects are permitted to give a varying number of responses of varying lengths. Variability in response length makes statistical comparison extremely difficult.

Croanback commenting upon projective tests wrote that assessment encounters trouble because it involved harzardous inferences, in which assessors considerably beyond known relationships between predictor and criterion variables makes judgement. There is little theoretical basis of expecting fantasy, as revealed by projective techniques, to be directly related to overt manifestations of personality such as academic work or work efficiency. Eysenck conducted a research on Rorschach and concluded that it has no validity for differential diagnosis, for understanding conflicts, or fantasies for psychotherapy, personality description of behaviour or evaluating or predicting the outcome of psychotherapy.

USES OF PERSONALITY TESTS IN GUIDANCE

Personality tests can play an important role in providing all types of guidance in schools. They, generally, serve two important purposes (*a*) they help to screen well adjusted and poorly adjusted students in home, school and society who are not otherwise easily detected through observation and interview. Such poorly adjusted students can be provided personal and educational guidance for their proper adjustment.

The second important purpose of personality tests is that they enable the individual to critically examine his personality characteristics. The individual may make improvement in his personality.

In the end it will not be out of place to mention that personality tests help in predicting future developmental trends in the personality of an individual.

ASSIGNMENTS

1. What do you mean by personality inventory? Describe any personality inventory.
2. Define interest. Describe strong Vocational Interest Blank and give in brief its uses in counselling.
3. Define Projection. Describe in detail either TAT or Rorschach Test.

REFERENCES

Mischel, W.: *Personality and Assessment* (1968).

Vernor, P.E.: *Personality Assessment* (London, Metheun, 1964).

Bell, J.E.: *Projective Techniques* (Longmans, Green and Co., NY. 1948).

Anderson, H.H. and Anderson, G.L. (ed.): *An Introduction to Projective Techniques* (Prentice Hall, NY. 1951).

Chapter 7

Appraisal of Students: Non-Test Techniques

The other techniques of appraisal of students for guidance purposes are called non-testing techniques in which a comprehensive assessment of the individuals' personality characteristics is made. It is a dynamic process that depends upon grasping the interaction of the individual's personal attributes with his environment. In the following section we will discuss non-testing techniques which provide qualitative assessment of an individual's personality in a comprehensive and reliable way.

1. OBSERVATION

Observation literally means looking outside oneself. It is the oldest and most commonly used analytical technique of assessing behaviour of an individual as well as groups of people. It is an important non-testing technique of appraisal which is being used in most of the studies. It provides useful data about an individual to confirm or refute tentative hypotheses. It is thought to be a reliable technique to evaluate the effectiveness of the steps that are taken to facilitate the individual's learning, development and adjustment, in home, school and society.

In spite of all this, observation is not magical, intuitive and "X-ray eye" that enables one to peer into the individual's inner-most self. Effective observation means grasping clearly, concisely and as completely as possible the essential behaviour of an individual within a given situation. Careful and systematically planned observation can supply meaning to a particular sample of behaviour which can be put into words for further clarification and study by other methods.

Human behaviour is complex and dynamic and constantly in the process of change. So assessment cannot be done quickly without effort. Therefore, observation may need to be carried on for a considerable time to determine how each of several small details fits into a larger design. It should be remembered that observation can play an important role in gathering reliable data if used by trained and experienced observer.

Limitations of Observation

1. It has been observed that unconscious biases in observation often occur because observers fail to admit their own feelings and limitations. They are unaware of fact that sometimes they unconsciously attribute their own behaviour tendencies to others.

2. Accurate observations demand an ability to evaluate objectively what is being perceived as well as an awareness of one's own feelings and behaviour. If the observer lacks objectivity to report behaviour as it really occurs, then his or her observations may be useless, since they tend to describe the observer more accurately than the individual being observed.

3. Adequate sampling of behaviour is another difficulty which the observers face.

4. Subjectivity of observed behaviour and inaccuracy in reporting are other problems that can destroy the usefulness of observation. Mental sets, interests and experiences often alter our perception of behaviour or situation because each of us tends to see the other's world as we have experienced our own.

Improving Observation

We can make our observations more reliable and objective if we follow the suggestions given below:

1. Since practice make a man perfect, observers should undergo rigorous practice in order to observe accurately and objectively. Practice in which two or more individual simultaneously observe the same behaviour and compare results will be most beneficial and reliable.

2. Decide in advance and precisely what is to be observed. The purpose and outlines of observation should be known to the observer in advance. It will be very useful if the objectives of observation are clearly specified and analysis of behavioural characteristics is made.

3. Observe only one pupil at a time. Few trained observers can observe with any degree of accuracy two or more pupils at one time.

4. In modern times, technical equipment like camera, tape recorder, films may be used to obtain a complete record of the multitudes of happenings that take place simultaneously.

5. Watch for significant behaviour and record your observation then and there. Do not leave it to memory. Better if shorthand is used.

6. Spread the observations over the school day. It will give a truer and more comprehensive picture of behaviour.

2. ANECDOTAL RECORDS

Observation may be of two types: unrecorded or recorded. Recorded observation is called anecdotes or anecdotal records. According to Cliford and Kenneth Hoyt "An anecdotal record consists of an objective description of pupil's behaviour in a particular environmental setting, an interpretation of the behaviour by the observer, writing the description, and a recommendation for future action based on the incident and its interpretation."

Jome E. Warters has defined anecdotal records as "a brief informal report by the teacher of an observation of a critical incident. The ancedotal record describes a sample of behaviour which may be positive or negative, but it must be the learner's behaviour that is described and not the teacher's interpretation of the behaviour". Briefly, then, we can say that an anecdote is a written account of a student's behaviour as observed in a specific situation.

Features of Anecdotal Record

All anecdotal records, generally, have the following features:

(a) The anecdotal records are objective, factual, recorded accounts observed behaviour.
(b) They are concise.
(c) They are continuous and cumulative.
(d) They are descriptive in nature.

Types of Anecdotal Records

Anecdotal records are of the following four types.

(a) The first type of anecdotal record contains only objective short description of the behaviour.
(b) The second type contains description and some comment.
(c) The third type contains description of behaviour with comments and interpretation.
(d) The fourth and the last type contains description of behaviour with comments, interpretation and recommendations for desirable future action.

Sample of Anecdotal Record

School ....

Name of pupil .... Class ....

Section ....

S. No.	Date	Place	Incident	Comments
1.				
2.				
3.				
4.				
5.				

OBSERVER

Characteristics of a Good Anecdotal Record

Following are the main characteristics of a good anecdotal record:

1. A good anecdotal record records the date and the situation in which the behaviour occurred with the name of the student.

2. It describes the behaviour of the subject, the reactions of others involved and the subject's reactions to these responses, in brief and informally.

3. It quotes what is said by the subject in the situation in an objective way.

4. It notes body postures, gestures, qualities of voice and emotional expression.

5. It describes the incidents sufficiently to present a behavioural moment in the life of the subject.

6. It reports both strengths and weaknesses accurately, objectively and dispassionately.

Advantages of Anecdotal Record

1. An anecdotal record describes the behaviour of an individual usually in diverse situations, and thus contributes to an understanding of the individual's personality characteristics.

2. An accurately recorded description of behaviour contributes more to the understanding of an individual than vague, unsupported or broad generalizations about the individual.

3. The anecdotal record encourages and stimulates teacher to become interested and informed about individuals. It may serve as a basis for pupil and parent conferences.

4. The anecdotal record supplements qualitative data and enriches interpretations of behaviour.

5. It provides very useful information to the guidance worker for counselling.

6. It provides useful data to pupil for self-appraisal.

7. Collection of anecdotal records may provide necessary information for validating various evaluative instruments.

8. The anecdotal record may be used by new members of the staff in acquainting themselves with the students. Moreover, teachers can help students better on the basis of this information.

9. The personal relationship between the pupil and the counsellor is improved by these records, for they show the pupil that the counsellor is acquainted with his problems.

10. The anecdotal record is very useful because it helps in the formation of better study habits.

11. The anecdotal record provides valuable information to the counsellor about the personality characteristics of individuals as manifested in different social situations.

Limitations of Anecdotal Record

1. An anecdotal record can be valuable only to the extent that the observational description is accurate and comprehensive.

2. The weakness of the anecdotal record lies in its subjective basis. Such records may create serious problems if access to them is granted to parents and students over eighteen years of age.

3. Typical incidents in the life of the subject are too likely to be observed and recorded. These incidents create impressions about the person out of proportion to their occurrence.

4. Recording and then preserving behavioural descriptions no longer typical of an individual may adversely influence other teachers toward the individual.

5. Anecdotal records take time to write and process. They place extra load and responsibility on teachers.

6. Most teachers tend to play up negative behaviour while perhaps overlooking the more positive factors of a pupil's conduct.

3. RATING SCALE

Rating scale is another important measure to evaluate the personality characteristics of individuals. This technique has been used since 1800 in navy, industry and Education to make comparative evaluation of individuals. The rating scale presents a list of descriptive words or phrases which are checked by the rater. The greatest use of rating scales in schools is to obtain personality ratings of students as regards their personality characteristics, for example, honesty, cooperativeness, self-reliance, leadership, industriousness and dependability etc.

Types of Rating Scales

Though there are many types of rating scales which are used by school teachers here we will describe only four types of rating scales.

1. *Numerical scales*. Generally, in numerical scales numbers are used to denote gradation and the meaning of each number is defined. For example, how would you rate cooperativeness? Numerical scales may be set up as 1. Ignore, 2. Rarely cooperative, 3. Sometimes cooperative, 4. Usually cooperative, 5. Highly cooperative.

2. *Descriptive scales*. In such types of scales, a series of phrases describing various degrees of the characteristic are rated. These phrases are, generally, arranged in order with instructions to the rater to rate the phrase that comes closest to describe the characteristic being considered. An example is given below.

How Would You Rate Industriousness?

(*i*) Indolent, expends little effort.
(*ii*) Frequently does not complete work.
(*iii*) Gets required work done.
(*iv*) Steady worker and occasionally does more work than required.
(*v*) Eager, usually does more than required.

3. *Paired comparisons*. The rater compares each person rated with respect to the trait to every other individual rated in general terms of 'equal', 'better' or 'worse'. Such a method tends to be somewhat cumbersome for large groups.

4. *Graphic rating scale*. The units or degrees are indicated on a continuum, with descriptive phrases placed appropriately under the lines, as for example.

Leadership

Actively avoids leadership	Prefers not to lead	Accepts leadership if asked	Occasionally prefers not to lead	Actively seeks out leader's role

Advantages of Rating Scales

1. They are a means to quantify observation of human characteristics. They may be conveniently used with children who cannot read and cannot evaluate their actions.

2. They are a means by which several observers can rate the same individual and can reach a certain agreement.

3. They are economic measures to evaluate a specific personality characteristic because they do not require any tool.

4. The rating scale is pragmatic in that although it may not be discovering, what is real in behaviour, it nevertheless does provide a ready means for judging the individual in different situations.

Limitations of Rating Scales

1. There are errors of personal bias of the rater, hellow-effect, central tendency and logical error etc. affect the rating.

2. It is very difficult to have experienced raters who can be objective and dispassionate in their ratings.

3. The last limitation of rating scale is to establish valid personality traits. It is not clear whether the situation controls and determines the behaviour or whether there do exist certain defineable personality traits which influence the environment.

4. CUMULATIVE RECORD

A cumulative record is a permanent record of progressive information about individual students, which gives complete and comprehensive information which will portray significant and representative characteristics of the individual over a period of years. It also shows trends and growth pattern in the individual. The information is used by the counsellor to help the student to make effective adjustment to school situations. The cumulative record may be useful in helping students understand themselves provided it has been prepared on scientific principles. It should be simple and well organized, containing only data which is reliable, valid and pertinent. A cumulative record is a permanent history of the individual consisting of relevant information on school achievement, health, test scores, attendance etc. and provides complete information of the growth of the individual.

Principles of Building Cumulative Record

1. It should be simple and well-organized containing data which are relevant, reliable and valid.

2. Advance planning should be made as regards the format of the cumulative record throughout the district to maintain uniformity to avoid repetition.

3. A degree of control should be exercised over some of the information in the records because of their confidential nature.

4. A cumulative record is maintained to help teachers, guidance workers, parents employers and other colleagues to understand pupils for improving instruction, employment, and to solve their problems. So it should be systematically maintained and carefully housed in an accessible place.

5. It should be maintained from primary to secondary stage.

Data to be kept in Cumulative Record

1. Personal data and family background information.
2. Medical and health information.
3. Date of school entry, school grade.
4. School-wise test results.
5. Transcripts from previous school.
6. Personality and behaviour trait ratings.
7. School activities.
8. Anecdotal record.
9. Autobiography written, class setting.

Uses of Cumulative Record

1. The cumulative record is used in guidance services to provide all types of counselling.
2. It gives a global picture of the individual.
3. Information can be used for in-service teacher training and for the school personnel.
4. Potentially harmful information concerning extreme behaviour should be carefully controlled and placed in the counsellor's confidential file.

(A sample of cumulative record has been given in the appendix).

5. INTERVIEW

Interview is an important technique of gathering information to evaluate the personality of an individual. Generally, we use interview in admitting students for different courses, training and for selecting candidates for various types of jobs.

In counselling the interview is usually predetermined. The interviewer very sympathetically asks questions and tries to gather complete information from the counsellee about his problems. In interview we emphasize two points — face-to-face interaction and collection of information for a definite purpose. The interviewer should be friendly, neutral and impartial in his reactions to the interviewer. The following suggestions will prove useful for guidance workers for conducting interview for the purpose of diagnosis and counselling.

1. A perfect rapport should be established before conducting the interview.
2. The interviewee should be made to feel at ease.
3. The interviewee should be assured that the information would be kept strictly confidential.
4. The interviewee should be encouraged to express his thoughts and feelings freely.
5. Avoid leading questions.
6. Listen without reacting emotionally.
7. Be courteous, patient and accepting.
8. Take notes or make a recording as unobtrusively as possible.
9. Attend not only to what is said but also to what is felt.
10. Adjust questions to the cultural and educational background of the interviewee.

Uses of Interview

1. *Collection of information.* The information gathering interview is used to collect information not easily and economically secured by other means. Individuals generally become very conscious to disclose and write their secrets but by an intelligently conducted interview secrets can be known.

2. *Supplementing.* The interview may be used to supplement information collected by other means.

3. *Verification.* The interview may be used to verify information collected by other means.

4. *Observation.* The interview may be used to interact face-to-face with the subject to know the background of overt behaviour. This gives an opportunity to study the mannerism, physical appearance and other non-verbal cues not obtained through other appraisal techniques.

Advantages of Interview

1. It is not only very useful in obtaining factual information but also information about attitudes, ambitions and other affective matters.

2. The fact-finding interview can be used to explore information needed for which previous data are not clear or for which underlying feelings need to be uncovered and understood.

3. The interview can be used to gather information about the future plans of the individual. his conflicts, tensions and frustration and problems of adjustment in home, school and society.

Limitations of Interview

No doubt the interview is an effective technique of gathering relevant information about an individual which may be of great use to provide guidance but it has certain limitations which are as follows:

1. *Subjectivity*. The interview is a subjective technique of collecting data which is influenced by biases and prejudices of the interviewer to a great extent.
2. *Training*. The success of an interview depends on the training and long experience of the individual.
3. *Time and money*. The use of this technique necessitates the expenditure of a lot of time and money.

6. AUTOBIOGRAPHY

The autobiography as a tool for understanding individuals was quite common several years ago but recently its use has fallen considerably. It reveals not only behaviour, but perhaps even more important personal attitudes and emotions behind the behaviour of an individual. The autobiography is a person's own written report of his or her life. As such it may provide insight into the 'inner person' the individual's experiences and knowledge about himself.

The autobiography may be divided into the broad categories-structured and non-structured. The structured autobiography is developed according to an outline or in response to specific questions. It may be more useful for work with pupils who are not very verbal. The unstructured autobiography is basically an account of the individual's life without regard to specific questions. It is freely written and does not force any answer or the inclusion of any particular topic.

Outline of the Structured Autobiography

1. Members of my family ....
2. My first year before school ....
3. My years in the elementary school ....
4. Places I have lived...
5. Trips I have made...

One of the limitations of autobiographv is that sometimes unauthorized people may read it. Many students have a natural reluctance to reveal to others, specially adults, what they think and feel and what they would like to be.

In spite of the above limitations, autobiography serves many useful purposes in guidance and counselling. It aids in the interpretation of facts obtained by objective methods and permits the clients to participate actively in the counselling process. It encourages the presentation of experiences too intimate to be revealed in a face-to-face situation by shy students. It is an easy method of recording information. It is invaluable in developing the longitudinal histories that are needed to supplement cross-sectional techniques. Finally, autobiographies can be obtained in groups with a minimum expenditure of the time of the counsellor.

7. CASE STUDY

The case study method is the oldest technique of summarizing data about an individual. It presents a comprehensive and cumulative picture of the total personality of an individual. The information employed in it is gathered from all available and reliable sources. Generally case studies conducted by school personnel are of pupils who have some learning difficulties or show some form of deviant behaviour. The main objective of the case study is to provide understanding of the child's total personality.

Definition

Before we give the definition of case study let us differentiate between two terms which are often confused by students, case history and case study.

According to Hayden, "a case history is a detailed itemization of data related to a given individual and usually covering a span of years. It includes all types of information from childhood to-date." A case study on the other hand is an analysis and writing-up of the data collected in a case history, including an analysis of the interrelationships in the data.

According to Hadley, "the case study contains all information gathered about an individual. It includes test data, interview data and the results of examination and observation. The main difference is that the case history includes only the past but the case study includes the past, the present and often even projects into the future."

Format of Case Study

Name School Date of Birth
Date Parents Siblings
Family
Physical history
Scholastic achievement
Aptitudes, interest, hobbies
General Appraisal
Recommendations.

Uses of Case Study

1. It is a reliable source of information.
2. It helps to summarize the large amount of information needed for the understanding of a particular pattern of behaviour.
3. It provides the counsellor information which makes it easy for him to understand the problem.

Advantages

1. It permits the understanding of an individual's problem in a global way. It gives more accurate evaluation of events.
2. It reduces the number of errors in diagnosis by ensuring that the counsellor thoroughly studies the facts the client presents.
3. It is very useful in isolating key factors in situations in which conflicting accounts confuse the case.
4. It can be very useful in predicting future behaviour.

Disadvantages

1. It is a time consuming technique.
2. In some cases the past information is very difficult to collect.
3. It may not always be sufficient as a basis for arriving at conclusions concerning the individual and thus for formulating a hypothesis.
4. The information in a complete case study goes beyond the scope of a school. Moreover, the school is not able to gather all the information needed for an adequate case study. After serious problems are diagnosed, the follow-up practices of schools are inadequate.

8. SOCIOMETRIC TECHNIQUES

Sociometry is a technique which measures the interpersonal preferences among the members of a group. The field of sociometry is very wide covering measurement techniques and methods and principles followed in making groups more effective in pursuing their goals and more personally satisfying to their members.

Purposes of Sociometric Techniques

1. Its main purpose is to study the structure of a group and discovering and analysing patterns of friendship within a group setting.

2. It may be used as a screening device to detect children whose behaviour in social settings is incongruent.

3. Sociometry can be used as a predictor for school dropouts. Sociometric technique may be used for the purpose of assessing school adjustment of students.

Advantages

The greatest advantage the sociometric technique is that it provides objective information about the functioning of individuals within their groups which is available from no other source. These techniques provide valuable information about how children are perceived by their peers, which supplement information gained from other sources. The knowledge gained helps to give a complete picture of the individual when it is viewed along with the information obtained from the other tools of the counsellor.

Limitations

1. Sociometry does not give a final answer to the problems. It merely gives counsellors indication or direction in their study of the individual.

2. Secondly, the whole body of sociometric theory has not been developed, not its postulates tested to the point that it is infallible. This is a relatively recently developed body of knowledge and a great deal more research is needed in order for it to fill its potential.

ASSIGNMENTS

1. Define observation. What are the advantages and limitations of observation ?
2. What are the uses of anecdotal records ?
3. Write notes on Rating Scales, Autobiography and Interview.
4. What is the importance of interview in the process of guidance?

REFERENCES

Traxler Arthur E.: *Techniques of Guidance* (Harper and Brothers Publisher NY., 1957),

Shertzer Bruce and Stone Shelley C.: *Fundamentals of Guidance* (3rd ed.) (Boston, Houghton Mifflin Co., 1976).

Aiken, Lewis R.: *Psychological Testing and Assessment* (Boston, Allyn and Bacon Co., 1976).

Chapter 8

The Informational Service

There have been many forces in 1970's and many more are expected in 1980's — which have been influencing and will continue to influence the career choice of an individual. Our country is a developing country which is rapidly heading towards technological development. Automation, consciousness about the rights and duties among the members of scheduled castes and tribes, increased use of technology, increasing specialization and the changing nature of jobs, complicate the task of decision-making and planning for an individual.

It becomes very essential for guidance services to provide maximum informational services to adolescents and adults which may help them to plan their future satisfactorily and may enable them to face the challenges of today and tomorrow in the society.

Students generally get information for their vocational planning from different sources. Some of the important sources are given below:

1. School Counsellors (in very few institutions).
2. Teachers.
3. Parents.
4. Close friends.
5. Newspapers.
6. Radio and Television.

NEED FOR INFORMATIONAL SERVICE

Why do we need informational services? The answer to this question is very simple i.e. we need these services to plan our future keeping into consideration the needs of the society, educational and vocational opportunities and our own abilities. The better informed the individual the more effectively can he plan his future career. The individuals, if they are informed of all job opportunities and qualifications needed, can plan their future more realistically and can be saved from tensions and frustrations. Following are the specific needs which informational services fulfil.

1. An informational service is fundamental if students are equipped with the basic knowledge needed to think through important personal issues-extent education, choice of occupation, maintenance of individuality with which they are confronted. Growing up in a complex and competitive world, going further in education, and undertaking responsibility impose great demands upon youth.

The goal of informational service is not only to import information but also to stimulate the students to appraise ideas critically, conditions and trends in order to derive personal meanings and implications for the present and the future. Becoming a functioning member of society requires that individuals seek out, recognize, and use all relevant information necessary for their development. The informational service appropriately designed and staffed will enable more individuals to realize their potentialities by becoming aware of them.

2. An informational service is fundamental if students are to become self-regulatory. Present-day youths are expected to assume more autonomous responsibility than their predecessors.

An essential condition of self-regulation is that individuals plan and know what they are doing as they do it and act correctly on the basis of known data. In other words, mature behaviour is based upon accurate information. It is stable but flexible. A good, active informational service must have (1) excellent current information, (2) the facilities for providing such information to students so that they can understand and use it. It is a fact that acquisition and use of environmental information is a growing feature of a developed individual. The individuals who possess information are able to conceive and pursue their purposes with intelligence.

3. An informational service is fundamental if students are to explore and become aware of the contingencies of stability and change that mark their development. People need to explore the positions which they are likely to occupy as they move through one or more possible pathways.

They must understand their choices and consequences and sequences of their choices. Lack of knowledge about self-development frequently leads to failure, rejection and defeat. Knowledge of self-development leads to positive images and encourages individuality.

Norris and her colleagues suggest the following objectives of the informational service for the secondary school. They are reproduced here.

(*a*) To evaluate one's self-perception of abilities and interests against actual occupational requirements.
(*b*) To identify and demonstrate job acquisition skills.

(*c*) To develop self-awareness and self-confidence in the individual's anticipated choice of occupational clusters.
(*d*) To demonstrate competency in skills basic to the chosen occupational cluster.
(*e*) To develop an appreciation for all occupations and the importance they have in society.
(*f*) To develop procedures to obtain needed abilities and experiences required in chosen occupational cluster.
(*g*) To develop in the individual the recognition of the relationship between personal values and the influence of others upon his occupational choice.
(*h*) To learn to lessen the discrepancy between where the learner perceives he is and where he wants to be.
(*i*) To learn to apply the decision-making process to the personal identification of tentative occupational choice.
(*j*) To become involved in the selection of an anticipated job or role based on individual attitudes, values, education and occupational awareness.
(*k*) To present understanding of broad fields of work.
(*l*) To develop means for aiding students to study intensively a few selected occupations or educational training facilities.
(*m*) To become fully acquainted with occupational and educational opportunities in the community.
(*n*) To develop tentative educational and occupational plans based upon through self-study.
(*o*) To present specific techniques to aid in meeting immediate needs confronting school leavers, such as obtaining employment, continuing an educational programme or establishing a home.

USES OF INFORMATION

Bear, and Rocher *et al*, on the basis of their survey have suggested the following uses of information:

1. *Assurance use.* Information may be used to assure the student of the appropriateness of his decisions.

2. *Evaluative use.* Informational service data may be used to check the accuracy and adequacy of students' knowledge and understanding of a decision.

3. *Exploratory use.* Information may be used to help students to explore and study all alternatives of possible choices or decisions.

4. *Readjustive use.* For students who have markedly inappropriate goals, information data may be used to help them reorient themselves to different levels of goals or objectives.

5. *Synthesis use.* Informational data may be related to other personal data such as tests. This encourages the synthesis of a pattern of behaviour.

6. *Information use.* Data are used to add to students' knowledge of occupation, choices, changing conditions, and the like.

7. *Verification use.* Informational materials may be used by students to verify and clarify choices, opportunities and decisions.

Barry and Woly have criticised the use of informational service on the following grounds. They have questioned the assumptions underlying the informational service that formal information is authentic and factual, that specific information about the work world is valid and applicable to future and that such information meets students' needs and produces important learning.

TYPES OF INFORMATION

There are three types of informations which are required for effective guidance services: educational information, vocational information, and personal-social information. Here we shall describe the three types of informations.

1. Educational Information

Norris and her colleagues have defined educational information as follows:

> Educational information is valid and usable data about all types of probable future educational or training opportunities and requirements, including curricular and co-curricular offerings, requirements for entrance, and condition and problems of student life.

The data collected will serve the following purposes for students, counsellors, teachers and parents:

1. School hours and regulations.
2. Available curricular offerings and subjects
3. Schools clubs and social activities.
4. Values of education.
5. High school units, credits.
6. Existing post-high school educational programmes.
7. The subjects required for entry into college or other post-high school educational institutions.

8. The costs of going to college or any type of post-high school training.
9. The education or training required for different occupations.
10. The characteristics of different colleges and other educational programmes.
11. Study habits and skills.
12. Scholarships, student loans, ways of financing post-high school education.
13. Accreditation of educational programmes.
14. Correspondence schools.
15. Student social life and cultural opportunities in post-high school educational programmes.

2. Occupational Information

Norris, Zeran, Hatch and Engelkes define occupational information as follows

> Occupational information is valid and usable data about positions, jobs and occupation including duties, requirements for entrance, conditions of work, rewards offered, advancement pattern existing and predicated supply of and demand for workers and sources for farther information.

Occupational information would include data relevant to the following items:

1. The labour force, size, composition, geographic factors, sex, race and age distribution, major industrial groups.
2. The occupational structure and major occupational groups.
3. Work trends including labour supply, population changes, public demands for goods, technological changes.
4. Labour legislation.
5. Sources of information for studying occupations.
6. Classifications of occupations.
7. Essential and critical occupations.
8. Duties of certain occupations, nature of work.
9. Qualifications necessary for employment in various occupations and methods of advancement.
10. Preparation needed for various occupations.
11. Methods of entering occupations and methods of advancement.
12. Earnings and other rewards of various occupations.
13. Conditions of work in various occupations,
14. Criteria for evaluating occupational information.

15. Typical places of employment.
16. Meaning of work.

3. Personal-Social Information

Norris and her colleagues cite the following example of personal social information as:

> Social information is valid and usable data about the opportunities and influences of the human and physical environment which bear on personal and inter-personal relations. It is the information about human beings which will help a student to understand himself better and to improve his relation with others. Included but not constituting the whole are such broad areas of information as understanding self and getting along with others as well as such specific areas — boy-girl relations, manners and etiquette, leisure time activities, personal appearance, social skills, home and family relationships, financial planning and healthful living.

The personal-social information service is concerned with the securing and the use of information which deals with such condtions and factors as the following:

1. Achieving self-insight and understanding.
2. Achieving mature relationships with the same and the opposite sex.
3. Understanding masculine and feminine roles.
4. Developing healthy personalities.
5. Understanding one's behaviour and one's characteristics.
6. Understanding how one differs from others and in what way one is like others.
7. Understanding others' behaviour and their needs.
8. Adjusting, accepting and understanding home conditions, family members and parental expectations.
9. Knowledge of dating practices, sex information, marriage responsibilities.
10. Physical and mental health development.
11. Personal appearance, manners and etiquette.
12. Social skills, financial planning and leisure time activities.

INFORMATIONAL MATERIAL

The informational materials may be secured from a variety of sources. The sources of published material are as follows·

(1) *Local sources.* Community serveys and job analysis published by industries, business, fraternal and civic clubs, professional organizations, chambers of commerce and the like.

(2) *State or regional sources.* The state employment division, departments of education, mental health organizations, state organizations, governmental agencies, manufacturing and industrial organizations.

(3) *National sources.* Such sources include commercial organizations, popular magazines, film distributors and the like. The following published materials are also excellent sources of information.

1. *Job descriptions.* These are the statements of the duties, qualifications and other important items relating to various jobs.
2. *Occupational descriptions.* These are statements which give complete and composite descriptions of occupations in a number of establishments.
3. *Occupational briefs.* These are brief statements about an occupation describing its history, wages, working conditions and methods of entry.
4. *Occupational monographs.* These are longer and more detailed statements.
5. *Books, bulletins.* Books, bulletins and personal social information appearing in books, bulletins and articles.
6. *College catalogues and educational directories.* Educational information needed by students can be found in the catalogues distributed by universities and colleges. They usually describe admission requirements, fees and tuition, scholarships, loans, degree and curricular faculty and staff etc.
7. Military service materials.
8. Visuals and auditory material.
9. Financial aid information.
10. College entrance examinations and scholarship examinations.
11. Study aids.
12. Personal and social information book, booklets and pamphlets.
13. Annotated materials.
14. Employment News weekly.

Evaluation of Informational Materials

Change is a marked characteristic of the world. There is a danger that informational materials may be out of date containing unreliable information and present misinformation. There are several statements of criteria against which informational materials may be compared and regularly evaluated for their authenticity.

Ohlsen has recommended the following criteria to evaluate the informational materials.

1. Who published the materials? Are they reputable publishers?
2. Who wrote the materials? Is the author qualified in this field?
3. What was the authors' motivation in preparing the material?
4. When was the material published? Is it still up-to-date?
5. Is the material well-written?
6. Is the material well-illustrated?

Innovative Informational Service

In the Western countries innovative methods and processes of providing career information have been developed and have been successfully used. We shall describe some of the important innovative methods.

1. *Computer.* Bohn and Super describe the following uses of computer in guidance:

(*a*) Educational and manpower development and planning.
(*b*) Extension of counselling by client access to data.
(*c*) Simulation of counsellors' function.
(*d*) Staff training and development.

Super also identified some major obstacles to the acceptance of computer-assisted vocational guidance systems.

(*a*) The counsellors' orientation and interest lie in working with people rather than using technology.

(*b*) The accuracy of the computer compared to the fallibility of the human counsellor was threatening.

(*c*) The threat of loss of control to counsellor because the machines set the pace of their work and directs problems to them.

(*d*) Computer support systems that simulate counselling life will become mechanistic.

2. *Simulation and gaming techniques*. The other innovative informational services are based on simulation and gaming.

(*A*) The life career game. Sarene S. Bookck developed it at John Hopkins University. According to him life career game involves both the education, labour and marriage markets. The major objective is to assist the youth to acquire a better understanding of these markets and to provide them with preplanning experiences believed beneficial to their future development. Teams (two to four) participate in game rounds during which they make decisions about the alternatives available to fictitious persons whom the teams represent. Each game round is used to depict a year in the life of the person represented. The game requires players to complete job application and college admission forms.

(*B*) *Occupational simulation kits*. Johnson and Myrick describe a simulation experience, making of life decision (MOLD) designed to help middle-school age students learn the decision-making process. The Local Schools and Local Markets are simulatory. All participants make their own decisions and give the probable consequences of the decisions for themselves rather than winning a point and being a winner or loser.

The participant takes the following six steps:

1. Completes a personal profile sheet describing his abilities and interests.

2. Becomes involved with small group procedures that assist him in self-appraisal.

3. Explores career fields and makes a tentative career choice based on his abilities and interests.

4. Plans on paper the next life, making decisions about his educations.

5. Receives feedback on his decisions such as grades earned in each course and whether or not he got a job for which he applied. The feedback takes into account such variables as ability, study time and change.

6. Uses the results and plans next year, for example, if a required course were failed it would have to be repeated for graduation, for tentative career plans could be changed and new directions pursued.

According to Johnson and Myrick, MOLD can be used to plan up to four years of a person's life. Each year takes approximately two hours to plan and receive probable consequences for the increased student's knowledge of educational and occupational information and that students enjoyed the simulation.

3. *Multimedia techniques*. Educational information services rendered by Vocational Information for Education and Work Project (VIEW) is an example of the simultaneous application of several types of media in disseminating information. It was developed by the San Diego Country Department of Education Project, which is a regional centre for collection, synthesis and dissemination of career information.

Phase 1: It is designed to assess the type of career information needed by students, counsellors and teachers to devise useful and appropriate methods for disseminating such information to local schools.

Phase 2: It was designed to develop an operational model system for 100,000 students in 70 school-districts located in San Diego Country.

The lable "VIEW" seems highly appropriate to the materials utilized because microfilm and electronic data processing cards are used for collecting, storing and disseminating information. This information is processed into an occupational brief entitled a "Viewsprint". The Viewsprint consists an aperture card (electronic data processing card) which contains a rectangular 35 M.M. microfilm frame. Completed cards can be prepared quickly by means of microfilm process or camera. The material used can be translated into any language. Schools using the system are equipped with microfilm reader-printer and reader and a flash filling aperture card storage tray.

VIEW is flexible, relatively easy to keep current, and intrinsically interesting information for students.

Principles of the Informational Service

1. The informational service is an essential part of the school guidance programme.

Adolescents in high and higher secondary schools face a number of problems in educational, vocational and personal life. All these problems need more and more information to enable them to make correct decisions regarding selection of courses and planning for future vocation. Informational services help more students to increase their chance of managing their future by providing meaningful data at strategic points.

2. The focus of the informational service is upon self-study and future trends and change.

Change is ever present. Trends in the labour force, shifts in the nature of occupations and new directions in educational programmes not only occur rapidly but are sometimes subtle and deceptive change cannot be held back.

The nature of informational service is also focused upon encouraging student self-study. One's personality and need structure are examined. Projections into different roles are encouraged. Educational, vocational and personal social information will be meaningful to students only as it is related to themselves and their environment.

3. Both group and individual techniques are used to convey informational data to students and to assist them in interpretation and using such data. Both approaches encourage self-analytical and

diagnostic methods. Both call for students to relate impression about themselves to environmental findings. The group approach builds upon inherent attitudinal and motivational factors.

4. The informational service is more than information giving. The informational service is not only confined in making available educational, vocational and personal social data but implies that attention should be given to individual's attitudes and emotional reactions to the information.

5. *Qualified personal to staff the informational service*. Service is essential. The quality of the staff will be reflected in the quality of service. Upgrading of staff and reassignment are responsibilities that guidance administrators must accept and carry out.

6. The informational service must contain provisions for its evaluation. Checks must be undertaken to determine how effective it is. Techniques used in the Service should be evaluated. Pupils', teachers' and counsellors' reactions to the service should be examined to determine if better ways can be found to achieve the objectives of the informational service.

ASSIGNMENTS

1. What are the needs of informational services?
2. What are the different kinds of informational services?
3. What are the sources of occupational information?

REFERENCES

Millar Carrol H.: *Guidance Services* (Harper and Row Publisher NY, 1965).

Super Donald E.: *Appraising Vocational Fitness* (Harper and Brothers NT).

Shertzer Bruce Stone Shelley C. *Fundamentals of Guidance* (IInd edition) (Houghton Miffin Co., 1976).

Chapter 9

The Study of Occupations

The study of occupations plays an important role in the process of vocational guidance. It is almost impossible to provide effective guidance without knowing the distinctive requirements of an occupation. Study of an occupation includes job description, job analysis, and worker analysis. A classification of occupations has been given in the appendix.

In this chapter we shall study these different processes.

JOB DESCRIPTION

A job description may be defined as a description of what the worker does and the conditions under which he does it. It generally includes the statement in detail of the actual activities which the worker carries out on the job. This statement should be comprehensive covering every significant feature of the work that the worker must do on the job.

The description of activities should not only be comprehensive; it should also be specific. It should describe the major activities of a job exactly and in detail.

The job description should also give an indication of the importance of each of the activities.

The report of the job description should be systematically organized in such a way as to facilitate identification of those activities and characteristic that represent critical requirement of the job as distinct from those that are relatively incidental features of it.

The following three indications of importance in a particular aspect of a job may be recognized:

(*a*) The proportion of his time which a worker devotes to an activity.

(*b*) The seriousness of the outcome if he fails to perform a particular activity satisfactorily.

(*c*) The likelihood of some workers' being unable to perform the particular activity satisfactorily.

A job description should indicate not only what the individual does but also the conditions under which he does it. It should provide an accurate picture of significant factors in the physical, social and psychological environment in which the work must be carried out.

One feature of job description is a statement and sometimes a description of the materials and equipment which the employee in the job needs. To acquaint the reader with job description, a proforma is given below:

A TYPICAL JOB DESCRIPTION PROFORMA

A. Identification Data:
   1. Job Title ....
   2. Department..
   3. No. of Employees with this job title ....
   4. Employees interviewed...
   5. Analyst...
   6. Date...

B. Job Summary (Brief outline):

C. Job Content:
   What?...
   How?..
   Why?...
   Skill?...

D. Minimum job requirements:
   1. Skill...
   2 Effort...
   3. Responsibility..
   4. Job conditions..

E. Comments and approval
   Supervision...
   Employee..
   Employee representative..
   Analyse...

The amount of details included in a job description will vary from job to job. Typically the lowest skilled jobs can be described very briefly and the same applies to jobs of the very highest level.

There are two opinions about job description. One opinion holds that job description should give minute details of the job making the boundaries of his job clear to the employee.

The second opinion holds that job description should be very general allowing the employee to interpret the job to the advantage of the organization. The philosophy underlying this approach is that the employee should not be constrained in his use of initiative by rigid job boundaries. In addition, the argument runs, an organization is a dynamic entity in which job requirements are always changing and consequently, any detailed list of duties becomes quickly obsolete.

JOB ANALYSIS

Job description gives only the general conditions under which the worker works on the job. It does not detail out the specific movements of the worker. For this purpose, job analysis is to be made. A knowledge of the job analysis is very essential for the guidance worker to provide vocational guidance to students.

Job analysis is very important and plays a vital role in the placement services and consequently increases the working efficiency of the workers, besides promoting smooth working relationships among the employees.

Job analysis is also important to select work position for the selected workers. It deals with the means of judging the job in relation to the personal characteristics of the individual. The problem of job analysis can be broken in the following aspects:

(*a*) Analysis of the job.
(*b*) Analysis of the worker.
(*c*) Matching the job with the characteristics of the worker.

Job analysis has been defined in different ways. It is a method that is meant to break down the job in terms of its requirements of the human abilities necessary for its performance and for constructing test.

According to Shartle, "job analysis refers to the procedures by which information is obtained concerning a specific job."

According to R.L. Thorndike, "Job refers to a category of employment in an organization rather than a specific single position. It may also refer to a programme of training preparatory to employment such as the training in medical school, engineering school, and the like."

The Scope of Job Analysis

A Job analysis yields the information such as the following:

A. Job name or title.
B. Present methods and procedures of work:
   1. Duties and tasks
   2. Materials that the workers use
   3. Tools and machines and description of the workplace
   4. Methods and procedures
   5. Responsibilities
   6. Supervision received and given
   7. Standard for output.
C. Physical conditions of the work environment:
   1. Place of work
   2. Conditions of illumination
   3. Conditions of ventilation
   4. Conditions of noise
   5. Hazards.

D. Relation of the job to other jobs:
   1. Helpers and assistants
   2. Co-workers
   3. Coordination work.

E. Conditions of employment:
   1. Methods of selection of employees
   2. Length and hours of work
   3. Amounts and methods of pay
   4. Permanency
   5. Opportunities for promotion
   6. Establishment of good relation between workers and management
   7. Defining and outlining promotional steps
   8. Investigating accidents
   9. Indicating faulty work procedure
   10. Maintaining, operating and adjusting machinery
   11. Time and motion studies
   12. Defining limits of authority
   13. Indicating cases of individual merit
   14. Indicating cause of personal failure
   15. Education and training
   16. Facilitating job placement
   17. Studies of health and fatigue
   18. Scientific guidance
   19. Determining jobs suitable for occupational therapy.

Lawshe and Satter gave four major uses of job analysis which are as follows:

1. The derivation of training content
2. The setting-up of personnel specifications
3. The improvement of job efficiency
4. The establishment of wage structure.

Purposes of Job and Worker Analysis

1. *The development of measures of job proficiency.* To develop adequate indices of success on a job it is necessary to take into account all the elements of the work involved. Without a systematic job analysis a complete picture of a job cannot be obtained. Any measures to evaluate the performance of employees should be worked out from a systematically determined set of job specifications.

2. *The functional organization of jobs.* In practically every government or industrial organization several persons deal with a given item, each processing it in relation to a given objective. For effective operation, work must go through definite channels, levels or points of

authority and responsibility be definitely established.

3. *Job evaluation*. The setting up of accurate wage scales for different jobs can be done through job description and specification. It is imperative to systematically obtain detailed specifications of the jobs to assign pay and allowance.

4. *The development of techniques for use in the selection of new employees, job-analysis*. Job analysis plays a vital role in the development of selective techniques. They are the best means of discovering the traits and personal characteristics leading to success or failure on the job. A good set of job and worker specifications are a valuable clue concerning the kinds of questions to be used in the employment interview and the application blank, and the types of tests that will probably be most effective in the selection of new employees.

5. *The development of more effective methods of work*. Methods and procedures of work are undergoing changes in the light of technological developments. To imnrove the effectiveness of methods of work one should begin by obtaining an adequate description of the current process of work. From an account of movements and operations involved in carrying out the work, points needing improvement may readily be detected.

6. *The development of more effective tool and equipment*. Job analysis is very important in the process of designing tools and equipment to improve the efficiency of the workers.

7. *The development of training programmes*. In organizing training programmes, generally two main problems are faced — what to teach and how to teach — job analysis and worker analysis provides relevant information on these two points. Such information will reveal the skills and knowledge, it will be necessary to develop in the training programmes. With information at hand on the nature of the different aspects of the work, training for the job can be arranged in optional instructional order according to their difficulty and the logical relationship existing between them.

Methods of Collecting Job Analysis Information

Industrial psychologists have evolved several procedures to analyse the components of a job. Following are some of the procedures which are used in job analysis:.

(1) *Observation method*. In this method, the job analyst observes the worker performing the job and collects the relevant information about the job in a proforma. A sample of a proforma is given below:

(*i*) Job-name or title
(*ii*) Classification title
(*iii*) Industry, plant, department, section

(iv) Number employed
(v) Hires, quits, job absences
(vi) Work performed
(vii) Supervision given and received
(viii) Level of difficulty (responsibility, knowledge, initiative, mental alertness and judgement)
(ix) Pay rate
(x) Hours and shifts
(xi) Output standards
(xii) Job combination
(xiii) Job relationship
(xiv) Machine tools, equipment, material used
(xv) Working conditions
(xvi) Social environment
(xvii) Physical demands
(xviii) Worker characteristics (dexterity, accuracy, experience and education required)
(xix) Previous experience required
(xx) Training required
(xxi) Selection method.

(2) *Job performance method*. In this method, the job analyst himself performs the operation involved in the job and prepares a detailed report on the basis of an analysis of his own activities. The actual participation in the job by the personnel psychologist provides him with the first hand information regarding the various operations and problems of the job.

(3) *Interview method*. In this method, the job analyst holds an interview with the worker and gathers necessary information about job. It is based on the assumption that the person who should know about the job is the person doing it.

(4) *Audio-visual method*. In this method photographic aids such as stills, TV and motion pictures are used to gather necessary information about the job. Computers are also used to make job analysis.

(5) *Questionnaire*. The use of questionnaire can be made to collect information about a job and the operations involved in it. The adequacy of this method depends on the cooperation of the workers and framing of the questions.

(6) *Use of materials of work and published manuals, and bulletins etc*. The job analyst can make use of the knowledge of tools, machines, printed forms and equipment etc. to analyse the components of a job. Previous studies and published information on the job may be helpful as tentative or printed job description.

(7) *Statistical analysis of test validities*. Statistical analysis of test validities can provide important information on various factors in a

job by using the technique of factor analysis. Analysis of validity data is also valuable in clarifying aspects of the job performance.

Techniques in Job Analysis

Though some of the information for job analysis can be obtained by various methods described above, a valid and complete account of duties the employee are expected to perform and methods used in carrying them out cannot be obtained without using special techniques for job analysis. In the following paragraph we will describe two important techniques.

1. The Analysis of Movements

Movements on a job may be of two types: slow and fast. Slow movements can be easily studied through observation of the employee on the job but rapid movements cannot be analysed without using special techniques because by the time the first movement is written down the worker would have completed that unit of work and be along on another.

To study rapid movements, a system of shorthand symbols is used by the analyst to jot down the movements of the worker in action.

Gilbreth developed a system of symbols and attempted to classify all movements employed in industrial work in 17 basic types, providing a symbol for each. These elements of movements are called therblings. Some out of the 17 therblings are given below.

S. No.	Symbol	Therbling
1.		Select
2.		Grasp
3.		Use
4.		Inspect
5.		Assemble
6.		Disassemble
7.		Position

The analysis of a total sequence of acts into its constituent movements is called Motion Study. Time and motion analysis shows not only which movements are being employed but also the time required to perform each of them.

Sometimes the analyst may use motion pictures for recording fast movements of the worker as he carries on his activities. When the film is projected at slow motion, it is a simple task to note the different movement and to jot down the corresponding therblings.

Another way of recording the hand movements of the worker on the job is by means of cyclegraph. A small electric light is attached to the hands or other moving parts of the worker and a photographic plate or film is exposed while he works. A total picture of the movements is obtained by this method. In addition we can use charts, simocharts, chronocyclegraphs for the study of operations at job-place.

2. The Analysis of Duties, Situations and Procedures

The nature of work involved in non-manual jobs makes it impossible to set down specific techniques that can be applied to all of them. With such jobs the analyst is interested in knowing the types of situations that confront the worker and the procedures he utilizes in dealing with these situations. The problem is to obtain complete and valid information. When dealing with positions in a highly organized occupation, it is relatively an easy task to obtain satisfactory information and to make sure that it is complete, since the lines of work are already laid down in definite channels, sequences and groupings.

The procedure of noting down functions as they are actually performed may be very revealing. Many unsuspected aspects of a job may be uncovered.

WORKER ANALYSIS

Worker analysis is as important as job analysis for two important reasons, namely, the determination of minimum requirements for the job and the determination of relative importance of various abilities, traits and other worker characteristics for the performance of jobs, Implicit in the first aim are two presumptions. First, it is presumed that there is a well-established point on the continuum of job proficiency below which individuals are clearly inadequate and above which they are clearly adequate. Second, it is presumed that for a worker characteristic with a minimum requirement greater than zero, all individuals, or at least most who fall below this minimum also will fall below the critical point in job proficiency, while all, or at least most, who possess more than the minimum amount of the characteristics in job performance is more reasonable point of view.

Estimated vs. Measured Worker Characteristics

There are two different ways of securing information about worker characteristics. First, a given job may be described in terms of the skills, abilities and other characteristics which the worker must have in order to perform the job successfully. This type of description of characteristics deemed necessary in the worker are estimated from the analyst's knowledge of the nature of the work or knowledge possessed by others.

Job specification or description or similar information obtained from unsystematic job studies form the basis of estimated worker characteristics.

The second type of description may be said to be concerned with measured worker characteristics in which objective description of the personal characteristics of individuals is made with the help of tests.

Both of these ways for describing worker requirement have certain advantages and limitations which will now be described.

The approach of worker estimated characteristics: *General versus specific meanings in worker requirements.* In the earlier studies of the analysis of worker characteristics only those traits, abilities, skills and other characteristics were listed which in the opinion of the analysts were important in the performance of the job. Such lists usually suffered from vague and abstract terms that rendered them useless for any precise evaluation. This deficiency has been remedied in modern approaches by using specific traits with more exact definitive descriptions and exemplifying them with samples of actual behaviour.

2. *Relating job requirements to specific job behaviour.* The important consideration for achieving specificity and hence meaningfulness, of worker requirements is to relate the requirements to specific behaviour on the job. For this purpose interviews are held with the workers.

3. *Critical requirement approach.* It has been studied by researchers that there are some kinds of behaviour that are especially critical in the sense that they are much more likely to lead to administrative action or judgements concerning the worker than is the goodness or poorness which characterizes his performance of the prescribed duties and responsibilities. Therefore, it is suggested that in doing worker analysis special attention should be given to the discovery of critical job behaviour of workers.

4. *Preparing a list of critical incidents.* Critical incidents that occur in connection with an individual's job can be uncovered by interviewing the individual, his supervisors, his associates or his subordinates. Questions to elicit relevant information regarding effective and ineffective behaviour are framed.

Techniques in Estimated Worker Analysis

A number of different techniques for worker analysis that yield quantitative estimations of the importance of various worker characteristics have been developed. The earliest systematic work was done by Viteles who prepared a list of skills, abilities and traits that might be important on any job and a scale on which the analyst could rate the degree of importance of each of these characteristics for the job in question. Viteles carefully defined the terms used in worker analysis. A sample of worker analysis schedule is given as follows:

WORKER ANALYSIS SCHEDULE
Job—Stenographer

S. No.	Characteristics	Amount of characteristics 0	1	2	3
1.	Strength				
2.	Dexterity of fingers				
3.	Dexterity of hands				
4.	Dexterity of foot and leg				
5.	Eye-hand coordination				
6.	Foot-eye-hand coordination				
7.	Perception of form, shape & size				
8.	Perception of speed of moving object				
9.	Keenness of vision				
10.	Colour discrimination				
11.	Sense of smell				
12.	Keenness of hearing				
13.	Sense of taste				
14.	Touch discrimination				
15.	Muscular discrimination				
16.	Memory				
17.	Numerical facility				
18.	Understanding of mechanical device				
19.	Division of attention				
20.	Oral expression				
21.	Written expression				
22.	Ability to make decision				
23.	Ability to plan				
24.	Initiative				
25.	Emotional stability				
26.	Ability to meet and deal with people				

DESCRIPTION OF SCALE VALUES

3 Very important
2 Moderately
1 Low importance
0 Not required.

Criteria for the Evaluation of Techniques of Estimated Worker Analysis

Procedures for estimated worker analysis differ greatly in the precision with which they evaluate worker characteristics. It is, therefore, necessary to have standards by which any technique can be assessed. Three important standards are the reliability, validity and independence of ratings.

Problems and Techniques in the Study of Measured Worker Characteristics

Objective test techniques. In the last seventy years psychological tests have been devised in almost all areas to assess objectively the human characteristics. By testing workers on a given job with standard psychological tests information could be obtained which would give indications of the relative importance of various abilities and traits. A job profile could be constructed from objective measurements.

No doubt the measured worker characteristics analysis technique is more objective and reliable but it is extremely expensive and time consuming.

Matching the Job Characteristics with Worker Characteristics

After making job analysis and the analysis of worker characteristics, the next step for guidance worker is to match both of them. The analysis is made with the aims of selecting certain individuals from among the most suitable applicants for a job. There are several difficulties which the guidance personnel face in matching the job with individual characteristics.

1. Job profiles are not available.
2. Job profile preparation is time consuming.
3. Testing material is not available.
4. *Worker resistance*. Sometimes workers resist the guidance of the guidance worker to accept a particular job for which their characteristics match.

ASSIGNMENT

1. Define job analysis. Describe the uses of job analysis.
2. What are the various methods of job analysis? Describe one of them.
3. Write short notes on the following:.
   (a) Job specification.
   (b) Job evaluation.
   (c) Worker analysis, and
   (d) Job description.

REFERENCES

Ghiselli Edwin E et al.: *Personnel and Industrial Psychology* (McGraw Hill Book Co. NY, 1955).

Blum Milton L.: *Industrial Psychology and its Social Foundations* (Harper Aim Row, NY, 1956).

Karan Harry W.: *Readings in Industrial Psychology and Business Psychology* (McGraw Hill Book Co. NY, 1952).

Husband T.M.: *Work Analysis and Pay Structures* (McGraw Hill Book Co. UK., 1976).

Currie R.M. *Work Study* (Pitman Pvt. Ltd., London, 1977)..

PART - III

Chapter 10

Fundamentals of Counselling

Counselling is the heart of guidance programme. Without it, guidance is incomplete. It helps students to resolve their educational as well as personal and vocational problems. It makes an effective use of the information collected about the individual or the group to provide insight into the problems for a better guidance programme. It may be viewed as an applied art that seeks deliberately to change the behaviour of an individual. This chapter is an attempt to present the basic concepts in counselling to acquaint the readers with the fundamentals of it.

DEFINITION

Counselling is a developing science whose terms and concepts have not yet been standardized. Concepts are interpreted and defined in several ways according to the mental attitude of the researchers.

Here we give some definitions of the concept of counselling as viewed by several researchers.

According to Webster's Dictionary, counselling is defined as, "counselling; mental interchange of opinions; deliberating together."

Strang defines counselling as, "face-to-face relationship in which growth takes place in the counsellor as well as the counsellee."

Traxier defines counselling as "the application of the personal resources of the school or other institutions to the solution of the problems of individuals."

According to Warner, "Counselling is a personal and dynamic relationship between two individuals — an older, more experienced and wiser, and a younger, less experienced and less wise. The latter has a problem for which he seeks the help of the former. The two work together so that the problem may be more clearly defined and the counsellee may be helped to self-determined solution."

Wiley and Andrew have given a comprehensive definition: "Counselling is a mental learning process. It involves two individuals — one seeking help and the other a professionally trained person who helps the first to orient and direct himself towards a goal which leads to his maximum development and growth in his environment."

E.L. Tolbert in his book *Introduction to Counselling* defined counselling as " . . . a personal, face-to-face relationship between two people, in which the counsellor, by means of the relationship and his special competencies, provides a learning situation in which the counsellee, a normal sort of person, is helped to know himself and his present and possible future situations so that he can make use of his characteristics and potentialities in a way that is both satisfying to himself and beneficial to society and furture can learn how to solve future problems and meet future needs."

We may summarize that counselling is a relationship between a professionally trained, competent counsellor and an individual seeking help in gaining greater self-understanding and improved decision-making and behaviour change skills for problem resolution and/or developmental growth.

The main objectives of counselling are to enhance personal development, to resolve the conflicts, the psychological growth toward maturity of its clients and to help them in the process of social adjustment by developing necessary social skills to meet the challenges of modern life.

Elements of Counselling

There are three distinct elements in the process of counselling which are as follows:

1. First, counselling involves two persons.
2. Second, the specific objective of counselling is to help and assist the counsellee to solve his problems independently.
3. And thirdly, counselling is a professional task and must be performed by professionally trained persons.

William, Cottle, a famous worker in the field of counselling, has differentiated five elements in the process of counselling. These are:

1. *Rapport*. The first element in rapport which involves establishing relationship of mutual respect between the two individuals, the counsellor and the counsellee.
2. *Communication*. Communication between the counsellor and the counsellee should be free and frank, without inhibition. Efforts should be made to increase the effectiveness of communication by using different devices such as depth interview.
3. *Qualification*. The counsellor should be a professionally qualified person with some practical experience and liking for people. This will enable him to understand the problems more adequately.
4. *Confidence*. The fourth element is directly related with the counsellee who starts with confusion and feelings of bewilderment and gradually progresses towards his goal of understanding his problems. In the process he undergoes a change in his attitudes and acquires insight into his problems. By and by the counsellee

gains confidence to tackle his problems and increases his capacity of adjustment to his environment.

5. *Counselling interview*. The last element is the couselling interview which is comprehensively planned by the counsellor to lead the counsellee to the desired goal. The counsellor tried to understand the problems of the counsellee and attempts to find out some remedy.

Mathewson in his book *Guidance Policy and Practices* sums up the basic elements which appear consistently in all counselliiig situations as follows:

1. Personal communication between the client and the counsellor is a professionally controlled or guided situation.
2. Appraisal and understanding of guided situation appraisal and understanding of the individual and of environmental aspects of the problem situation and its possible outcomes.
3. Evaluation and correlation of pertinent personal and non-personal factors in the problem situation.
4. Adjustive, orientational or developmental aid to the individual through conveyance of information; interpretation of data; provisions of the means or facility, for self-appraisal and clarification of motives and values; reference to environmental opportunity of other modes of assistance.

Comparison between Teaching and Counselling

Teaching	Counselling
1. Teaching is done in groups.	Counselling is one-to-one relationship, in which each individual is treated as unique.
2. Teaching centres round intellectual and academic areas.	Counselling centres round the adjustment areas.
3. Teaching uses lectures, audiovisual aids, excursions to present the subject matter effectively.	The Counsellor uses varied techniques such as diagnostic tools, occupational information, and tests to understand the psychological make-up of the individual.
4. Interview is never used as a technique in teaching.	Interview is the most frequently used basic technique here.
5. The information is related to teaching.	The information is related not to teaching but to other fields like occupations.

Counselling and Psychotherapy

Counselling and Psychotherapy have been used in the literature interchangeably because it is difficult to draw a clear line of demarcation between them, There is overlapping in the concepts and theories of both. Another difficulty to differentiate between counselliing and psychotherapy is that of the definitions offered by various authors. The definitions of counselling would in many cases by acceptable as definitions of psychotherapy, and vice versa.

All agree that counselling and psychotherapy involve a special kind of relationship between a person who asks for help with a psychological problem and a person who is trained to provide that help. The nature of the relationship is essentially the same and the techniques used are also the same. There is difference in the objectives however. The objectives of counselling are as defined by the Committee on Definition, Division of Counselling Psychology of the American Psychological Association "to help individuals toward overcoming obstacles to their personal growth wherever these may be encountered and toward achieving optimum development of their personal resources."

Now let us examine one of the most recent definitions of psychotherapy as advanced by Stephen J. Morse and Robert I. Watson Junior in their recent book *Psychotherapies* (1977). They define psychotherapy as "special form of interaction between two individuals, in which the patient initiates the interaction by asking psychological helps and in which are therapist structures the interaction using psychological principles to aid the patient in gaining more control over his or her life through changing thoughts, feelings and actions. The therapist's role is to help the patient learn new behaviour. The techniques for facilitating this learning process are quite different from one form of therapy to another, but all therapy is essentially a learning experience for the patient."

Tyler, attempting to distinguish counselling from psychotherapy, states that it is not the job of the counsellor, "to remove physical and mental handicaps or to get rid of limitations". He further says that the activity of the therapist "is aimed essentially at change in developmental structures rather than at fulfilment." While counselling does not attempt to repair damage done to the client in the past, to stimulate inadequate development of some stunted aspect of his personality but is the process of "helping a -person to gain a clear sense of personal identity alongwith acceptance of limitations.

The distinctions that are being made by many including Tyler as well as Vence and Volsky, well-known workers in the field, are as follows:

1. Counselling applies to work with so-called normal individuals whose problems are related to the development of their potential while psychotherapy refers to work with individuals who are deficient in some respect.

2. A second distinction is that if the setting is medical what is done is called psychotherapy while if the setting is non-medical, it is called counselling.

3. A further distinction is made in terms of the nature or content of the problem that the client brings to the counsellor. The so-called reality-oriented problems such as educational and vocational problems, and choices have been considered to be the province of counselling while problems that are inherent in the personality of the individuals are the province of psychotherapy. Here for the convenience of understanding, a comparison is given between counselling and psychotherapy.

TYPES OF COUNSELLING

Generally counselling is classified into the following four types:

Comparison between Counselling and Psychotherapy

	Counselling	Psychotherapy
1.	It is concerned with normal anxieties.	It is mostly concerned with neurotic anxieties.
2.	It operates in the educational set-up.	It operates in a medical set-up.
3.	It uses tools and techniques that can be used in schools.	It uses tools that can be used in any situation.
4.	Psychology is not the only basis for studying behaviour.	Psychology is the only basis for studying behaviour.
5.	Socio-economic status of the individual is considered important.	Socio-economic status of the individual is not considered important.
6.	It is broader rather than deeper in scope.	It is deeper rather than broader in scope.

1. *Crisis counselling.* Brammer (1973) states: "Crisis is a state of disorganization in which the individual faces frustration to important life goals or profound disruption of his life cycle and methods of coping with the stress..."

It is our common experience that almost all individuals, at some time in their lives, have witnessed or experienced crisis situations such as loss of loved one, inability to cope with life situation, family crisis, drought, unemployment, failure in examination and so on. When a crisis becomes serious and prevents the individual from consciously controlling himself then the individual seeks help and treatment from qualified persons.

The counsellor needs to accept the situation and maintain personal poise and self-assuredness. This type of confidence in the counsellor can help to reduce anxiety on the part of the client at that time, through reassurance and expression of hope to the client. The counsellor can deal with this immediate situation and then in future aid the client in a developmental sense to deal with crisis situation in his life.

2. *Facilitative counselling*. Ailan Hoffman *et al*, describe facilitative counselling as "the process of helping the client to clarify a concern, then through self-understanding and acceptance to devise a plan of action to work on the concern, and finally to act on it in a self-responsible manner." This type of counselling is also called remedial or adjustive which means to correct a fault or an undesirable behaviour of the client. Remedial counselling is often interpreted as aiding an individual to progress from deficient stage to a functional one.

Facilitative counselling is mainly concerned with choosing academic options, planning a career, getting along with family members, fellow workers or classmates, and identifying individual strenghts, interests and aptitudes. Regardless of the counselling approach professionally trained and competent counsellors can help individuals to gain self-understanding and change their behaviour through the framework of facilitative counselling.

3. *Preventive counselling*. Preventive counselling differs from other types of counselling in that it is primarily programmatic as well as related to a specific concern. Such counselling could involve, for example, an elementary school sex education programme with the purpose of alleviating future anxieties about sexuality and sex relationship. The students are better prepared to handle problems when they actually appear in their lines.

Carkhuff and Friel (1974) mentioned another programmatic counselling for self-awareness which related to future career choices and career preparation.

In preventive counselling, the effort of the counsellor is to present information to a group or an individual to prevent the occurrence of problems in future.

4. *Developmental counselling*. Developmental counselling is an ongoing process that occurs throughout an individual's lifespan. This type of counselling focuses on aiding clients in achieving positive personal growth at any stage of their lives. Developmental counselling aims at helping the individual to become aware of himself and the ways in which he is reacting to the behavioural influences in his environment. It further helps him to establish some personal meaning for his behaviour and to develop and clarify a set of goals and values for future behaviour. Out of such awareness and understanding of his past learning history and his environment, an individual is better able to identify those environmental influences that will best facilitate the kind of future

development that is goal-oriented for him. Developmental counselling which can be contrasted with adjustment or crisis counselling is not always problem-oriented in terms of assuming that the child has some difficult problems. Instead the goals are the development and methods of utilizing one's capacity. Developmental counselling truly focuses on helping the individual.

NATURE OF PROBLEMS

1. *The problem is deviant behaviour*. "Ram is always causing trouble in my class." On the parents report that their son is aggressive. In these cases the goal of counselling is set for others than the clients.

2. *The problem is expressed as feeling*. The clients usually present their problems in the form of descriptions of feelings; problems are not specifically defined and analysed.

3. *The problem is the absence of a specific goal*. Many people are unable to make up their minds as regards their goal. Sometimes we see that the problems which clients report have no goals. People troubled by the absence of a goal may be encouraged to explore how other people have solved their particular problem.

4. *The problem is a choice conflict*. Another problem that is sometimes difficult to translate into behavioural objectives is a choice conflict between two desirable alternatives.

The problem is that the desired behaviour is undesirable. There are rare circumstances a client may desire to achieve goals that the counsellor is unwilling to help him achieve. Generally, the following categories of problems are handled by counsellor.

Problems Handled by Counsellors

(A) *Behavioural deficits*. Children and adults develop a number of behavioural deficits which are corrected through counselling. The common deficits are shyness, delinquency, depression, sexual dysfunction and speech defects, etc.

(B) *Behavioural excesses*. Excess smoking, gambling, alcoholism, drug addiction, temper outbursts, and physical aggression.

(C) *Inappropriate behaviour*. Child misbehaviour, compulsive fire setting, enuresis, encopresis, exhibitionism and homosexuality.

(D) *Fear and anxieties*. Treatment of phobias, test-anxiety, school phobia, fear of social rejection and generalized anxiety.

(E) *Physical problems*. Insomnia, tension, headaches, and physical conditioning.

(F) *Promoting wise decision-making*. One of the important goals of counselling is to prevent the occurrence of maladjustment by giving proper counselling and training to family members, teachers and administrators.

Brief History

Human beings have been communicating with one another from time immemorial. However, it is very difficult to say exactly when this communication became counselling. Shartzor and Stone (1974) indicate that if counselling's traditional definition of giving of advice is accepted, then the point at which man first sought and received verbal aid or instruction from another marked the advent of counselling. Belkin (1975) traced the history of counselling to Greek philosophers such as Plato and Aristotle who formulated the basic concepts of counselling. The British philosophers of 17th and 18th centuries were also concerned with counselling in that they wrote and discussed how one might perceive and relate to individuals and society. The author of the present book feels that formalized counselling was present in ancient India. There is sufficient evidence in Sanskrit literature of different types of counselling. There are several examples when kings and rajas, in times of crisis, sought the counsel of old rishis and visited their hermitages for the solution of their problems. Afterwards counsellors were appointed in the courts to counsel the monarchs in the time of crisis.

Significant Influences

Some of the important influences which affected the development of formalized counselling in the West in the last 60 years are as follows.

One of the most significant influences has been the belief in the dignity and worth of each individual. There has been increasing desire in the individuals to control their own destiny. Following are the specific reasons which have fostered the rise of formalized counselling in the USA and other advanced countries of the world.

1. *Social conditions*. Socially, people have been moving from rural to urban settings.

2. *Migration*. People have been migrating in a great number from one location to another.

3. People are becoming more and more conscious of social inequities. Leweis (1970) indicates that life and its related problems become much more complex in the area of social relationship. People have lost close relationships. Family is disintegrating and close neighbourhood friendship is dying. The individual has turned increasingly to educators, social workers and psychologists for their aid.

4. Economically, the world has seen increased industrialization and diversification. Unemployment has created severe problems for individuals and societies.

5. International tensions and conflicts have brought uncertainty and grief to our citizens.

6. Scientifically, inhabitants of our earth have made tremendous progress in such areas as transportation, medicine, communication,

and agriculture. Psychological testing movement during the last two centuries also contributed in the development of counselling. Important dates in the history are given below:

1870: Establishment of first psychological experimental laboratory in Germany.
1890: Sigmund Freud began the use of psychoanalysis in treating emotional illness.
1895: George Merril established the first systematic vocational guidance programme.
1895: A psychological counselling clinic was established.
1905: Binet and Simon devised a standardized general intelligence test.
1908: Frank-Parson encouraged work in vocational guidance.
1909: Clifford Bears wrote, "A Mind That Found Itself."
1913: NGVA was founded.
1939: E.G. Willianson published "How to Counsel Students."
1942: Carl Rogers published, "Counsellings and Psychotherapy."
1951: The American Personnel and Guidance Association was founded.
1953: B.F. Skinner published, "Science and Human Behaviour."
1954: The Journal of Counselling Psychology was published.
1962: G. Gilbert Wrenn published "The Counsellor in a Changing World."
1964: "Toward Effective Counselling and Psychotherapy" was published by Charles True.
1969: John Krumboltz *et al* edited "Counselling: Cases and Techniques".
1973: Robert Carkhuff published, "The Art of Helping."
1978: John J. Pietrofesa *et al* published "Counselling: Theory, Research and Practice."

ASSIGNMENTS

1. Define counselling and give in brief the main elements of the process of counselling.
2. What are the different types of counselling? Describe them briefly.
3. Trace the history of counselling.

REFERENCES

Pietrofesa, John J.: *Counselling: Theory, Research and Practice,* (Rand Me Naily Du Series Chicago, 1978).

Patterson, C.H.: *Theories of Counselling and Psychotherapy.* (Harper and Row, NY, 1973).

Chapter 11
Group Counselling

Man is a social animal. He is born in a particular social environment. The personality of the child is shaped by the members of the group he associates with. It is a universal fact that the tendency to form small group is at its peak in adolescence. The likes, dislikes and other behaviour of an adolescent are patterned by the members of his group.

Guidance workers and counsellors have been using the knowledge of small group dynamics to provide proper guidance and counselling for the last several decades. Group counselling is a new approach for the school counsellor. It gives him a new avenue of approach but it also demands of him a new set of skills and a new kind of understanding. Group counselling utilizes the dynamic phenomena of group interaction, group cohesion, patterns of leadership and group leadership.

GROUP COUNSELLING DEFINED

Group counselling has been defined in different ways. C.G. Kemp in his book, *Foundation of Counselling*, says: "Persons in all walks of life sense the need for — means of gaining new understanding regarding the significance and purpose of life itself. Hence the interest and increase in the use of what is now known as group counselling."

Stone defines group counselling "as a process in which one counsellor is involved in a relationship with a number of counsellees at the same time." The number of counsellees may vary from four to eight, but six has been recommended as the optimum number of counsellees by most of the workers in the field.

Mahler has defined group counselling as a social experience that deals with developmental problems and attitudes of individuals. In his words, it is "The process of using group interaction to facilitate deeper self-understanding and self-acceptance. There is a need for a climate of mutual respect and acceptance so that individuals can loosen their defenses sufficiently to explore both the meaning of behaviour and new ways of behaving. The concerns and problems encountered are centered in the pathological blocks and distortions of reality."

According to Cohn (1964) "Group counselling is a dynamic, interpersonal process involving the use of counselling techniques with normal individuals. The members of the group mutually explore, with the counsellor, their problems and feelings in an attempt to modify their attitudes and values so that they are better able to deal with their developmental and educational situations. The counselling group is composed of six to ten peers working with a professionally trained counsellor in a non-medical setting."

Robert W. Hyes says: "Group counselling is the counselling process which focuses on the potentially therapeutic aspects of group cohesion, group interaction, the development of learner behaviour, and group structure, allowing members, in conjunction with a trained counsellor, to explore their conscious thoughts and behaviours in order to reach greater self-understanding as a basis for developing more appropriate personal, social, vocational and educational behaviour patterns."

Goldman defines group counselling as "a meeting of counsellor with a group whose members exhibit various anxieties, concerns and/or needs. It is distinguished from teaching by the fact that the latter usually deals with academic content which comes from outside the group and which is presented by a person, usually the teacher, to the group. It is further distinguished from group guidance in that the latter group counselling process may vary, but it usually is a collaborative one dealing with various attitudes, opinions, and concerns, school-related and otherwise, which originate from within the group."

Gazda described the following fundamental characteristics of group counselling.

(*a*) It focuses on conscious thought and behaviour.
(*b*) It involves such therapy functions as permissiveness, orientation to reality, catharsis, mutual trust, caring, understanding and acceptance.
(*c*) It is composed of members who are basically normal.

Here are certain important concepts which have been used in group in group-counselling which used to be clarified.

Group. A group is not just a collection of people. For a collection of people to qualify as a group, they must relate to one another in many ways. They must share some common attitudes,. values and accept one other. The word group has been differently used. Gibb has given three uses of the term as follows:

Comparison between Group Guidance and Group Counselling

	Group Guidance	Group Counselling
1.	Group guidance is recommended for all school students on a regularly scheduled basis.	It is recommended only for those who are experiencing continuing or temporary problems.
2.	It attempts to change attitudes and behaviour by providing information and stressing cognitive or intellectual functioning.	It makes a direct attempt to modify attitudes and behaviour by stressing affective involvement.
3.	It is applicable to classroom size groups.	It is applicable to small intimate size.

1. Objects or persons which are in some sense together.

2. A group may be defined as a collection of units having qualities in common. A social group by this concept would be a collection of individuals who are perceived to have common characteristics.

3. A group is characterized by the interaction of its members in such a way that each unit is changed by its group membership. The important point is that the members have a psychological relationship to one another.

Here we are concerned with the third usage of the group. Such a group has four distinctive characteristics:

(i) There is dynamic interaction among the members.
(ii) Members have some common goal.
(iii) Members are present with their own consent.
(iv) The group has capacity for self-direction.

Cartwright and Zander (1968) suggest that many of the following statements characterize individuals in a group.

(*a*) They engage in frequent interactions.
(*b*) They define themselves as group members.
(*c*) They are defined by others as belonging to the group.
(*d*) They share norms concerning matters of common interest.
(*e*) They participate in a system of interlocking roles.
(*f*) They identify with one another as a result of having set up the same model object or ideal in their superego.
(*g*) They find the group rewarding.

(h) They pursue promotively interdependent goals.
(i) They have a collective perception of their unity.
(j) They tend to act in a unitary manner toward the environment.

Group dynamics. It is a term which refers to the interacting forces within groups as they organize and operate to achieve their objectives. Group dynamics may be defined as a field of inquiry concerned with advancing knowledge about the nature of groups, their development and the interrelations of individuals, other groups, and larger institutions.

Coffey, an eminent scholar in the field of social psychology, suggests that the focus of group dynamics is the study of forces within the group that produce group productivity or the ways and means that members invest themselves in problem solving. Some other psychologists use the term to indicate group process and procedures and the roles enacted within a group.

Group process. It is continuous, dynamic and directional in movement. It refers to two or more people working together on some need or problem toward some end or goal.

Thomas Hoppins points out: "In social behaviour the movement is largely from individual to individual, whereas in group behaviour there is a tangible qualitative interdependence of each group member with others which operated in three ways: individual to individual, individual to whole, and whole to individual."

This quality in the relationship of individuals is the group and the way they work together to produce it is the process .... Group process is the way people work together to release an emergent quality, called psychological climate, group morale, espirit, decorps, or cooperative units, through which each discovers and develops his inner capacities, realizes better the nature of his self, releases more of his past experience, and learns how to create this emergent quality in all life situations.

Group Task Roles

The main task of the group is to select, define and solve common problems. The following roles are identified in relation to functions of facilitation and coordination of group problem-solving activities.

(a) The initiator-contributor. He initiates new ideas or a changed way of solving common problem.

(b) The information seeker. He seeks relevant information and facts pertinent to the problem.

(c) The opinion seeker. He asks for a clarification of the values involved in a suggestion.

(*d*) The information given. He offers facts which are authentic or relate to his own experience.

(*e*) The opinion giver. He states his beliefs or opinions.

(*f*) The elaborator. He spells out suggestions in terms of examples and offers a rationale for suggestions already made.

(*g*) The coordinatory. He shows or clarifies the relationship among various ideas and suggestions.

(*h*) The orienter. He defines the position of the group with respect to its goal.

(*i*) The evaluator critic. He critically evaluates the practicality of a suggestion or some unit of group discussion.

(*j*) The procedural technician.

(*k*) The recorder.

PURPOSES OF GROUP-COUNSELLING

The following are the purposes of group counselling:

1. *Psychological security*. Every human being desires to be liked and accepted to his group, but people differ greatly in their degree of sociability. Some people have association with more groups than others. Group membership, particularly in adolescent, provides psychological security. Group participation enables adolescents to develop a mutual capacity for interpersonal interaction. The needs of students may be met by various activities, of which many are common and universal, for instance, affiliation and acceptance. The importance of the satisfaction of these needs is very helpful in the adjustment and development of the individual. All adolescents have a keen desire to be accepted by peers, and to be loved by others. Students have to develop some competency in dealing and working with others.

2. *Outlet for emotions*. Group counselling is helpful in developing different roles in students. Students can sometimes assume the role of leader, and at other times they can revolt against group members without severe guilt feelings being attached to the revolt. Group counselling experiences provide adolescents outlets for such needs as status, security and mature emotional expression.

Malher states that students who have completed a group counselling experience appear to be able to transfer their learning to subsequent group interaction. In classes they are more likely than before to speak up and to offer their own ideas and beliefs. Moreover, with increased confidence in their own perception, they tend to meet the unexpected with a great deal of more zest and less fear.

3. *Development of confidence.* Group counselling is also helpful in developing confidence in adolescents through free mutual discussion with their peers.

According to Ohlsen, adolescents benefit with group counselling. in that they learn that their peers have problems tool: (1) that, despite their fault, which their peers want to help them correct, they are accepted; (2) that at least one adult, the counsellor, can understand and accept them; (3) that they are capable of understanding, accepting and helping their peers; (4) that they can trust others, and (5) that when they can express their own real feelings about themselves and others, as well as about personal beliefs, it helps them to understand and accept themselves.

To channel such needs in fruitful social direction is one of the functions of group counselling experiences. A fundamental purpose of most group counselling experiences is to develop members' insight into their problems and feelings and help them to arrive at some understanding of the causes of their problems. Members of counselling groups talk about themselves, the things that disturb them, and what they can do to improve themselves. Effective group counselling facilitates the individual member's understanding of their problems and mastery of those skills which are needed to solve the problems.

4. *Training for expression.* Students through group counselling learn to express themselves in actions, feelings and attitudes. Initially, communication may be between individual group members and the counsellor but the counsellor soon shifts this interaction to the other group members. Students learn that they may interact and discuss with group members as well as the counsellor and that the group will help each member express personal feelings.

Summarizing the purposes of group counselling, we can say that in group counselling under ideal conditions, group members serve as multiple counsellors for each other in that they assist one another in the expression of emotions, interpret feelings, give support and exert some influence on behaviour. Dinkmeyer has given the following goals of group counselling:

(*a*) to help each member of the group know and understand and to assist with identification seeking process.

(*b*) as a result of coming to understand self, to develop increased self-acceptance and feelings of personal growth.

(*c*) to develop increased self-direction, problem-solving and decision-making abilities, and to transfer these abilities to use in regular classroom and social contacts.

(*d*) to develop social skills and interpersonal abilities which enable one to cope with the developmental tasks in their personal social areas.

(*e*) to develop sensitivity to the needs of others which results in increased recognition of responsibility for one's behaviour; to become able to identify with the feelings of those significant others in our world as well as to develop a greater ability to be emphatic.

(*f*) to learn to be an emphatic listener who hears not only what is said but also the feelings which accompany what has been said.

(*g*) to be congruent with self, and be able to offer accurately what one thinks and believes; to say what one means to be a congruent sender.

(*h*) to help each member formulate specific goals for himself which can be measured and observed behaviourally and help him make a commitment to move toward those goals. The main objective of group counselling is to assist individuals in coming to a fuller realization and acceptance of self and others. While this goal is not achieved by all, members who participate in such a group experience may gain, according to Waters, an increase in self-confidence, an improvement in social skills and a reduction in tension.

BASIC INGREDIENTS OF GROUP COUNSELLING

Counselling groups contain certain basic ingredients that are meaningful to those experiencing the process. There are certain stages in group counselling and the ingredients are present in varying degrees in each stage.

1. *An Exploratory stage*. The members of the group indentify themselves and describe the goals they seek. The counsellor and members of the group create an atmosphere in which they feel safe and secure and not threatened.

2. *Transition stage*. At this stage, members of the group begin to self-disclose. By so doing feelings of threat are experienced by the members.

3. *An action stage*. Self-disclosure by members brings reinforcement and members feel confident.

The major components of group counselling are as follows:

1. *The facilitative conditions*. The counselling group must possess certain qualities which help in building proper environment and confidence among the members of the group. These qualities are empathy, unconditional positive regard, non-possessive warmth and genuineness. The counsellor and group members are expected to provide these qualities to each other. These qualities play an important

role in the early phase of group counselling in developing sound relationship among the members.

2. *Self-disclosure*. Self-disclosure of here and now feelings, attitudes and beliefs is generally actively sought in group counselling. Members express their feelings and thoughts only when there is perfect understanding and trust.

3. *Feedback*. A basic ingredient of group counselling is the feedback a member receives from other members. Feedback consists of telling members how they are being perceived when they interact with one another.

4. *Leadership qualities*. The counsellor is supposed to possess qualities of a good leader. He should be capable of influencing people in getting their cooperation to reach the goal.

5. *Group norms*. It has been reported by researchers that in a group situation members identify each other. They become sensitive to one another's opinion, they often seek with member's approval and disapproval. The counselling group is very effective because of pressures it exerts on individual members. In a group there is hightened suggestibility. Group norms regulate the performance of a group.

Group Counselling in Action

Group counselling was developed by Jacob Moreno in the years (1930-40) to study the problems of individual members of the group and aid them in solving their problems. The following technique may be used in group counselling.

Selection of students. The classroom teacher and the principal can help to identify the disruptive students, under-achievers and others who have problematic behaviour. School records may also be consulted to locate the students who have problems.

The following points should be kept into consideration while forming a group.

(i) Groups should be carefully balanced.

(ii) Members should have a common problem but with different levels or degrees of the problem.

(iii) Maturity of the members should be considered.

(iv) Period of time.

(v) Identification of members with each other and with the counsellor.

Size of group. The size of the group depends on several factors: maturity of the students, the level of adjustment and the problem to be discussed. Researchers have recommended the optional size to be six to eight for adolescents.

Physical setting. Group counselling session can be organized in regular classroom, conference rooms and small offices.

The room should be as plain as possible without any pomp and show. The size of the room for six to eight students should be 15' x 15' with a round table and be free from external noise and distraction.

Length of the session. The length of group counselling session will depend on the age of the students. For adolescents, group counselling sessions seem most effective when they are of 35 to 45 minutes' duration.

Initiating counselling. The group counselling interview should be initiated by briefly explaining the purpose of meeting by the counsellor. The members should be made familiar with the rules of the game. They should feel free to express their problems. Cyclostyled material on the rules of game may be distributed among the members.

Rules of the Game

1. Group counselling is a cooperative job. We must all work together to help each other solve problems.
2. Look at your problems honestly.
3. Try to listen to others patiently.
4. Stick to a topic, do not get sidetracked.
5. Speak freely whenever you have something to say.
6. Have trust in other members of the group.
7. Do not feel that you have to come to a group solution or agreement. The purpose of the group is to explore problems together.
8. One of the best ways you can help others is to let them know that they are not alone in what they feel. If you have experienced the same feeling, tell them.

Atmosphere. The atmosphere for group counselling situation must be permissive. The members should be free to express their problems but permissiveness should be followed within certain limits and restrictions. It should not become anarchy. The counsellor must be experienced by the students as an accepting and facilitating adult.

The control of the topics snould be in the hands of students. The students should take the decision to change the topics and, if necessary, to recognize the group.

Duration. Group counselling seems to be most effective on a one-period per week basis running from fifteen to twenty weeks.

It is important that group counselling sessions should be decided on the basis of the needs of the particular school. Group sessions should be started in the month of July or August. The counsellor should not be too concerned if there is lack of observable difference in behaviour or attitude early in the counselling process because the process of change is very slow in group counselling.

ADVANTAGES OF GROUP COUNSELLING

1. Group counselling enables the counsellor to have contact with more students. In dealing with the several students simultaneously, it spreads the effect of the counsellor and at the same time preserves his effectiveness.

2. Students readily accept group counselling since other students are present. They do not view themselves as different.

3. Participation in group counselling enables adolescents to develop the capacity for mutual interaction. Through group counselling, pupils experience relationship with others in life experiences. Counselling groups provide outlets for such needs as status, security and mature emotional expression. It makes effective use of the social setting and peer identification.

4. Group counselling is economical in terms of the time and money.

5. Group counselling provides life-like and realistic social experiences useful for modifying personal habits.

6. Often the establishment of counselling groups within the school may facilitate individual counselling and other new opportunities to meet the needs of the students.

LIMITATIONS OF GROUP COUNSELLING

1. Group counselling is not applicable in case of children below the age of ten years because they cannot communicate effectively through verbal expressions. Group counselling needs ability to talk, to listen, and the ability to work in the abstract to work with ideas and feelings rather than things.

2. Some authors are of the opinion that group counselling can only be used as an adjunct to individual counselling. It cannot be independently used.

3. The areas where group counselling can be used have not been clearly defined. Counsellors must conduct research studies and define the areas where they are most effective.

4. Current research studies on group counselling in schools leave essentially unanswered many of the elemental questions related to the use of group procedures, for instance, kinds of problems to be dealt

with, composition of groups that leads to greatest effectiveness and the most appropriate group size for dealing with particular problems.

ASSIGNMENTS

1. What is group dynamics? Explain in detail the operations involved in group dynamics.
2. What are the advantages and limitations of group counselling?

REFERENCES

Pietrofese John, J.: *Counselling: Theory, Research and Practice*, (Rand McNally College Publishing Co., 1978).

Krumboitz John D. (ed): *Counselling Methods* (Helf Rinehart and Winston, NY. 1976).

Hansen James C. and Cramer Standley H. (ed): *Group Guidance and Counselling in the Schools*, (Appleton Century Crofts, Meredith Co. NY, 1971).

Chapter 12

Theories of Counselling/Psychotherapy

In the last seventy years several theories of counselling have been developed which explain human behaviour from different angles. The terms counselling and psychotherapy have been used interchangeably in the literature. This has been done in this chapter also. We shall present selected theories of counselling. But before we describe specific theories of counselling let us first define a theory. A theory is a set of stated postulates or assumptions, which are related to each other and are internally consistent. It not only predicts new facts or relations but organizes and integrates what is known in a meaningful framework. It is comprehensive, simple and stimulating.

CRITERIA OF A GOOD THEORY

A good theory must have the following characteristics:

1. *Preciseness and clarity*. A theory should be precise and free from ambiguity. Clarity of a theory means ease of relating it to data or practice or the ease of making predictions from it and specifying methods of testing them.

2. *Importance*. A theory should not be trivial, it should be significant. It must have wide applicability and relevance to life.

3. *Simplicity*. Simplicity is another important characteristic of a good theory. This would involve a minimum of complexity and few assumptions. Hall and Lindzey propose that parsimony is important only after the criteria of comprehensiveness and verifiability have been met.

4. *Comprehensiveness*. A theory should be complete, covering the area of interest and including all known data in the field.

5. *Operational*. A theory should be capable of being reduced to procedures for testing its propositions or predictions. Its concepts should be precise enough to be measurable.

6. *Empirical validity or verifiability*. A good theory must be supported by experience and experiments involving the testing of predictions. That is in addition to its consistency with, or ability to,

account for what is already known. It must generate predictions that are confirmed by new date. The theory should be verifiable.

7. *Stimulating*. A theory must provoke new thinking and the development of new ideas or theories.

CLASSIFICATIONS OF THEORIES OF COUNSELLING

1. **Dynamic Counselling**
   Psychoanalytic Counselling.
2. **Humanistic Psychotherapy**
   (*a*) Client-centred therapy.
   (*b*) Gestalt analysis.
   (*c*) Transactional analysis.
   (*d*) Rational therapy.
3. **Behaviour Counselling**
   (*a*) Systematic desensitization.
   (*b*) Modelling.
   (*c*) Operant Conditioning.
   (*d*) Trait and Factor Theory.

Only major theories of counselling have been selected for brief description to acquaint the readers with the fundamental concepts of each of them. Since all theories are rooted in personality theories, the approach followed in this chapter is as follows. First a very brief description of the fundamental concepts of the personality theory is given. This is followed by the process of counselling developed on the basis of the personality theory which in turn is followed by goals and researches being conducted in the field.

1. DYNAMIC COUNSELLING

Dynamic counselling began with Sigmund Freud's (1856-1939) development of psychoanalysis as both a theory of personality and as a technique of treating mental disorders. Since the development of classical psychoanalysis, several schools of dynamic psychotherapy have emerged which are either a direct result of Freud's psychoanalysis or they have developed in reaction to it. Despite theoretical differences, however, the therapeutic practice of the various schools is quite similar. In this chapter we shall trace the origin of the different psychodynamic theories and therapies and then common techniques of dynamic counselling.

Tenets of Classical Psychoanalysis

Instincts. Freud was the first psychologist who emphasized the importance of instincts as the determinant of human behaviour. He proposed two instincts: (*a*) eros, love and self-preservation; (*b*) thanatos, the death instinct.

Psychic structure: Libido is the source of psychic energy which is primary driving force of personality. He conceived of three levels of psychic energy which are id, ego and the superego.

Id. It is inborn and operates on the principle of immediate gratification of needs. It seeks pleasure. It cannot differentiate between good and bad.

Ego. It operates on the principle of reality. The ego is called the executive of personality. It formulates the plan for the satisfaction of needs and executes it, keeping into consideration the principle of reality. It often integrates the conflicting demands of id, the super ego and the external world. Freud remarked that "The poor ego....has to serve three harsh masters and has to do its best to reconcile the demands of all three."

Superego. It is the agency which internalizes the parental influences and norms of the society in early childhood experiences. It represents the ideal rather than the real and strives for perfection.

Topographically, the mind is divided into three parts — conscious, subconscious and unconscious. Freud, for the first time, attempted to explore the unconscious part of human personality. He proposed that the greater part of personality is buried in the unconscious of which we are not aware and is not accessible except under special conditions.

According to Freud, the human organism is a complex energy system which derives its energy from the food it consumes. The three parts of the psychic structure are in constant interaction and clash between id impulses seeking pleasure and inhibition imposed by the superego.

The personality develops through a definite sequence of psychosexual stages such as oral, anal, phallic and genital. The person's experiences at each stage leave some characteristic impressions and imprints that influence his personality development.

According to Freud, human behaviour is determined largely by unconscious psychological forces. The cause of mental abnormalities can be explored in childhood experiences. He further discovered that many unconscious thoughts, feelings, memories and impulse seem to be concerned with sexuality. Neurotic conditions can be removed if the patient becomes conscious through free association and other techniques.

Jung's Analytic Psychology

Jung (1875-1961) was a close associate of Freud and worked with him upto 1912. He separated himself from Freud and developed his own approach. He never accepted fully the theory of infantile sexuality that Freud considered the touchstone of psychoanalysis.

According to him the mind of man has two major aspects: the conscious and the unconscious. The unconscious has two levels: (*a*) personal unconscious and (*b*) collective unconscious. "The personal unconscious," says Jung, "contains lost memories, painful ideas that are repressed, subliminal perceptions, by which are meant sense-perceptions that were not strong enough to reach consciousness, and, finally, contents that are not yet ripe for consciousness."

The collective unconscious or the objective psyche does not derive from personal experience and is not a personal acquisition but is inborn. It has "contents and mode of behaviour that are more or less the same everywhere and in all individuals. It is in other words identical in all men and thus constitutes a common psychic substrate of a suprapersonal nature which is present in every one of us."

The other important concepts are archetypes, persona, shadow, anima and animus.

Archetypes. The collective unconscious is made of universal idea which are called archetypes that appear in dreams, myths and fantasies. They are also ways of thinking and experiencing, of understanding, of behaving. They have been formed, "during the thousands of years when the human brain and human consciousness were emerging from an animal state." There are some principal archetypes that appear in almost everyone's life.

Persona. It is a complicated system of relations between the individual and society, fittingly enough a kind of mask, designed on the one hand to make a definite impression upon others and on the other to conceal the true nature of the individual.

The persona is that face we put on to society. Briefly, we can say that it is the outer attitude that the person adopts in response to cultural expectations.

Shadow. The shadow personifies everything that the subject refuses to acknowledge about himself and yet is always thrusting itself upon him directly or indirectly, for instance, inferior traits of character or other incompatible tendencies.

The contrasexual part of a man, the anima, is his unconscious feminine aspect and the contrasexual part of a woman, the animus, is her masculine aspect. The thrill of being in love is the excitement of finding a lost part of oneself.

The self, according to Jung, is an organizing agency of the personality. It plays an important role in unifying and stabilising personality characteristics.

Adler's Theory of Individual Psychology

Alfred Adler broke with Freud at the same time as Jung. He developed individual psychology. The term individual psychology was chosen by Adler to stress the uniqueness of the individual as a self-consistent unity striving for the overall goal of mastery of the environment rather than a passive element worked on by drives, subject to a conflict between conscious and unconscious forces common to all persons.

Adler developed his own system that is called individual psychology. According to individual psychology the development of man is inclined toward social interest. We find neurotics, psychotics, suicides etc. only when social interest is throttled.

The main concepts of his theory are:

(a) He emphasized the importance of childhood experiences in the development of personality.

(*b*) Each individual is a unified, self-consistent whole striving toward a social goal. Every choice made by the individual in life is a movement toward that goal.

(*c*) Lifestyle develops gradually and includes everything of living. It is the unique quality of the personality which differentiates one person from the other. All aspects of an individual's life and details of his behaviour organize around his life style.

(*d*) Neurosis is the result of attempts to compensate for the inferiority feelings that are caused by every person's childhood feelings of weakness and helplessness. To compensate people strive for power over others and for unrealistic goals that Adler called "fictive goals". Striving for power and superiority may be achieved by openly struggling for power or by becoming ill and thus manipulating the environment.

Neo-Freudians

Erich Fromm, Erikson, Karen Horney and Harry Stack Sullivan, deviate from classical psychoanalysts but explain their theories with the psychoanalytic approach of Freud. They rejected the 'libido' theory of pansexuality. And they emphasized that social experiences and cultural factors are more important than biological and intrapsychic factors in explaining human behaviour. According to them individual's adaptation to his environment is the crucial behavioural variable. Interpersonal relationship is important in the development of character. Anxiety and maladjustment are caused because faulty and distorted interpersonal relationships add relationship to society.

The Technique of Psychodynamic Psychotherapy

In psychodynamic psychotherapy, the patient is asked to lie on a couch with the analyst sitting in a chair behind him. The patient is asked to talk about whatever comes to his mind without direction from the psychoanalyst. The patient is encouraged to be spontaneous and to speak about whatever he chooses.

Transference

Freud discovered an unusual result of his non-directive and unobtrusive method. Patients began to behave with Freud in much the same way that they had behaved with significant persons, such as their parents in the past.

This unavoidable process of treating the therapist like other significant persons was called transference neurosis. The transference is the result of infantile needs, conflicts and feeling; it is not a presently realistic relationship to the therapist.

Counter-transference. It is another critical factor which the therapist must take into account. When the therapist transfers his feelings to the patient, this is called counter-transference. All persons have some conflicts and pains in common. Thus, patients' explorations of his conflicts as well as his real world personality are bound to revive some of the therapist's own conflicts.

Resistance. Patients sometimes resist talking freely. This behaviour is termed as resistance which may be caused by many reasons.

Goal. The fundamental goal of dynamic psychotherapy is understanding and insight through the process of real human relationship.

2. HUMANISTIC PSYCHOTHERAPY

In the preceding section, we have described dynamic psychotherapy. This section will deal with humanistic psychotherapies: client-centred therapy, Rational Emotive, Gestalt, and transactional analysis.

The humanistic psychotherapies are not bound by common techniques nor are they a unified school of psychotherapy. They represent a general approach to understand human beings psychologically. Humanism mean the study of the person, the individual as a whole with aim of helping him to live a happier life, a more self-actualizing and more creative existence. It completely accepts people with their human limitations. It emphasizes their ability to create and direct their own destinies and it views them as holistic, goal-directed individuals.

Client-centred Therapy

Client-centred therapy or non-directive counselling was developed by Carl Rogers in 1942. Since then this theory has been continuously developed on the basis of studies in human growth and change. As the term non-directive counselling implies, the major role is played by the client in the counselling process.

Theory of Personality

The theory of client-centred therapy is based on certain assumptions regarding personality.

Every individual is capable of dealing constructively with his problems provided that he is made aware of them. Therefore the responsibility remains with the client. The individual has a basic tendency to grow, to actualize his potentialities and this growth leads to personally and socially satisfying behaviour.

The organism is composed of all that the individuals are: their physical being, their thoughts and their behaviour. The organism is at all times a total organized system in which alteration of any part may produce changes in any other part. Individuals, then, react to the total perceptual field which is their reality. As a person interacts with the environment in his perceptual field, the self-concept starts developing — that is the, "I" and "me" of personality. Perception of experience is influenced by a need for positive regards, which Rogers states in a universal need in human beings, pervasive and persistent. Since this need for positive regard can be satisfied only by others, the self-concept is the learned sense of self and based on the individual's perception of the regards they have received from outside the self. Parents and other significant people impose conditions of worth that must be met before they give their children positive regards. These conditions become an integral part of the children's self-regard system; conflict, then, arises when individuals must choose between the need for positive regard and a need that is not in accord with the significant other's conditions of worth. In such a situation, individuals are likely to perceive needs as bad as, and in opposition to, their being a good person. Any experience that is not consistent with the self-concept is seen as a threat, because it would disturb the self-concept by being contrary to the conditions of worth that one has incorporated. The source of anxiety or tension is the discrepancy that exists between the experiencing self and the conceptualization of self when the event is contrary to the self-concept.

Counselling Process

The success of non-directive counselling depends on the relationship between the counsellor and the counsellee. The counsellor offers positive regard with no strings attached and no conditional clauses. "The counsellor chooses to act consistently upon the hypothesis that the individual has a sufficient capacity to deal constructively with all those aspects of his life which can potentially come into conscious awareness". (Roger, 1951).

The non-directive counselling proceeds in the following stages:

(*a*) The client comes for help. (*b*) He expresses emotionalized attitudes freely. (*c*) This leads to the development of insight. (*d*) The client terminates the contracts.

Goals. The following changes can be expected after client-centered counselling. The clients become:

(*a*) more realistic in their self-perceptions.

(*b*) more confident and self-directing.

(*c*) more positively valued by themselves.

(*d*) less likely to repress aspects of their experiences.

(*e*) more mature, socialized, and adaptive in their behaviour.

(*f*) less upset by stress and quicker to recover from it.

(*g*) more like the healthy integrated well-functioning person in their personality structure (Rogers).

Research. Researches conducted by Rogers and Dymond and Baskin indicate that as the counselling relationship progresses, there is a decrease in the amount of client defensiveness, an increase in congruence between the self and experience, and a tendency for the client to see himself as the focus of evaluation. Carkhuff and Bersenson (1967) report that clients will move into self-exploration which will lead to positive changes. Carkhuff has developed a new model which is called "Carkhuff Model" based on Rogerian Theory.

Rational-Emotive Therapy

Rational-emotive therapy was developed by Albert Ellis. According to him, human being is both rational and irrational. Irrationality is the cause of emotional problems, such as guilt, anxiety, anger and depression. Emotions cannot be separated from ideas.

He has developed his own model of behaviour which is called A, B, 'C' Model. 'A' is the activating event, 'B' is the belief system and C is the emotionat consequence. Here model 'A' is not the cause of 'C', rather 'B' is the cause.

Ellis states that "every human being who gets disturbed really is telling himself a chain of false sentences. That is the way humans seem almost invariably to think in words, phrases, and sentences and it is these sentences which really constitute his neurosis." Ellis has identified the following eleven irrational ideas which lead neurosis.

1. It is absolutely essential for an individual to be loved or approved by every significant person in his environment.

2. It is necessary that each individual be competent, adequate and achieving in areas of interest, if the individual is to be worthwhile.

3. Some people are bad, wicked, or villainous and these people should be blamed and punished.

4. It is terrible and catastrophic when things are not the way an individual wants them to be.

5. Unhappiness is a function of events outside the control of the individual.

6. If something is dangerous or harmful, an individual should constantly be concerned about it.

7. It is easier to run away from difficulties and self-responsibility than it is to face them.

8. Individuals need to be dependent on others and to have someone stronger than themselves to lean on.

9. Pet events in an individual's life determine present behaviour and cannot be changed.

10. An individual should be very concerned and upset by other individual's problems.

11. There is always a correct and precise answer to every problem and it is catastrophic if it is not found.

The Counselling Process

The main purpose of R.E.T. counselling is to demonstrate and convince the client that self-talk is the source of disturbance and to re-evaluate this self-talk in order to eliminate it and subsequent illogical ideas. The process of R.E.T. is as follows:

In the initial interview the responsibilities of counsellor and client are defined. The client is responsible for practising any learning acquired during the counselling sessions. Practising means homework.

Goal. The major goal of R.E.T. is to make the client aware of his irrational thoughts and aid him in the process of adjustment.

Gestalt Therapy

Frederick Perls is the name associated with the development of Gestalt therapy. Before we describe the theory of personality, let us see the basic principle of Gestalt psychology. The brain always tries to organise stimuli into wholes, since isolated parts of anything have no meaning. The other important principle is that stimuli have meaning only as they are organized in the mind and that the above principles are the ways in which one organizes.

Theory of Personality

Theory of Personality is based on the following assumptions:

1. Individuals are a totality consisting of interrelated parts. Individuals are also part of their environment and cannot be understood apart from it.
2. Individuals choose how they respond to internal and external stimuli.
3. Individuals have the capacity to govern their own life effectively.
4. Individuals cannot experience the past and future. They can only experience themselves in the present.
5. Individuals are basically neither good nor bad.

The motivating force in Gestalt therapy is self-actualization which smacks of Carl Rogers. There is difference, however, in that Rogers views self-actualization as a potentiality with futuristic satisfaction whereas Gestalists state: "Becoming is the process of being what one is and not a process of striving to become" (Kempler). The emphasis in Gestalt therapy is on the here-and-now.

The Counselling Process

Gestalt counselling is active, conformative and concerned with what is experienced in the "now"'. The past is memory, the future is a fantasy.

Much of gestalt counselling involves retrieving "What has been disowned by the clients by having them experience these splits as they exist. One split that is often seen is what Perls describes as 'topdog' and 'underdog' which can coexist in one personality. The underdog is the Mickey mouse.

The topdog is the super mouse. The topdog is apologetic and defensive. Perls states, once we recognize the structure of our behaviour which in the case of self-improvement is the split between the topdog and the underdog and if we understand how by listening, we can bring a reconciliation of these two fighting clowns, then we realize that we cannot deliberately bring about changes in ourselves or in others.

In Gestalt counselling a two-change method is used to bring awareness of this split. A client sits in open chair and role plays topdog speaking to underdog. He then switches chairs and responds underdog to topdog.

This method is also used in the resolution of unfinished business which is a gestalt that has not had closure. Non-verbal behaviour is important in gestalt therapy as a contract to what is said and as an emphasis on what is said. Other gestalt tèchniques include:

Personalization. It means changing impersonal comments stated with "You" to non-personal ones stated with (I). The client is helped to assume the responsibility for his own actions rather than replying to external control. Projection is the process by which clients associate with someone else that part of themselves that they are unwilling to own. The counsellor has the client's role to play that other person to see if the projection actually fits them.

Goals

The major objective of gestalt counselling is the integration of the individual, a bringing together of all parts she or he has disowned, along with recognition that the individual is self-regulating. Increasing awareness is of paramount importance and awareness alone is curative.

Transactional Analysis (TA)

In the end under humanistic psychotherapy we will describe the most recent theory of Transactional Analysis developed by Eric Berne in the sixties. Transactional Analysis, (TA) as defined by Eric Berne is "a theory of personality and social action and a clinical method of psychotherapy based on the analysis of all possible transactions between two or more people on the basis of specifically defined ego-states." Transactional Analysis (TA) is very useful for any one who wants to be a real person. A real person is one who acts spontaneously in a rational and trustworthy way with decent consideration for others." Those who do this are autonomous.

Basic concepts. A major Transactional Analysis (TA) concept is that people can be autonomous. They do not have to be enslaved by their past. Change is a continuing process for those who want to be real people. Real people are autonomous and autonomous people, according to Berne, are able to demonstrate "the release or recovery of three capacites."

Awareness, Spontaneity and Intimacy

Awareness is knowing what is happening now. Autonomous people are aware. They peel away the layers of contamination and hear, smell, see, touch, taste, study and evaluate for themselves. They perceive the world through their own personal encounters rather than the way they were taught to see it.

Aware people listen to the messages of their own bodies. They know their own world of feelings and fantasies are not afraid or ashamed of them. They also hear other people. They attempt to make genuine contact with other people. . . .

Aware people work as an integrated personality. They can spontaneously choose from the full spectrum of parent behaviour and feelings.

They are spontaneous — flexible, not foolishly impluslive. They behave according to the situations most appropriately. Spontaneous people are liberated. They make and accept responsiblity for their own choices. They learn to face new situations and to explore new ways of thinking, feeling and responding. They constantly increase and re-evaluate their repertoire of possible behaviour.

They use or recapture their ability to decide for themselves. They make their own decisions rather than remaining at the mercy of their face.

In addition to the qualities of awareness and spontaneity, autonomous people are also capable of intimacy. They attempt to be open and authentic. They also attempt to see others in their own uniqueness, not through the distortions of past experiences. People who do not experience awareness, spontaneity and intimacy are not in touch with their potential. TA enables these people to change.

A basic concept is the belief that people are of value and their personalities and lives are enriched and enhanced by the release or recovery of autonomy, which includes awareness, spontaneity and intimacy.

Brief History of TA

The development of the basic concepts of Transactional Analysis was initiated by Eric Berne who was dissatisfied with traditional method of psychoanalysis to cure psychological disturbances. He was in search of a new theory and method that would be more effective than traditional methods of psychotherapy and counselling.

Eric Berne started his work in Army Medical Corps as a psychiatrist in 1941. He practised group therapy in army and succeeded to a great extent in curing mental disturbances of armymen. The development of TA can be traced back to 1949 when he wrote six articles on intuition.

His first book, *Transactional Analysis in Psychotherapy* was published in 1961. He wrote several other books which deal in detail his concepts on Trasactional Analysis. *Games People Play* was published in 1964, *Principles of Group Treatment* in 1964 and *Principles of Group Treatment* in 1968. The study of TA started in the small town of Cornet (California) in 1953. He used to hold regular seminars of professionals to discuss clinical material. The TA Bulletin with Berne as editor came into existence in 1962. The Bulletin created interest in the members to share information.

The International TA Association was formed in 1964. The journal on TA is a quarterly published by ITAA presenting theory, methods and research materials, on Transactional Analysis (TA).

Berne died in 1970. Throughout his life he dedicatedly worked on the theory of Transactional Analysis (TA) and produced a great amount of literature which has created enthusiasm among the workers.

Theory of Trasactional Analysis (TA)

TA theory is very comprehensive. It is not possible to describe the theory in a single chapter. A brief summary is therefore given here to acquaint the readers with the fundamental concepts of the theory. TA is concerned with the following four types of analysis:

(*a*) Structural Analysis.
(*b*) Transactional Analysis.
(*c*) Game Analysis.
(*d*) Script Analysis.

(*a*) *Structural analysis.* Structural analysis is segregation and analysis of the parent, adult and child ego states which comprise individual personality. The goal of this procedure is "to establish the predominance of reality-testing ego states and freeing them from contamination by archaic and foreign elements." Parent ego states are the incorporation of the specific parent figures people have when they are young. Each individual has his unique parent ego state. This ego state is outwardly expressed toward others in prejudicial, critical and nurturing behaviour — behaviour which is identical or very similar to that of the original parent figure.

The child ego state contains all the natural feelings, needs, impulses, and potentialities of an infant. It also contains creative, manipulative, intuitive capacities as well as the adapted feelings and behaviour learned during childhood, such as compliance, rebellion and procrastination.

The adult ego state is not related to a person's ego. It is concerned with autonomous collecting and processing of data and the estimating of probabilities as a basis for action. It organizes information, in adaptable manner and functions by testing reality and computing dispassionately. The following chart shows the structure of personality.

P = Parent ego state.
A = Adult ego state.
C = Child ego state.

These three ego states are manifested in the behaviour of the individual. When people act, think or feel as their parent figures once did, they are in the parent ego state. When they are living in the here and now, gathering facts, computing them and acting on the basis of facts, rather than on the basis of parental traditions or childhood feelings, they are in the adult ego-state. When people feel, act and respond to others as they learned to do when they were little, they are in their child ego state, using, however, the increased facilities they have gained while growing up. Shifts in ego, states, according to Berne, may be accounted for "by using the concept of psychic energy or Catheoxis, on the principle that at a given moment that ego state which is cathected in a certain way will have the executive power. There are three states of catheoxis, unbound, bound and free.

(b) *Transactional analysis*. Transactional Analysis is used to distinguish from the theory of Transactional Analysis as a whole. Berne says that the goal of this phase is social control, that is, the control of the individual's own tendency to manipulate other people in destructive or wasteful ways, and of his tendency to response without insight or option to the manipulation of others.

Transactional Analysis (TA) consists of determining which ego state in one person is transacting with which ego state in another and in what ways — what is the transactional stimulus and what is the transactional response.

A transaction consists two or more strokes. Strokes may be positive like a smile or friendly greeting or negative like a frown or sacrastic greeting. They can be unconditional like "I love you or conditional like" I love you if you. Hello is a single stroke. A hello in return is another stroke. The two strokes make up a transaction. There is a stimulus and response.

Patterns of stimulus and response are categorized into three basic kinds of transaction which are as follows:

(i) *Complementary transaction*. These include Adult — Adult stimulus and response pattern as follows.

P	P
A	C
C	C
Client	Therapist

(ii) *Crossed transactions*. These may occur between any ego states. When a message sent from one person gets an unexpected response, the vectors cross communication is usually broke off or someone feels misunderstood or hurt or angry. Gestures, facial expression, body postures, tone of voice, words, all contribute to the meaning of any transaction, crossed or otherwise.

P	P
A	A
C	C
Client	Therapist

(iii) *Ulterior-transactions*. These transactions are as the name suggests hidden. Along with the spoken words is sent a non-verbal message. Very often the verbal stimulus and the non-verbal stimulus are quite different.

There are two types of ulterior transactions, angular and duplex. There is a covert message under the surface of the ostensible social transaction. Communication may or may not continue after ulterior transaction.

(c) *Game analysis*. Game analysis is the analysis of a series of overt social transactions that are accompanied by covert ulterior transactions which lead to a well-defined pay off. The goal of this phase is for clients to gain awareness of the psychological games they play, how they initiate those games and how they get hooked into them by others. The goal also includes awareness of how games can be broken up in favour of more satisfying ways of structuring time.

A game is an ongoing series of transactions, seemingly complementary, covertly ulterior which lead to a well-defined pay off. Pay offs are usually negative feelings, such as fear, anger, sadness, inadequacy, etc. for one or both the players.

Psychological games are similar to card games, it takes two or more to play. All games have a beginning which is the initial stimulus, a set of rules and expected plays, and a conclusion. People tend to have favourite games that they play over and over again. Thus they collect the old feelings from childhood at the end of the game.

There are three different modes of playing:

(*a*) A first degree game is one which is socially acceptable in the agent's circle.

(*b*) A second degree game is one from which no permanent irremidiable damage arises but which the players rather conceal from the public.

(*c*) A third degree is one which is played for keeping and which ends in the surgery, the courtroom or the morgue.

The pay off at the end of first grade game is like a small prize such as a temper tantrum or crying jag. At the end of the second degree game, the prize is bigger and often involves a quitting of some kind, quit school, quit a job, quit a marriage etc. The third degree game player, like a big game hunter, usually is going for a broke — homicide or suicide.

(*d*) *Script analysis*. Script analysis is the analysis of life-dramas that people, usually without awareness, act out compulsively. The goal of this phase is the discovery of scripty behaviour which is based on early childhood decisions. Because the decisions made in these scripts often interfere with autonomy, the focus is on redecision that will put a better show on the road.

Although people are not usually aware of it, their psychological scripts, like those of stage plays, contain not only the themes, but also the role they expect to play, the roles they expect others to play, the dramatic actions, climax and denonuement.

Generally speaking, it is people with destructive, non-productive or banal scripts who enter treatment, since those with constructive scripts seldom feel the need for it.

Advantages of Transactional Analysis (TA)

1. *TA is a self-help psychology*. Mostly the literature in the field of psychotherapy and counselling is highly technical which is beyond the understanding of lay persons: TA theory is simple and can be understood by non-technical persons. Persons can help themselves by reading the basic concepts of TA.

2. *TA is non-threatening psychology*. TA deals with observable behaviour of the client such as verbal expression, tone of voice, facial expression and body postures etc. Traditional theories deal with unconscious sexuality, death drives — often seem so threatening that many people avoid getting help.

3. *TA psychology of change*. TA is basically a psychology of change. It is aimed to change what people want to change in their behaviour.

4. *TA is immediately effective.* Traditional therapeutic systems are lengthy. They take long time to understand the problems of the client and solutions of the problems also take too much time. On the other hand, in TA therapy people gain insight about themselves, their needs and the ways they can change.

5. *TA is for all.* TA is meant for both sick and healthy persons. Healthy persons can learn to feel better about themselves and can learn to communicate more authentically with others. TA can be used in cases of severe emotional problems, mental retardation and delinquency.

6. TA can be used by families, children and parents for their benefits.

7. TA is also an on-the-job communication tool. TA is an important technique in understanding the problems of labourers, in business and industry. It improves human relations, decreases staff turnover and increases staff morale as well as productivity.

Transactional Analysis Process

The success of Transactional Analysis treatment largely depends on the setting of the room where the session is held. The furniture, the colour of the curtains and walls, the dress of the therapist all constitute the setting.

In the initial interview, the therapist very carefully tries to assess the ego state the client seems to be in. The therapist makes the analysis of the initial transactions and draws certain conclusions. TA can be used in individual therapy but much of its power comes from its use in groups. Transaction Analysis interview records are kept for future references. Brief notes or summary of the interview is recorded in standard forms. A specimen as follows.

Name *Address*

Initial Session — Date .... *Reference Source*

Positions	Symptoms	Current Parent situations figures	Childhood
	Client's complaints		
Contracts to be made and completed.	Dates.		

Contract Theory and Techniques

The establishment and completion of contracts is one of the important TA techniques that can be used for effective therapy.

A contract is bilateral agreement between the therapist and client. It is a specific statement in operational form of the individual or interpersonal problems to be solved.

Mechanisms of TA Psychotherapy

The first stage of TA relationship is that of meeting a confused client with a benevolent parent. The therapist seeks the information he needs in order to establish a contractual relationship. The main objective of the first stage is to create a safe environment in which the client may begin to reown his adult.

The TA is usually carried out in a group. The initial stage also serves to develop the group into a community of meaningful others. Improved communication between group participants is hoped for and the therapist works to ensure the free flow of effective communication.

In the second stage, the TA therapist explains the clients' behaviour to him using the information obtained during the first stage. The TA therapists' tools here are structural analysis, transactional analysis, script analysis and game analysis. The specific objective of this stage is to familiarize the client with the vocabulary and principles of TA. The therapist may use various techniques to make the client aware of his internal areas of conflict and explore his understanding of them. The third stage is marked by confrontation. The therapist tries to keep the client in the present timeframe while eliciting a commitment to some action. It is during this stage that clients begin to appreciate their own value in the therapeutic progress. The TA clients come to accept their own adult as the true base of support for life activity.

The client's self-conditioning is further enhanced by the fulfilment of therapeutic contracts.

Goals. TA aims to free people from their froggy feelings and behaviour and helps in improving the communication process. It can be used for everyday problem-solving both for mentally healthy people and the mentally disturbed.

Behaviour Therapy

Behaviour therapy is a term which is used to describe a number of psychotherapeutic methods which have been developed in recent years from the discoveries made in experimental psychology laboratories. Though procedures vary to a great extent in different behaviour therapies they all have a common theoretical basis.

The dynamic and humanistic therapies described above were evolved from the clinical efforts of therapists seeking to help clients, but behaviour therapy evolved from basic, non-clinical research often done on animals. Behaviour therapy relies largely on experimentally derived principles of psychology especially learning principles, to help change maladaptive behaviour.

According to Krumbolty, behaviour counselling is "based on laboratory of conditioning for describing behaviour and specifying the conditions under which it is acquired, maintained and eliminated."

Basic Concepts

1. Overt behaviour is the only subject of study and there is no need to hypothesize any inner determining agents such as id, ego and the superego. Introspection and concept of symptoms have been completely eliminated.

2. All behaviours are learned by conditioning in the environment. Learning is inferred from a subject's behaviour.

3. Behaviour is a function of the interaction of hereditary and environmental variables.

4. All behaviour is lawful and unadaptive behaviour is learned and unlearned according to the same principles as adaptive behaviour. Changes in behaviour can be brought by systematic and gradually introduced changes in the environment.

5. Counsellors are concerned with specific, precise and current problems.

6. A number of techniques can be applied in behavioural counselling, for example, reinforcement, modelling, role playing simulation and counter-conditions etc.

Behaviour counselling as a technique is based on the principle of learning. The most important contribution to behaviour counselling has been made by Pavlov, B.F. Skinner, Wolpe and John D. Krumboltz who believed that neurotic behaviour is acquired and is subject to the established laws of learning.

Theory of Personality

Behaviourists emphasize the importance of environment in the development of human personality. Some of the behaviourists adhere to the "tabula rasa" theory of John Locke. People are born into this world neither intrinsically bad nor good but neutral. The behaviour of the child develops in constant interaction with the external environment.

Techniques of Behaviour Therapy

1. Desensitization based on relaxation.
2. Conditioning (classical and operant).
3. Training in assertive behaviour.
4. Use of sexual responses.
5. Extinction based on negative actions.
6. Avoidance learning.
7. Anxiety relief responses.
8. Modelling.

Theory of Learning

Behaviour therapy, as already stated, is based on the principles of learning. So it will be worthwhile to know the operations of learning. First we describe the favours experiment conducted by Pavlov on dogs. The paradigm of the experiment is given below:

1.	UCS (Food)	UCR (Salivation)
2.	CS + UCS (Bell + Food)	 Do
3.	CS (Bell)	CR (Salivation)

Classical conditioning is a process when a neutral stimulus in combination with a natural stimulus acquires all the characteristics of the natural stimulus.

The other theory of learning was developed by B. F. Skinner of Havard University. His theory is known as theory of operant conditioning. The theory states that if spontaneous behaviour results in the satisfaction of some need, frequency of that behaviour increases. The model of operant conditioning presented by Skinner differs from classic conditioning model (Pavlov) in that the unconditioned stimulus follows a spontaneous behaviour.

As easily recognizable mode of learning is that of imitation. Children learn many things by imitation in early childhood.

Childhood-imitative learning is a vicarious progress whereby behaviour is learned through the observation of a model. Thousands of adolescents in our country have been imitating the lifestyle of western civilizations.

A more basic model of learning is that of modelling. Most behaviour is influenced by models in everyday life. Modelling extends the concept of imitation in that it involves a planned demonstration. Some writers make a distinction between imitation and modelling on the basis of subject's action. Imitative learning does not involve teaching a new behaviour. The emphasis is on copying. Modelling implies direct teaching of a certain action.

Some standard concepts. Behavioural counselling involves a number of principles which need clarification. Here we are mentioning some concepts which help to understand behavioural counselling.

Reinforcement. Reinforcement can be positive or negative. In positive reinforcement we do something to get something and in negative reinforcement we do something to avoid something.

Generalization. Human beings and to some extent animals are capable of generalizing their learning experiences from one situation to another. In the progress of generalization, an individual responds to a stimulus similar to another stimulus. For example, if one responds with a smile to the arrival of a loved one, one would respond with a smile to the arrival of yet another loved one. It is necessary, however, to be able to discriminate between similar situations. If the loved one arrives in tears, it would be inappropriate to respond with a smile. The act of arrival remains the same but it does not elicit the same response.

Discrimination is necessary to separately evaluate the responses evoked by generalization. Shoping is the moulding of the standard concepts previously mentioned. By this process a new behaviour is learned using the principles of reinforcement, extinction, generalization and discrimination.

The counselling process. Before starting the counselling process, the counsellor should establish rapport to determine the client's problems and gain his cooperation.

Blackham and Silberman have suggested the following steps to facilitate behavioural counselling.

(i) *Problem definition.* The counsellor should specifically define the problems. All the circumstances surrounding the inappropriate behaviour should also be identified.

(ii) *Developmental and social history.*

(iii) *Specification of counselling goals.* The counsellor should decide in advance the goals of counselling. The client and the counsellor come to an agreement as to what the problem actually is. It is the counsellors' responsibility to decide if the goal is within his realm of expertise and in accord with ethical behaviour.

(iv) *Selection of methods.* The techniques used in the counselling will vary and remain consistent with the client's goals.

Krumboltz states counselling consists of whatever ethical activities a counsellor undertakes in an effort to help the client engage in those types of behaviour which will lead to resolution of the client's problems.

Some of the Strategies

(*a*) *Relaxation*. The client is taught how to eliminate muscular tension in the body as a way reducing tension.

(*b*) *Desensitization*. If a client has described several anxiety producing situations, it is possible to rank them from the lowest to the highest in terms of disturbance. The client is instructed in relaxation technique, and when this is accomplished, each anxious situation is presented starting with the one that produces the least anxiety. As the situation is recalled by the client he is reinforced by the relaxation process, until there is no anxiety.

(*c*) *Assertive training*. There are occasions when the clients do not have adequate interpersonal relationships because of their inability to express their feelings. The counsellor encourages the client to reveal his feelings. With reinforcement and shaping, the appropriate assertive responses can be practised in the sessions. The next step is to encourage the client to use these responses outside the counselling situation. The feedback the client receives from others will serve as a positive reinforcer for this behaviour which in turn reduces the feelings of anxiety and inadequacy.

Goal. Behaviour therapy is the most modern method of treating disorders of behaviour. Changes in the behaviour of the client are gradually effected which can be observed and measured in an objective way. It permits precision and a systematic planning of the therapeutic procedure required in individual cases. The goal is to change particular behaviour efficiently and specifically.

Research. A number of research studies have been conducted and are being conducted using the various techniques of behaviour therapy. The prominent workers in the field are Wolpe, Lazarus Eysenck and Cooper who have tested the effectiveness of behaviour therapy on large groups of patients having various types of problems.

Issues in Behaviour Therapy

Though thousands of research studies have been conducted with great success all over the world using the various techniques of behaviour therapy, critics of behaviour therapy have raised a number of issues which need consideration to improve or modify the theory and procedures of behaviour therapy. The major issues are as follows:

1. The first issue is that behaviour therapy is superficial. It does not go into depth of the causes of maladaptive behaviour. It only deals with the symptoms and leaves basic cause of the neurosis untouched. Therefore it is considered that it brings about only temporary alleviation

of symptoms. There is always danger of the patient being relapsing into his original condition.

The issue has been discussed and resolved by Wolpe and Lazarus who claim that the objection of critics against behaviour therapy as superficial is baseless and unfounded. They have reported a number of cases of severe neurosis who have successfully been treated by them without any relapse.

2. The second observation of critics is that behaviour therapy is symptom-oriented. To some extent the observation is correct. Behaviour therapy has also been criticized on the ground that it nearly smothers the neurotic symptoms. It is said that new symptoms will necessarily arise to replace extinguished behaviour patterns.

3. The major issue in behaviour therapy is the extent to which the therapist dehumanizes his client by mechanically controlling the therapeutic interaction and to some extent the client's life. Behaviour therapy has been accused by critics of being antihumanistic because it treats persons as machines and because it does not treat whole persons but only restricted part of the symptoms.

4. A very crucial issue which has attracted the attention of all people in recent years is the concern that powerful behavioural techniques especially operant techniques and aversice conditioning will be used for improper purposes such as changing undesirable political and social behaviour that the subject does not wish to change. Behaviour therapy can be used to overbear the "Will" and thus the dignity of the individual.

5. Another important issue raised in recent years is whether and to what extent behaviour therapists should attempt to integrate the theory and practice of the dynamic therapists within one holistic therapeutic framework. Some psychologists feel that dynamic theory has much to offer to understand human behaviour and behaviour theory offers more effective techniques for behaviour change. Therefore it is suggested that an integrated dynamic and behavioural approach should be used in the treatment of behavioural disorders.

6. A last but an important issue is regarding the application of the principles of learning evolved from the experimental studies conducted on infrahuman within a restricted environment of psychology laboratory.

According to London, learning principles do not have systematic application to behaviour disorders and in any case even the most basic principles are open to dispute.

Trait and Factor Theory of Counselling

Trait and factor theory of counselling was developed in the beginning of the present century with the progress in the development of measuring tools for intelligence personality, interest and aptitudes. The theory is based on the assumptions that human beings, have specific traits of personality. A trait may be defined as "a continuous dimension of which individual differences may be arranged quantitatively in terms of the amount of the characteristics the individual has." Traits develop gradually in the process of interaction in the environment. Traits have specific properties by which they are distinguished from other personality characteristics. The important properties are, sealability, inferred from the behaviour, universality, inferred from the behaviour flexibility. Traits are learned behaviours, they are higher order habits and they have functional utility. G.W. Allport, Cattell and Eysneck have developed theories of personality based on traits.

More recently psychologists have started on isolating various factors which constitute intelligence. Therefore, Guilford Spearman, Vernon and Thorndike have devoted their research studies to isolate the factors.

The Counselling Process

The counselling theory of trait and factor theory of personality is very simple and objective in approach. The counselling is provided on the measured characteristics of the individuals. The counselling theory gradually developed into four distinctive phases which are briefly described as follows:

(*a*) The first phase started with the construction of a varieties of test and inventories to measure the educational, vocational interests and tests of aptitudes and achievements. The tests were used to provide guidance to the individuals.

(*b*) The second phase was marked by the construction of adjustment inventories covering a wide range of activities in addition to educational and vocational problems of the clients. The second phase of development includes the development of client adjustment inventory. This approach emphasized an objective analysis of the individual client's measurable attributes.

(*c*) The third stage of development in the trait approach counselling was brought by factor analysis of human abilities notably by Spearman Burt, Thurstone and Guilford etc. Ginzberg and Anne Roe developed theories of occupational choice and career development.

(*d*) The fourth stage of counselling was introduced by the concept of career patterns. Davidson and Anderson studied career patterns of the workers in occupational hierarchy. Psychologists like Super and Ginzlurge have classified personality as work-oriented and pleasure-oriented.

Comparison of Different Therapies

	Dynamic	Humanistic	Behaviour	Trait and Factor
1.	Causes lie in the unconscious.	Self-concept is the organizing factor of personality.	Overt symptoms are important.	Individuals differ in ability interest and aptitudes.
2.	Symptoms as evidence of repression.	Self functions in the phenomenological world.	Symptoms are determined by individual differences.	Individual differences can be measured on a continuum of defined traits.
3.	Defence mechanisms are the indicator of maladjustment.	Self tends to maintain and actualize itself.	Faulty learning is the cause of maladjustment.	Individuals can be made aware of their abilities.
4.	Treatment explores the past history of the patient.	Treatment emphasizes the importance of present.	Present is important.	Symptoms are indicators of faulty utilization of traits.
5.	Treatment emphasizes the unconscious behaviour.	Symptoms are threat to self concept.	Cure is achieved by treating symptoms.	All problems are not caused by lack of information.
6.	It is subjective in approach.	It is also subjective.	It is purely objective.	It is also objective.
7.	Treatment is through free association and drawn analysis.	Treatment is concerned with the development of self.	A variety of techniques are used.	—

Goals. Trait-factor counselling aims to:

(*a*) select appropriate educational and vocational career based on measured abilities.

(*b*) find out the areas of maladjustment with the help of inventories.

(*c*) acquaint the individual with his strengths and weaknesses with the help of tests.

Research. Research studies are being conducted to isolate the exact number of abilities involving intellectual functions. It is expected that in near future counsellors would be able to provide better guidance and counselling facilities based on measured factors of personality.

NEW TRENDS IN COUNSELLING

Here we will describe some of the major trends in the counselling process in the western countries. No doubt counselling services in our country at present are at the initial stage but in the present age of information technology counselling services need to be improved and strengthened to provide effective services to the larger population.

1. The first important trend which has developed after 1947 is of mobility both in terms of residence and job opportunity. Due to industrialization, the population started migrating from one area to the other, many people are moving from rural to urban, from east to west, south to north and vice versa. The migration of population may be due to many factors, for example, job dissatisfaction, lack of employment opportunities in an area, job transfer, reservation of jobs for scheduled castes and scheduled tribes. All these factors have necessitated the migration of population from one part to the other.

2. The second important trend is that due to industrialization and westernization, our traditional values are constantly shifting and our clients are affected by them. Traditional attitudes toward work and leisure use of time have changed and are continuing to change.

The moral values of India are also in a state of flux — Greater permissiveness is emerging in the areas of sexuality and drug use.

The women's liberation movement has affected males and females alike. As women assume a more equal status, this will influence their working and family relationship. As women's roles change, there will continue to be a noticable effect on the roles and attitudes of both men and women.

3. Another issue that reflects the values within our society deals with the conflict of material gain or of service to others on the part of our citizens. Clients will differ as to their emphasis upon each of these values. Counsellors need to be aware of these values as held by their clients in order to work successfully with them.

The status of the family as being a traditional and unalterable institution is changing very fast. The number of divorces and separations is increasing. There are also more remarriages taking place, inter-caste, and inter-state marriages are being encouraged.

Within families themselves, there has been less contact with older generations.

The fact that more wives and mothers are working than ever before influences the relationship within families. In instance where being the money provider has meant being the head of the household, men have been greatly disturbed when they were unemployed and the wife was the sole financial support of the household. Acceptance of this type of relationship, nevertheless, has been increasing in our society.

Parental authority seems to be challenged by young adults more frequently and at earlier ages than previously.

There is great need on the part of clients for counselling regarding marriage, family and parental concern.

4. In the recent past counselling services are more accepted by the public. More and more people are using counselling as a method of helping themselves and their families.

Parents, teachers and administrators are becoming more and more convinced of the importance of counselling in aiding students to solve their problems.

5. Counsellors are working within more specified areas of concern. There is a trend toward specialization on the part of many counsellors. Senior retired citizens need specialized counselling regarding retirement plans, financial matters and housing etc.

6. Another trend is that counsellors are being asked to be more accountable for their services. The trend toward accountability in education and the request for observable results has influenced many counsellors. Counsellors are presenting their services to clients in the form of systematic and programmed approaches, for an easier evaluation of activities carried out and progress made.

7. Counsellors are becoming more directive and assertive. This trend is directly related to counsellor accountability. Counsellors are becoming less inclined to allow clients to proceed at their own pace and make decisions based on self-insight and self-understanding. This movement of counsellors to become more action-oriented might also include counselling techniques, such as behaviour modification, in that change can be seen.

8. Group counselling as technique is being increasingly accepted and used by counsellors. Group counselling has been widely advocated and adopted as an economical and an effective way of aiding clients. The goals of aiding clients to become self-understanding and self-

acceptant and to develop self-direction and self-responsibility are the same in both individual and group counselling. Counsellors are training parents, teachers, students and community social workers using counselling and related skills to handle problems of the general population.

9. It is expected that in the near future computerized technology and audio-visual aids will be increasingly used by counsellors. Counsellors have often tried to be encyclopaedias of information for their clients in terms of providing data about educational and occupational opportunities, employment openings and referral agencies. They have often been burdened with the clerical duties of record keeping, storage and retrieval.

Automation has aided and will continue to aid counsellors in dealing with these tasks. All types of information regarding educational and occupational opportunities are now available in the form of films, cassettes, computer print-outs and at computer terminals that have access to computerized programmes.

ASSIGNMENTS

1. Define a theory. What are the characteristics of a good theory?
2. Differentiate between client-centred and directive counselling.
3. Describe in detail Behaviour Counselling Theory.
4. Define Transactional Analysis and describe in brief the fundamental concepts of TA.
5. What are the new trends in counselling?

REFERENCES

Pietrofesa, John J.: *Counselling: Theory, Research and Practice.* (Rand McNally College Publishing Co. USA, 1978).

Peek Dabid and Whitlow David: *Approaches to Personality Theory,* (Methuen and Co. Ltd. London, 1975).

Rothney John W.M: *Adaptive Counselling in Schools* (Prentice Hall INC Englewood Cliffs W. J., 1972)

Patterson, C.H.: *Theories of Counselling and Psychotherapy* (Harper and Row Publishers, NY, 1973).

Ellis, Albert: Humanistic Psychotherapy, (McGraw Hill Book Co., NY, 1973).

James Muriel and Contributors: *Techniques in Transaction Analysis* (Addison-Wesley Pub. Co., Philippines, 1977).

Berne, Eric: *Principles of Group Treatment* (Grove NY, 1968).

Chapter 13

The Counselling Process

It is not possible in this chapter to give a detailed account of the counselling process. We will give only a panoramic description of how it is actually practised. No doubt, different theories of personality prescribe different processes of counselling which differ to a great extent in practice but there are certain common techniques which are invariably followed by all workers in the field.

CHARACTERISTICS OF THE COUNSELLING PROCESS

General characteristics of counselling process are as follows:

1. Counselling is a person-to-person relationship. It involves two people (Counsellor and Counsellee) in interaction which is highly confidential and unobserved by others.
2. There is mutual participation in the process of counselling. The mode of interaction is usually verbal communication.
3. The counselling process is structured around the felt needs of the counsellee. It continues till the behaviour of the counsellee is modified to enable him to handle his problems independently. The process, generally, takes too much time because the behaviour alteration is a very gradual process.
4. The main emphasis in counselling is on self-direction and self-acceptance. It is a process in which counsellee freely and frankly expresses and explores himself the issues which are of concern to him.

Approaches to Counselling Process

In the preceding chapter we discussed the major theories of counselling and the counselling process they adopt to solve the problems. All the theories, generally, follow the following three approaches, which are described below:

1. *Directive approach.* It is a process of counselling in which the counsellor directs the activities of the counsellee. This approach is based

on the assumption of viewing his problems objectively. He needs help from others who are more experienced and knowledgeable in analysing and solving his problems. Children and adolescents who are emotionally immature and inexperienced need constant help when they are faced with a problem. This approach which emphasizes the importance of the counsellor in the process of counselling was developed by E.G. Williamson and Darley. The counsellor is responsible for solving the problems of the counsellee. He identifies the problems and analyses them for the individual and explains diagnostic picture to the counsellee. He suggests the treatment to be given to the counsellee. Great stress is laid on the need for careful diagnosis and prognosis. The interview is conducted assuming direct leadership by the counsellor. He takes firm control of the interview and most of the time he leads it.

The approach of direct counselling is based on the assumption that in the society more able persons are capable of directing less able. The focus in the process of direct counselling centres round the problems, not the individual. The directive approach of counselling has been criticized on the following points.

(a) It is a counsellor-oriented approach. It does not develop self-confidence and self-direction in the counsellee.

(b) It develops submissiveness in the counsellee. It makes him dependent on the counsellor wherever there is a problem.

2. *Non-directive approach*. This approach has already been discussed in detail under the theories of counselling. As the name suggests, the major role is played by the counsellee. The counsellor plays a secondary role in the whole process of counselling. The approach of non-directive counselling is based on the assumption that every individual is capable of solving his problems provided that he is made aware of the problems, and that the individual has a basic tendency to grow, to actualize his potentialities and that his growth leads to personally and socially satisfying behaviour.

The main task of the counsellor is to help and encourage the counsellee to think himself to face his problems. It emphasizes the emotional aspect of the counsellee's personality.

3. *Eclectic approach*. A third approach which uses the middle course was developed by F.C. Thorne. This approach of counselling neither exclusively adopts the directive nor non-directive counselling approaches but a combination of both. In the initial phase, in collecting relevant information, the counsellor may be directive but later one he may switch over to non-directive approach whenever the situation warrants. He may use simultaneously both the approaches in the treatment of a case.

CONDITIONS FOR COUNSELLING RELATIONSHIP

It is universally acknowledged by all psychotherapists and counsellors that counselling relationship plays an important role in the whole process of counselling. The counselling relationship is characterized by some specific conditions which are described below:

(a) *Acceptance*. Acceptance is the first requisite condition for successful and effective counselling. The counsellor should willingly accept the basic nature of the client and the client should demonstrate the feeling of acceptance towards the counsellor. Here it is important that the counsellor has the upper hand in the counselling process. It means that he can win the confidence of the counsellee by expressing his basic feelings in a fashion that is conducive to demonstrate his acceptance of the client. The counsellor should not conceal his feelings. He should be straightforward in dealing with a counsellee.

(b) *Trust*. Trust is another important condition of counselling relationship. It involves confidence in another person. If the counsellee has trust in the counsellor, then he can express his personal problems and can risk with him. A counsellor should be able to trust others. If he is unable to trust others in his own living, it is difficult to transfer this lack of trust outside the counselling relationship to one of trust in it. It is likely that he will behave counselling relationship much as he would in other relationship. Lack of faith or confidence in the counsellee can be exceedingly detrimental to the relationship.

It is said that trust begets trust. The counsellor by his behaviour can create trust and faith in the counsellee.

(c) *Understanding*. If the above two basic conditions of acceptance and trust have been established in the counselling relationship then understanding of each other's behaviour and feeling is possible. Understanding is an abstract concept which is difficult to comprehend. It is more than hearing the content or feeling of another's experience and understanding. The counsellor must try to understand the total personality of the counsellee.

DIMENSIONS OF THE COUNSELLING PROCESS

1. *The internal vs. external*. The process of counselling involved two types of variables: internal and external. Internal aspects of a counsellee's life have great influence on his behaviour as expressed in various experiencing situations in the environment. These include his own beliefs, values, attitudes and needs which account for the individual's behaviour. The external variables include the total environmental influences which affect the behaviour of the individual.

These may include home, school and society and all persons who come in contact with the counsellee.

(*a*) *Beliefs.* Beliefs are represented by those opinions, ideas or concepts we accept and use in our day-to-day living. They can be identified and enumerated. There are two categories of beliefs: abstract and concrete. The belief in God is an example of abstract belief and concrete belief as too much sugar is bad for the teeth.

A belief is something that we have confidence in, that we trust. It represents some deliberate thought and reason. Beliefs including ideas are an important part of one's internal reference and they are continually used in our day-to-day behaviour in the many life-situations and task which we encounter.

Both the counsellor and the counsellee may find themselves verbalizing beliefs in the form of convictions, sentiments, ideas or concepts.

(*b*) *Values.* The social, moral and ethical standards of our society have in one way or another contributed to the development of our own particular value system. It is important to remember that each of us is continually being exposed to different standards and values as these are represented by different groups in the social strata.

Every counsellor has his own value system. He has considered aspects of worth in many different areas such as family, religion, work, love, money and politics. Our values in these areas are represented by those aspects that we find desirable and worthy.

According to Luis E. Raths *et al*, valuing involves three processes — choosing, prizing and behaving. These processes indicate the manner in which the individual selects from the many alternatives available those things which he believes are of worth to him. Those which he has chosen, which he comes to value or esteem. These individually represent a value and these in combination represent our value system. The priority of any value, that is the worth that we attach to it, the place we accord it in our total value system and the manner in which we act on it, very definitely affects our behaviour.

Indian society is divided into various broad groups and sub-groups, which have different value systems. There is great variation in individual value systems in our heterogeneous society. In the process of counselling, both the values of the counsellor and the counsellee are constantly in operation: both value systems are tested and explored. The counsellor is faced with values and behaviour which may be the same as his or different from him or foreign to him. Thus he is constantly reacting internally to the expression of values of others.

There may be some problem in creating basic conditions of the relationship when the counsellee's values differ from those of the counsellor.

(c) *Attitude.* Attitudes influence our behaviour to a very great extent. Attitude is an enduring learned predisposition to behave in a consistent way toward a given class of objects; a persistent mental and/or neutral state of readiness to react to a certain object or class of objects, not as they are but as they are conceived to be (*English and English*).

(d) *Needs.* Needs have been classified in different ways by psychologists. Here we will give the classification of needs as developed by Maslow in his theory of human motivation. His "theory of hierarchy of needs is as (*i*) basic physiological needs (*ii*) security and safety needs (*iii*) love and belongingness needs (*iv*) self-esteem or prestige needs (*v*) aesthetic needs (*vi*) self-actualizing needs.

In the process of counselling, human needs should be considered, both in terms of their relationship as it develops between the counsellor and the counsellee and in terms of the help that can be afforded to the counsellee in assessing and understanding his own needs and their effect on his behaviour.

(e) *Abilities.* Abilities play a very crucial role in the process of counselling, particularly in relation to various aspects of educational and vocational planning. Students, no doubt, are generally guided on the basis of test scores on standardized instrument but equally important is the potential for growth in self-assessment and self-understanding.

(f) *Interests.* Interests are often expressed in the counselling situation by the counsellee. Self-expression of one's likes and dislikes indicates the internal frame of reference providing many avenues of self-exploration to follow. The counsellor can help the student examine his interests in detail; it takes some time to help a student process an interest.

2. *The feeling vs. the content.* The internal-external dimension of the counselling process as described above deals with the individual's beliefs, attitudes, abilities etc. and the external environmental influences which affect his behaviour. The feeling-content dimension derives from the fact that an individual is concerned with his feelings about himself in his environment (feeling) and with his experiences in his environment (content).

In a counselling situation, content descriptions and discussions are essential and often necessary to establish a base for the communication process. An individual's feelings of the event and about what was said are equally important to explore. Sometimes, in the excitement of recounting an episode, a counsellor can read much feeling while the student is telling what happened and very frequently, the content of the story will be punctuated with significantly direct statements of feelings.

The counsellor learns to utilize techniques that help the counsellee to express both feeling and content. The expertise of the counsellor depends as much on his ability and insight to judge how to help the counsellee explore the situation as on the techniques which he emploves in moving the session along.

3. *The self and self-disclosure*. The last dimension of counselling process is the self-disclosure. The main objective of individual counselling is to help the individual to explore his self. This requires a good deal of self-disclosure which is not done quickly but is a very slow and continual process that depends on the human aspects of the relationship and the manner in which these are characterized in their counselling relationship.

ASPECTS OF THE COUNSELLING PROCESS

(A) *The communicative aspects of counselling practice*. Communication between the counsellor and the counsellee is an important condition for successful counselling. In the process of communication, the counsellor can play an important role by applying his insight and tact in exploring the problems of the counsellee.

Francis Robinson has suggested the method of how a counsellor can guide and lead or control the counselling process. The following are the specific techniques arranged in order of the degree:

(*i*) Silence (*ii*) Acceptance (*iii*) Restatement (*iv*) Clarification (*v*) Approval (*vi*) Summary clarification (*vii*) General leads (*viii*) Tentative analysis (*ix*) Interpretation (*x*) Urging (*xi*) Depth interpretation (*xii*) Rejection (*xiii*) Assurance (*xiv*) Introducing a new aspect of a problem.

Another communicative aspect of the counselling process is the non-verbal behaviour of the counsellee which is manifested in gestures, position of the body, body movements and facial expression. The counsellor can glean much evidence by assessing the nature and depth of relationship by observing the movements of the counsellee, eye contact, the position and use of hands, facial expression and a number of other non-verbal expression of comfort, hostility, anxiety and nervousness.

Gladestin has developed a chart of non-verbal behaviours which are generally shown by the counsellee in counselling situations.

He has grouped all types of behaviours in the following three categories:

1. Body movements.
2. Voice qualities.
3. Vocalization.

These can be used in modifying and controlling the behaviour of the counsellee by neutral acceptance of understanding mild approval or disapproval and strong approval or disapproval.

(B) The structural aspects of counselling process. The counsellee comes to the counsellor with some purpose in his mind. The purpose may not be very clear in his mind. The counsellor has to consider the structural elements in relation to the practice of counselling.

The Initial Interview

Preparation. Before conduction counselling the counsellor should take necessary preparation keeping into consideration the magnitude of the problems of the counsellee. The first is to study thoroughly the previous record and other material bearing relevance to the case without drawing inferences and jumping to conclusions.

If unable to do so the counsellor should go into the initial session without extensive preparation.

There are certain assumptions that can be made about the process of counselling in the initial interview. It can be assumed (*i*) that the counsellee needs help (*ii*) that nothing specific needs to be accomplished beyond the structure required by the counsellor (*iii*) that initial session is merely a stage more frequently a beginning one.

Tyler suggests three objectives for the initial interview: (*i*) getting a sound counselling relationship started (*ii*) opening up the psychological realms of feeling and attitude with the person and (*iii*) clarifying the structure of the helping process.

Buchheimer and Balogh divide the initial interview into the following three phases:

(*i*) Statement of the problem;
(*ii*) Exploration;
(*iii*) Closing and planning for the future.

Cattle and Downie list four specific purposes of initial interview: "One of these is to establish a good working relationship between the counsellor and the client which will last throughout counselling. Another is to validate and expand the data about the client collected prior to the interview. Still a third is to observe the client directly and to collect information which will show client feelings about values, interests, attitudes and goals. In addition this first interview is used to establish the structure within which counselling will take place."

In take procedures. The first contact with the counsellor should always be very personal. The counsellor should be friendly and hospitable. He should be courteous with the client and should observe punctuality in his programmes. In the first meeting the counsellor should talk about general problems. He should try to make him feel at ease and comfortable.

Establishing rapport. The major purpose of the first interview is to establish rapport with the client. The first interview is very critical in many instances in determining whether or not the client will continue. The counsellor should effectively observe and attend to the client. This will help in establishing rapport. In the first interview question-asking should be kept to a minimum.

Termination of initial interview. The first interview is meant to develop rapport with the client. The interview should be terminated in a facilitative manner. The counsellor can use a variety of statements to close the session.

Tyler (1969) points out:

> The initial interview is the hardest part of our task — the part that demands from us the most intensive concentration. Each person constitutes for us a new adventure in understanding. Each is destined to broaden our own lives in directions as yet uncharted. Each initial interview renews our appreciation of the challenge and the fascination of the counselling task.

Structuring the counselling relationship. Structuring the counselling relationship is a continuous and on-going activity and may occur at various states in the counselling. It is a means of accommodating the 'person' of the two people involved in the relationship. It is a process of helping both understand each functions.

The counsellor talks about the life expectations of the counsellee and his perceptions of them. He pinpointedly locates the discordant expectations.

Duration of counselling. The duration and frequency of contacts with the counsellee in the counselling process varies from individual to individual depending upon the nature and magnitude of the problem.

Another important factor is the number of students who are to be served by a school counsellor. Therefore the questions of duration and frequency of contant should be considered by the counsellor himself.

Counselling Notations and Records

Counseliing may be considered a working record of the counselling relationship. They may be incorporated in the student's record file. Counselling notes are helpful in recalling the general tenor or essence of the previous session, in recalling specific conversation or topic or insight or progress.

Record notations are particularly helpful in secondary school counselling as evidence of the contact and nature of it.

Diagnosis. Diagnosis of the problems of the counsellee means to locate the causes of the problems. In counselling a number of theories have been developed in the last fifty years which apply different approaches in diagnosing the problems.

Bordin suggested five diagnostic categories that prevented the client from solving his own problems. They are (1) dependence, (2) lack of information, (3) self-conflict, (4) choice anxiety, (5) no problem.

Apostal and Miler developed a two-dimensional diagnostic classification plan. Problem-goal dimension (1) vocational (2) emotional (3) educational.

Cause dimension included (1) lack of information about self, (2) lack of information about environment, (3) motivational conflict within self, (4) conflict with significant others, (5) lack of skill.

The *use of educational and occupational information.* Most of the problems of adolescents in India are due to lack of educational and occupational information. The counsellor should make available information for decision making self-directing activities.

Selection of tests. The counsellor should very carefully select the tests for administration. Tests should be selected on the basis of their reliability and validity.

Legal and ethical consideration. The counsellor should be familiarized with the legal implications of his professions. He should also work and follow the ethical standard as set from time to time by the National Association of Counsellors.

ASSIGNMENTS

1. What are the necessary conditions for counselling process?
2. What are the important dimensions of counselling process?
3. Write an explanatory note on the counselling interview.

REFERENCES

Munson, Harold L.: *Foundation of Developmental Guidance* (Allyan and Bacon Boston, 1971).

Pinto, Diana V.: *Counselling: Theory, Research and Practice,* (Rand McNally College Pub. Co., Chicago, 1978).

Chapter 14

Role of the Counsellor and the Teacher in Counselling

Since the development of systematic theories of counselling, numerous researches have been conducted on the personality characteristics and professional preparation of counsellors. All books on counselling invariably list the personality traits which have been considered essential for counsellors to perform their duties successfully. Traditionally, personality traits such as fairness, sincerity, intelligence, alertness and interest in other people were considered important to success in counselling, but very recently, the emphasis has shifted from personality attributes to the way the counsellor uses himself in his human communication.

Here we will describe the characteristics of the counsellor, role of the teacher and the administrator in the process of counselling.

Characteristics of a Good Counsellor

The personality characteristics of the counsellor are very important for him to carry on the counselling process efficiently and successfully. The characteristics that distinguish the counsellor have become the focus of much investigation in the last 30 years. National Vocational Guidance Association (NVGA) has emphasized the following characteristics — interest in people, patience, sensitivity to other attitudes and reactions, and emotional stability and objectivity and that they respect facts and are trustworthy.

Hamrin and Pulson conducted a study on the characteristics of counsellors and have listed the following in order of preference:

1. Understanding, 2. Sympathetic attitude, 3. Friendliness, 4. Sense of humour, 5. Stability 6. Patience, 7. Objectivity, 8. Sincerity 9. Tact, 10. Fairness, 11. Tolerance, 12. Neatness, 13. Calmness 14. Broadmindedness, 15. Kindliness, 16. Pleasantness, 17. Social intelligence 18. Poise.

The Council of Student-personnel Association in Higher Education has recommended that a personnel worker must have the following characteristics:

1. Abiding interest in students, 2. Faith in students' capabilities, 3. Understanding of students' aspirations, 4. Interest in educational process, 5. Good physical and emotional health, 6. Willingness to serve others, 7. Ability to function at irregular hours, 8. Respect for others, 9. Patience, 10. Sense of honour.

The Association for Counsellors Education and Supervision has suggested the following characteristics :

1. Belief in each individual, 2. Commitment to individual human values, 3. Alertness to the world, 4. Openmindedness, 5. Understanding of self, 6. Professional commitment.

Robert E. Farson in his article "The Counsellor is a Woman" published in *Journal of Counselling Psychology* 1954 has concluded that counsellor characteristics were fundamentally those that society traditionally attributes to women-tenderness, gentleness, receptiveness and passivity.

Kazienko and Neidt surveyed the characteristics of male enrollees in 25 Counselling and Guidance Institutes throughout USA and reported the following:

1. *Self-concept.* Serious, earnest, patient, soft-spoken, aware of personal self-centredness, more domestic than social, not mechanical minded.

2. *Personal motivation.* Concerned about possessing a measure of security but rejects need for wealth.

3. *Values leading to happiness* ... and shrewdness as leading to personal contentment, feels persons should have the right to be different.

4. *Feelings about other people.* Views people as possessing an adequate measure of intellectual ability.

Weitz has conducted research on counsellors' personality traits, and has listed three personality traits that can facilitate counselling. These are: security, sensitivity, and objectivity. Security, states Weitz, is a ".... sense of self-acceptance. This involves a frank recognition of strengths and weaknesses". "The secure person," he adds, "....accepts other people as they are, recognizing within the limits of his perceptions, their needs, and expects to be accepted on the same terms by them and as he usually is,".... "The sensitive person," according to Weitz,".. is capable of understanding and appreciating a wide range of psychological behaviour. This must be construed to include both the cognitive and affective levels of human understanding". Lastly, Weitz characterizes the objective person as,"....capable of distinguishing between objective and symbolic behaviour, yet understands the intimate relationship between these two."

A counsellor should not make hasty judgements about others. He should be capable to transcending the certainties and uncertainties of his own life. Briefly then, it can be said that he must possess a balanced personality.

Counsellor's Role and Function

Here we shall describe the role of the counsellor as viewed by different categories of persons.

1. *Pupil perceptions.* According to students a guidance counsellor programme adds something of value of their school. They expect that a counsellor must know something about courses and curricula and educational and vocational opportunities. Van Riper conducted a survey on counsellor role and reported that "the counsellor was rather easily identified as a person who helped with educational plans somewhat identified as a person who helped with school problems and not clearly identified as a person who helped with school problems. . . ."

Several studies conducted on counsellor's role lead to the conclusion that students do not view the counsellor as an effective source of help except in the area of educational and vocational decision-making. It is further concluded that counsellors have failed to convey to students feelings of acceptance and understanding.

2. *Teachers' view of the counsellor.* Now let us see how teachers view the role of school counsellors. A survey was conducted by Darley on the attitudes of teachers. He summarised the result of his study as follows :

(a) Counsellors are administrators and the nicest thing you can say about administrators is that they are a necessary evil which may be but better not eradicated.

(b) Counsellors provide ancillary services and are therefore expendable.

(c) Counsellors coddle and pamper those who would, and perhaps should flunk out.

(d) Counsellor's pretense of confidentiality is merely a shield to hide behind when the welfare of the institution is involved or their activities are challenged.

Lewis and Florence conducted another survey on the attitudes of teachers towards the role of school counsellors and their conclusions reflect some of Darley's conclusions.

Teachers have harsh and hostile attitudes towards school counsellors. There are many reasons of it. It is difficult for most classroom teachers to accept the need for human relations specialists in school. To admit that counsellors are necessary and earn their keep is to imply that teachers have certain weaknessess that they are reluctant to face.

3. *Administrators' opinion of counsellors.* Hart and Prince report that conflict exists between counsellors, perceptions of their roles and that which administrators expect them to do.

Administrators do not believe that counsellors are particularly competent to assist students with personal and emotional problems. Principals thought that counsellors were second rate, in both their preparation and their personal characteristics. Counsellors failed to get close to students and that the counsellor's jargon bored students, was unrelated to their concern and made them distrustful. Several studies have reported that counsellors frequently function as clerks. The administrator views the counsellor as a Jack of all trades.

Counsellor's Functions

In the preceding paragraphs we saw that students, administrators and parents have different attitudes as regards the role of the counsellor. Some of the counsellor's functions will be reviewed here. Wrenn has prescribed the following functions:

1. *Counselling.* This includes counselling with students on matter of self-understanding, decision-making, and planning, using both the interview and group situations.

2. Counselling with staff and parents on questions of students' understanding and management.

3. Studying changes in the character of student population and making a continuous interpretation of this information.

4. Performing liaison functions between the school and community.

The following ten functions have been described by the American School Counsellor Association in 1964 for School Counsellor:

1. *Planning and development of the guidance programme*. It is the basic responsibility of the counsellor to plan the various activities involved in guidance programme.

2. *Counselling*. The counsellor shows concern for educational, vocational and personal problems of the students. He attempts to solve their problems.

3. *Pupil appraisal*. The counsellor collects data about individual students through non-test technique and test techniques.

4. *Educational and occupational planning*. The counsellor aid the students in self-evaluation, self-understanding enabling them to. make decision consistent with their immediate and long range educational goals.

5. *Referral work*. The counsellor also helps the students to acquire a better understanding of the world of work in the community.

6. *Placement*.

7. *Parent help*.

8. *Staff counselling*. The counsellor works with all members of the school staff by providing appropriate information, materials and consultative assistance in supporting teacher efforts better to understand the individuality of each pupil. He contributes to curriculum development and cooperates with administrators and teachers in the refinement of methods for individualized learning.

9. *Local research*. He conducts researches in the local communities in order to find out the needs of the community.

10. *Public relations*. The counsellor holds conferences with parents or guardians about the students' growth and development.

He provides the parents with accurate information about educational and career opportunities.

He assists the parent/guardian in forming realistic perceptions of the students' aptitudes, abilities, interests and attitudes as related to educational and career planning, academic achievement, personal and social development and total school progress.

Counsellor's Functions Related to Counselling

1. Assist the pupil to understand and accept himself as an individual, thereby making it possible for the pupil to express and develop an awareness of his own ideas, feelings, values and needs.

2. Furnishes personal and environmental information to the pupil as required regarding his plans, choices or problems.

3. Seeks to develop in the pupil a greater ability to cope with and solve problems and an increased competence in making decisions and plans for which he and his parents are responsible.

Functions in Planning and Development

(*a*) Assists in defining the objectives of the programme.
(*b*) Assists in developing plans of action.
(*c*) Assists in continued guidance programme and development.
(*d*) Assists in identifying the guidance needs of pupils.
(*e*) Evaluates the programme.
(*f*) Assists other members of the staff in evaluating their own contributions to guidance services.

Commission on Guidance in American Schools has suggested the following responsibilities of the school counsellor:

(a) Counsels with students on matter of self-understanding, decision-making and planning, using both the interview and group situations.

(b) Consults with staff and parents on questions of students understanding and management.

(c) Studies change in the character of the student population and making a continuing interpretation of this information available to school administration.

(d) Performs a liaison function between school and community counselling resources.

THE TEACHER

The teacher can play an important role in making the guidance services more effective by virtue of his being in close touch with the students. No doubt, to some extent every teacher is a counsellor when he counsels students about the selection of courses, developing good reading habits and suggesting remedies for the personal problems of the students but every teacher is not supposed to be an effective counsellor. A teacher must bave some specific qualities to be a good counsellor. Following are the characteristics and functions of a teacher-counsellor.

In our country, there is a lack of qualified counsellors. We can give orientation to our teachers till we have qualified competent counsellors.

Role of the Teacher

The teacher's role is that of being a good teacher. This means that the teacher organizes learning experiences first in terms of the abilities and needs of the group, then within that framework adapts instructional content, method and personal relationship to the optimum learning potential of each youngster. Guidance services provide information about those students who have some problems. The teacher plays an important role in the total guidance programme: He contributes to and draws benefits from the programme of guidance. He supplies the following information:

(*a*) The marks of the students indicating achievement in each subject.

(*b*) The report which includes any outstanding achievement of the student in and outside the school.

(*c*) He can, on the basis of his observation and interaction with the students, report the cases which need immediate help. The student with problems should be reported in the form of an anecdote or note describing a list of behaviours of the student.

(*d*) The teacher can inform the students of educational and occupational opportunities available in helping the child to plan his future career.

(*e*) The teacher can render invaluable aid by participating in case conferences.

(*f*) The teacher also has a definite duty in the counselling programme. His primary responsibility is working with students who have problems related to learning in the particular course. This may include individual contact. The teacher is the primary referral agency. The student whose difficulties do not respond to classroom treatment is referred with information to the counsellor.

ASSIGNMENTS

1. What are the roles and the characteristics of the school counsellor?
2. What is the role of the teacher in the process of counselling?

REFERENCES

Morse, Stephen, J.: *Psychotherapies* (Holt-Rinchart and Winston, May 1977).

Pinto. Diana V.: *Counselling* (Rand McNally College Pub. Co. Chicago, 1978).

PART - IV

Chapter 15

Placement and Follow-up Services

PLACEMENT

Placement is an important service in any guidance programme. Without placement, a guidance programme is incomplete because until and unless an incumbent is placed in a good job where he can utilize his maximum abilities and skills, and a continuous evaluation of his progress is made, the services are meaningless.

Placement refers to "assigning of a worker to the job for which he is judged best fitted". The term 'fitted' means the individual's satisfaction as well as his abilities in relation to the job. There are two types of placement services: (a) Educational placement and (b) Vocational placement. We will describe them in the following pages.

Functions of Placement Services

1. *Determining needs revealed by drop-outs and follow-up studies.* In our country, the largest number of drop-outs is at the higher secondary school stage. The reasons of drop-outs may be many. How can the school prevent the high percentage of drop-outs? This question can be answered by placement workers who may gather information from drop-outs as regards their problems and also evaluate the total school programmes to minimize the percentage of drop-outs.

2. *Counselling of former pupils.* Pupils who dropped out return to the school in future for guidance. The counsellor can aid such drop-outs by suggesting them courses which can help them in bringing efficiency in their work.

3. *Curriculum planning.* Placement services help in planning, modifying and reconstructing the curriculum in the light of the data collected from the field.

4. *Occupational information.* Placement personnel may collect information on problems peculiar to various jobs. They can provide useful information to the teacher of the occupations, on job getting technique, and trends in occupations.

Phases of Placement Services

1. In the first phase, the general character of educational or occupational life is explained to the student and he received necessary education pertaining to occupational life.

2. In the second phase, the student is oriented to some educational or occupational field in which he is interested and about which he has sufficient educational experience.

3. In the third phase, the student is enabled to understand his own interests and aptitude and to relate them to the educational or occupational areas under his study.

4. The fourth phase of placement service deals with the actual choice of an educational course or an occupation. It is the most important phase of placement service. The individual needs skilful guidance and counselling in choosing a job for himself. This is the stage when the guidance worker thoroughly evaluates the personality characteristics of the individual.

5. In the fifth phase, the individual takes up the job and begins to perform actual duties.

6. The last phase of the placement service is follow-up of the job course provided to the individual.

TYPES OF PLACEMENT SERVICES

A. Educational Placement

Educational placement consists of helping students select appropriate curriculum, the subjects within a special class for gifted and slow learners and the like. Traditionally the curriculum followed needed upto 8th class in our country is uniform. Educational guidance is needed in class IX to select a suitable course out of the five groups. Arts, Science, Commerce, Agriculture and Technical Education.

The new pattern of education (10+2) recently accepted in the country provides a uniform curriculum upto 10th class and after 10th class, different streams are provided for the students.

Placement within a curriculum after the 8th or 10th grade level is extremely important because of its eventual influence on future career of the pupils.

Educational placement within school is concerned with placing students in school activities that will add to their development as individuals.

Placement helps the youth to meet their needs for social development, civic participation and personal growth. It helps in their selection of activities that contribute to their development in line with their interests and help them engage in more or in fewer activities as warranted. Educational placement may help pupils select the special courses that are suitable to them.

Some Characteristics of Educational Placement

Educational placement involves assisting pupils to obtain information in relation to higher educational and training opportunities.

It is the process of assisting the individual to reach the next step in the sequence of educational or training experiences which he accepts as appropriate for himself. It is more comprehensive than job placement.' Following are the major characteristics of educational placement.

1. *Educational placement affects all pupils.* Educational placement is a continuous process which aids all pupils to adjust to the new grades and the next school. The teachers and the administrators are concerned with adjustment of pupils in their present grade and school and also to prepare them for the next school. The personal information which teachers gather and record about each pupil accompanies him to the next grade and school in order to facilitate his adjustment by understanding his interests, aptitudes and academic achievements etc.

2. *Articulation between schools palacement.* Assisting the individual to progress from one school to the next is a placement function. For discharging this function successfully, the cooperation of the sending and the receiving school is essential. The teachers should make clear to the individual with the opportunities open to him for further education and training. This function of placement services needs active cooperation between the schools.

3. *Placement in training situations.* In our country, pupils may be divided into three categories (a) those who pass Higher Secondary or Intermediate and enter college, (b) those who pass Higher Secondary or Intermediate examination and seek employment, (c) those who drop out of school to work or to seek employment.

Some pupils will seek assistance to get admission to some technical or professional institutions while some others may need on-the-job training, etc.

The services involved in the placement process should be concerned with providing information, counselling and placement in accordance with the needs and interest of individual pupils.

4. *Placement in co-curricular and community activities.* Some of the educational opportunities which may serve pupils are found outside the school's instructional programme and others exist beyond

the four walls of the school. Certainly, the co-curricular activities offer opportunities for exploring pupils' interests and aptitudes. Likewise many community activities offer developmental experiences for pupils. It is the responsibility of the school to identify co-curricular activities in the school and the community which offer desirable experiences for pupils. Once these activities have been explored, the school needs to recognize the functions of placement. Aiding pupils to utilize those who promise to serve the needs, and interests of individual is the responsibility of the placement worker.

The school should help pupils to relate their interests to co-curricular opportunities and to see that those activities which serve their needs and interests are made easily available to them.

B. Vocational Placement

Vocational placement includes assisting the youth to secure part time and full time employment after their school career is over and placement in post-high school education and training situations. The university educational guidance and vocational guidance department (A list of universities which have department and bureaus of vocational guidance is appended at the end of this book) can play an important role in providing information on the labour market at local, state and national levels. But types of services which are provided at present in the university bureaus to the vast majority of students are not of great use because the bureaus have no separate accommodation, meagre resources and one or two members of staff who are not duly qualified to provide guidance services in the universities.

Some Characteristics of the Job Placement Service

Effective job placement services are an essential part of the total guidance services. The placement personnel must keep themselves in touch with the job opportunities and referral agencies in the community to perform their duties efficiently. The following are some of the characteristics of job placement services.

1. *Placement activities should be well-coordinated*. The job placement services should be well-coordinated to avoid unnecessary duplication of services. The teacher, employer, community agency and job placement personnel should occasionally hold meetings to discuss the problems of job placement. Job placement consists of the following phases:

(*a*) *Orientation to occupational fields*. This step introduces the individual to job families requiring similar aptitudes, interest abilities and preparation.

(*b*) Relating self to occupational life. This step involves learning about one's own aptitudes and interests and how they are related to a given occupational area. The individual is made available the information about a wide range of occupations. Both group and individual methods may be used in carrying out this phase.

(*c*) *Choosing an occupational area*. The individual is aided to match his abilities with the requirement of an occupation and assisted to choose an occupation suiting to his abilities and interests.

(*d*) *Job placement*. After completing all the above stages of placement services, the next steps are evaluating choices, confirming relationships of personal aptitudes and interests to occupational requirements, locating job opportunities, and referral to potential employers, directly or through cooperating agencies.

(*e*) *Follow-up*. This is the last step which determines the appropriateness of his choice.

2. *Publicizing the placement services*. The students could be given information related to educational and vocational opportunities. Placement services may be publicized through handbooks, school newspapers, teaching in the class and career conferences, information corner, use of audio-visual aids and meetings with employers etc.

3. *Cooperation with community agency*. If placement services are to be made effective and successful then it is essential to enlist the cooperation of various community agencies.

4. *Providing reliable job information*. The school should provide reliable job information to the students.

5. *Using information about pupils*. The placement service should rely on the information collected in school after collecting reliable data about students.

6. *Providing counselling services*. Regular counselling should be given to those who need it. It may be organized on individual basis or on group basis.

ORGANIZATION AND ADMINISTRATION OF PLACEMENT SERVICES

Efficient organization of placement services depends on the attitude and willingness of the principal of the school. If the principal is convinced of the utility of placement services and realizes their importance in the total educational programme and if prepared to meet the expenses, then the programme can be successfully organized. The principal should decide questions about the needs, facilities, occupation, areas of services, participation of teachers and counsellors, type of clients, and ratio of placement services workers to pupils. The placement services will be most satisfactory if the following principles are kept in view.

1: Organization should be in harmony with existing school orgniazation.

2. Functions of the service should be predetermined.

3. The service objectives and policies should be in harmony with the purpose and training objectives of the school.

4. An advisory committee of administrators, teachers, counsellors and placement workers should be formed to recommend policies on (*a*) objective, (*b*) clearance of information, (*c*) research activities, (*d*) follow-up and evaluation.

5. Duties of the placement workers should be clearly specified. The major duties of placement workers are to (*a*) select placement personnel, (*b*) serve as liaison between the school and the employers, (*c*) interpret the school programme to the employer, (*d*) advise school on the needs for curriculum revision, (*e*) coordinate placement services with the other agencies, (*f*) conduct field visits, (*h*) contribute towards a programme of follow-up.

FOLLOW-UP

This is the last step in guidance, services which determines the appropriateness of occupational and educational adjustment of the pupils.

Follow-up is an important aspect of guidance service. Without proper follow-up guidance services are meaningless. It means continuously to evaluate the progress and adjustment of the individuals after giving them counselling regarding courses or vocation. Follow-up may be classified into the following types:

1. *Incidental follow-up*. This type of follow-up is carried on by teachers and counsellors as part of their normal duties. Counsellors and teachers hold interview to get information about the results after counselling and the improvements made by counsellees.

2. *Remedial follow-up*. This type of follow-up is meant for chronic cases which have received intensive remedial help in certain fields. Case histories are prepared and on the basis of the findings, counselling is provided.

3. *Systematic follow-up*. This type of follow-up is to be found where schools have evolved a systematic procedure for following up pupils from one unit of the school to the next higher one. For example, primary school, junior school, high school or to make the follow-up study of those who have entered the world of work.

4. *Follow-up for school leavers.* This type of follow-up is meant for school and college leaving pupils. The school follows up the pupils after they complete their education. They are aided to get adjusted in their post-school environment.

FUNCTIONS OF FOLLOW-UP SERVICES

The concept of follow-up as a service suggests the need for maintaining continuous contacts with students who complete their education and with drop-outs in order to collect useful information, to improve school programmes and to meet the needs and aspirations of the students in a changing society. In our country follow-up services hardly exist except in some professional institutions. The schools, colleges, and universities should seriously think of introducing follow-up services to reduce the problems of the coming generations of students. The follow-up services perform the following functions.

Service Function

(*a*) Keep in touch with all school, college and university students for years to aid them in making adjustments.
(*b*) Keep the institution informed of the difficulties former students encounter on jobs or in other institutions.
(*c*) Locate and offer assistance to unemployed, discouraged or those students who dislike their work.
(*d*) Improve co-operation between high school and college.
(*e*) Locate occupational opportunities and keep the school in touch with current occupational trends, requirements and opportunities.

Guidance Functions

1. Collect and supply teachers, counsellors and administrators information about the problems of former students.
2. Supply the information on the demands of different occupations. Information on the skills needed by workers for available jobs provides a basis for modifying the school's occupational training programmes.

Curriculum Research and Revision Function

1. Evaluate the effectiveness of the school curriculum to modify or expand in the light of the experiences of school leavers.
2. Assist in adapting the school programme to the needs of the pupils and the community.

3. Evaluate specific portions of the school programme such as guidance services, instruction etc.
4. Provide information for pupils and teachers to aid in understanding the school's aims and achievements.

Purposes of Follow-up Surveys

1. To obtain information as to how well students do after completing their education in vocational, educational and social adjustment.
2. To help students realize the problems that lie before them.
3. To gain an appraisal of school programmes and services.
4. To obtain ideas for improving school services.
5. The last purpose of the follow-up of school leavers is to gather information of general interest concerning those who have left. Such follow-up studies are intended to help all social agencies, including schools to deal with the problems of youth more intelligently.

Procedures in Follow-up Studies

Before initiating follow-up studies, the guidance worker or researchers should keep the following points in view.

1. The purpose of the study should be specifically detailed out. There should be no ambiguity left as regards the objectives and the type of data to be obtained for the study.

2. The uses of such data should be specified in the beginning and also the instrument to be used for data collection should be carefully selected, keeping in view the objectives of the studies.

3. The researchers should decide the method of processing the data and method of reporting the findings to the appropriate agency. Generally, two main procedures are used in gathering information in follow-up studies, survey through questionnaires and interviews. Both procedures have certain limitations which are very difficult to overcome. One of the limitations of questionnaires which has been reported by all researchers is that the half of those whom questionnaires are sent do not return them. This creates sampling problems. Exkert suggests that "to detect certain kind of bias, such as lesser cooperation from persons who failed to make satisfactory adult adjustments, it may be necessary to interview a random sampling of non-respondents and compare findings with those already secured from respondents". Interviews are time-consuming, costly and seldom practicable in the case of individuals who have left the community.

In both questionnaires and interviews, the replies to questions of opinion about the values of training received in school may be somewhat too favourable. Everyone tends to remember pleasant experiences and to forget the unpleasant ones. When one has been out of school a few years, his memory of school life tends to be coloured by sentiment and he is liable to exaggerate the values derived from the school programme.

A representative sample of each group is interviewed in order to obtain more extensive and detailed information that can be included in a questionnaire.

Responsibility for making follow-up studies is decentralized so that each class is advised to follow up his own class as they leave school.

The adviser's analysis of the data is made available to other school functionaries and is combined with those of other advisers in order to give a complete picture for the school system.

Conclusions concerning causal relationships are drawn with caution.

Characteristics of Follow-up Plan

Traxler in his book *Techniques of Guidance* has given the following salient characteristics of a follow-up plan.

1. It is planned to serve the needs of both the individual and the school.
2. It begins before the students leave school.
3. It is continuous.
4. It includes all school leavers.
5. Each class is followed up for at least five years.
6. Procedures are used to ensure the return of questionnaires from 80 per cent of those to whom these are sent.
7. The significant items for each individual's return are transferred to his cumulative record card.
8. The follow-up plan is coordinated with a post-school counselling service.
9. So far as possible, the cooperation of lay citizens is obtained in collecting, studying and using the follow-up data.

PLANNING BETTER FOLLOW-UP STUDIES

Follow-up studies are very important to evaluate the outcome of schools. In our country, very few studies have been conducted on educational and vocational follow-ups. Everyone feels that follow-up studies are very valuable to improve the existing programmes. To attain greater value and to justify time and money required to be spent, follow-up studies should be conducted following a scientific procedure which is given here.

1. *Follow-up studies be carried to their logical conclusion*: Generally a follow-up is conducted in three phases — (a) The first phase involves the systematic collection of data from former students using standardized or self-made tools. (b) The second phase involves the analysis and interpretation of the information collected and the results of the study should be presented to all persons involved in the study. (c) The third phase is important because it is concerned with planned modifications in the educational programme on the basis of the findings of the study.

2. *Follow-up studies be conducted at regular intervals*: If schools are really interested in improving their curricular programmes in accordance with the fast-changing socio-economic conditions then it becomes imperative to conduct follow-up studies at regular intervals. The interval may be of two, three or five years which may be decided keeping into consideration the resources of the school.

3. *Follow-up study be school projected, not one-man projected*: Follow-up study should be taken up by a team of teachers and students and if possible some interested persons from the local community may also be involved in the study.

4. *Follow-up study results must be handled effectively*: This is an important step in the follow-up study. If the findings and conclusions of the study are not effectively reported and publicised among the members then it can nullify the great deal of effort spent in gathering facts. Better methods of reporting data to professional and lay groups need to be developed in order to gain their understanding and support.

5. *Technical aspects of conducting follow-up studies deserves greater attention*: This is the last step which deserves special attention of the experts. This deals with the technical aspects of tools to be used for data collection. Tools to be used should be objective and reliable.

ASSIGNMENTS

1. Define Placement. What are the functions of placement service?
2. Describe the administration and organization of placement services?
3. What do you mean by follow-up? How will you improve follow-up studies? Suggest some measures.

REFERENCES

Stoops Emery: *Guidance Services* (McGraw Hill Book Co. NY, 1959).

Erickson, Clifford E. (ed.): *A Basic Text for Guidance Workers* (Prentice Hall Englewood Cliffs NY, 1955).

McDaviel H.B. (et al): *Readings in Guidance* (Henry Holt And Co. New York, 1959).

Chapter 16

Role of Family and Community in Guidance Services

GUIDANCE AND THE FAMILY

All psychologists agree that the personality of an individual develops by constant interaction between biological inheritance and environmental forces. The first social environment is home which plays a most important role in shaping the personality pattern of an individual in early infancy. The child's likes, dislikes, stereotypes about people, expectancies of security and conditioned emotional responses all shaped in early childhood which have lasting effect on his future adjustment.

There are several empirical studies which prove that any type of deprivation in early infancy results in consequences which are detrimental to the harmonious development of personality. The home can help to reduce the personal social problems of children by providing a conducive environment for growth. The parents who provide a good moral pattern help in the adjustment of children more than the parents who provide a poor model for imitation. In the last forty years, due to scientific discoveries, socio-economic change and scientific inventions, the role of family is fast changing. The joint family system is being disorganized gradually to meet the needs of the changing society.

A larger number of women are entering in different jobs. Families are becoming more mobile. But even though family life is changing very fast, it plays an important role in the guidance of children.

The home, community and school are interdependent and their functions are interrelated. No programme of guidance can be successful without the cooperation of home. The guidance worker can aid better in solving the problems of pupils if he develops liaison with home by getting the following information.

1. Knowledge of socio-economic status of the family, education of parents, profession.
2. Needs and activities of the child and his relation with siblings.
3. Problems of the child, and his emotional relation with children.
4. Parents' behaviour with the child.
5. Type of home, physical facilities, religion.

Collection of relevant information is not enough to provide guidance to the pupils. Active cooperation and participation in the process of guidance is very essential. The home can cooperate in the following ways:

(*a*) by providing accurate information about the problems of the child in home, his interests and hobbies etc.
(*b*) by providing conducive environment in the home for developing good relations among different members of the family.
(*c*) by providing physical facilities in the home.
(*d*) by providing information regarding the problems of adolescents freely and frankly.
(*e*) by cooperating with the counsellor.

School-Home Cooperation

The home and school should supplement the activities and functions of each other. Both should work in close unison. If school and home maintain close contacts with each other, both can be mutually benefited. The school and home reinforce each other in their reciprocal task of educating and socializing the pupil. The existing conditions in our country are very unfortunate. The school and home are moving in diametrically opposite directions. There is no mutual relationship between home and school. Whatever values, habits and attitudes the school endeavours to inculcate in the young children are washed off in the external environment due to lack of proper reinforcement.

Guidance Services and the Home

Aurbuckle on the basis of his study of parents reports that such study groups result in (1) better parental understanding of adolescents, (2) greater awareness of the guidance process, (3) sharper awareness of social needs and educational aspirations of youth, (4) more efficient parent-counsellor guidance conferences. Parents should be involved in the whole process of education, in order to focus on building stronger family relation by helping parents understand themselves, their children and family communications. If parents are well-informed about the characteristics of children and problems emerging at different age levels they would be able to solve conflicts between the child and the family members.

The school and home are, of course, two of the strongest forces in the lives of children. The strength of these two can be markedly increased if the schools work cooperatively with home to reduce the factors that disrupt youth and to reduce the number of children who already show undesirable behaviour. The schools occupy a central position in providing guidance to youth. They have close and continued contacts with every child over a period of time. They receive children early in life and have as their central objective assisting them directly to become a well-integrated useful citizen. An effective programme of guidance will only emerge if parents, teachers and counsellors cooperatively plan the strategy.

Guidance services can provide parents with educational and vocational information that will make them better informed in their planning situations with children. It results in sounder expectations and decisions.

No doubt, furtherance of the relationship among the parents, the school and the community is an extremely important outcome of the guidance programme. But in our country majority of the parents are illiterate who cannot be held responsible for providing guidance to their children. Moreover, parents in our country are not interested in establishing a relationship with the school. The school is working independently and in isolation without taking the community into confidence.

ROLE OF COMMUNITY

Community guidance responses consist of those services available from individual agencies and organizations which, through study and analysis of each individual attempt, provide formal and informal experiences to encourage growth toward the individual's highest potential developmental level.

The size and composition of a community, its wealth, its values and leadership affect the resources of the community, which in turn affect the growth, development and behaviour of children. The school does not and obviously cannot provide all the necessary services required by guidance personnel especially teachers and counsellors to ensure a complete guidance programme.

Methods for Becoming Acquainted with Community Resources

Each community has its own resources which may be of great use in providing guidance services to the pupils. The following methods may be used to collect information about community resources.

1. *Publications*: School, community and public libraries offer the most readily available sources of gathering information. Telephone and business directories, newspapers, files and brochures provide information.

2. *Survey*. Survey is another method of collecting information from the community. Association of parent-teachers, chambers of commerce and local colleges can be canvassed for help and cooperation. Pupils may be utilized for gathering occupational information from the community.

3. *Workshops, field trips and work experience*: Colleges and universities may offer either on-campus or extension courses to help familiarize teachers and counsellors with community resources.

In our country agricultural universities are doing valuable services by establishing extension departments, field trips, and workshops. Special days may be fixed to gather information from the community.

Types of Community Resources

There are some family welfare services which have been recently instituted in our country. The main objective of these services is the welfare of the individual and the community. These services need to be strengthened in our country.

Community Services

The parent-teacher associations, neighbourhood clubs and other informally organized groups of parents of handicapped children are but a few of the organizations providing a positive influence for improving home relations.

Information about Special Education Services

The school charged with the responsibility of educating the children and youth of the nation must not only be skilled in dealing with learning problems but must also serve as a source of information for those who are ineligible for schooling or who seek equivalent or additional training. This is the responsibility of the teacher-counsellor and psychologist working together for developmental and remedial instruction. The school psychologist should keep in his file information about schools of exceptional children. Information about special programmes should be available to parents.

COLLEGE-COMMUNITY RELATIONSHIP

The college-community relationship has acquired a new dimension in our rapidly changing society in recent years. If we are interested in improving the community, it becomes imperative to involve it in the programme of the colleges and seek its active co-operation to initiate new programmes to strengthen the relationship.

Keeping into consideration the importance and urgency of the problem the United States Educational Foundation in India (USEFI) organized four regional seminars in Delhi, Pune, Chennai and Bhubaneshwar in the months of October and November 1979.

The theme of the seminar was "College and Community". The participants, mostly professors of education, and principals of colleges, discussed, with a team of American experts (Presidents of Community Colleges), the various problems involved in strengthening college-community relationship. The seminarians made recommendations for the UGC, the USEFI and principals.

Though the recommendations have been made in the context of higher education, they are also applicable to higher secondary education. Here we will describe only those recommendations which fall within the purview of the principals.

IDENTIFICATION OF WAYS AND MEANS

1. Work and service should form part of the academic curriculum and should be given credit by the university.
2. Career courses should form part of the curricula for credit and universities should be moved to implement this recommendation.
3. These career courses could be given in addition to the present academic load of students or they may replace courses which have been less relevant.
4. Colleges and universities intending to do work in community relations should first identify the need of the community so that need-based programmes could be started in consultation with community leaders. There should be flexibility so that the courses could be stopped as soon as the needs have been fulfilled.
5. Courses started by the college should as far as possible be self-financed. Resources of the community should be tapped to the maximum. Funds from the community could also be collected depending upon the type of factories in the area.
6. Coordination with the existing voluntary and governmental organizations should be ensured.
7. Autonomy should be given to colleges to try new experiments and introduce new courses within the present curricula.
8. Teachers engaged in community service should be given orientation, particularly in their pedagogical approach. There should be total involvement of the staff and the students. They should be prepared to face setbacks. Sometimes the institution,

teachers and the students may be accused of creating problems in the community, since change leads to resistance.

9. Colleges should think themselves as instruments of social change. They should invite the people living in the region to share ideas whenever possible.
10. Two or three colleges in a given area should make a cooperative attempt, using available resources, equipment and expertise to run vocational courses.
11. Both non-formal and formally structured approach to vocational education should be experimented with or the job experience should form a necessary component of all vocational education.
12. Universities and colleges should institute degree courses and post-graduate courses in extension work, community development and vocational education.
13. The concept of guidance throughout life and at one's own pace should be made known to all and efforts should be made to implement programmes to make this possible.
14. All new colleges should be vocationally-oriented.
15. The teacher training institutes and colleges should restructure their programmes to teach new methods of pedagogy and educational technology.
16. Universities/colleges should set up multiple centres throughout the community to render useful services.
17. Funding should be both local and governmental. The community should be involved in the funding as much as possible.
18. Socio-economic surveys should be conducted in order to assess the needs of the community.
19. Extension service department should be opened for guiding and coordinating services to the community.
20. Lead colleges should be made community colleges.
21. NSS should be integrated with the college curriculum.
22. USEFI should sponsor more programmes of this nature and help provide resource persons.

FORMULATION OF PLANS FOR ACTION

1. The curriculum for special courses should be prepared with the help of experts from outside the academic community if necessary.
2. Credit should be given in monetary or non-monetary form to the faculty for their services to the community.

3. Colleges should adopt a village or group of villages and help to solve their problems with mutual consultations.
4. A journal on college community relations should be established.

ROLES OF TEACHERS, STUDENTS, PRINCIPALS AND COMMUNITY LEADERS

1. Teachers with only an academic background will need orientation before they can be involved in college community relations, and some organization should take up this task.
2. Full time extension officers should be appointed both at the college and at the university level.
3. Full use should be made of the expertise of managers of industries or other professionals for teaching and drawing up curriculas, and extension services should be made compulsory.
4. The members of the teaching faculty and administration should be helped to develop positive and creative attitudes towards extension work, community service and career education.
5. The college administration, faculty and students must learn to listen to the people around, understand their problems and needs and then work out effective programmes suited to local needs.
6. Students should be involved in adult education and they should live in villages.

ASSIGNMENTS

1. What is the role of family in the process of guidance?
2. What are the resources of the community which are helpful in guidance?
3. How will you enlist the cooperation of community to improve guidance services?

REFERENCES

Miller, Carrol H: *Guidance Services* (Harpar and Row Publishers, Y. 1965).

Erohlick Cliffer P: *Guidance Services in Schools* (McGrow Hill Book Co., Ny., 1958).

Erickson Clifford H: *A Basic Text for Guidance Workers* (Englewood Cliffs Prentice Hall, Ny.,1955)

Chapter 17

Organization of Guidance Services

The organization of guidance services is gradually acquiring importance in our country. Sporadic efforts in the past on individual basis are being replaced by formalized guidance services. Educationists are now convinced that organized guidance services should be available in all higher secondary schools to prepare adolescents to develop their abilities to the maximum in a democratic society. Needless to mention that in the last two decades several revolutionary changes have taken place in our society. The enormous growth in our population, use of technology in all sectors — medicine, business, industry and increased job opportunities for skilled and semi-skilled professions — all these have necessitated the introduction of guidance services.

The reader may now ask a simple question: What are the advantages of organized guidance services? Some of the advantages are enumerated below.

Advantages of Organized Guidance Programmme

1. *Coordination.* It makes possible coordinating work of staff members, guidance personnel and social worker so that instead of divergent, unrelated types of activities, the work of each person will relate to that of others in an integrated pattern.

2. *Avoidance of duplication.* The unnecessary duplication of effort can be easily avoided. An organized programme makes it possible to plan for the most pressing needs. It increases the efficiency of the services.

3. *Maximum utilization of services.* Organization facilitates the use of skills, training and interest of individual staff members and utilizes their services to the maximum.

4. *Economy of time and effort.* A third advantage of organization is the economy of time and effort by the principal as well as the staff members involved.

5. *Spirit of cooperative participation.* Finally, an organized approach to guidance should result in increased cooperation among the staff. A member is able to know the responsibilities of others as

well as his own and can participate as a team member in promotion of guidance services.

Characteristics of a Good Guidance Programme

Guidance programme should be organized on certain principles if it is really meant to provide efficient services to the pupils. Following are some of the characteristics of a good guidance programme.

1. A modern guidance programme is keyed to the purposes of education. A good programme should be aimed to achieve the purposes of education.

2. A good guidance programme assists children to resolve conflicts arising from modern society. Many conditions which affect adolescents are given below:

(*a*) changes in the role of home and family.
(*b*) shifts from rural to urban modes of living.
(*c*) conflicts in social values.
(*d*) rapid scientific development and the lag in adaptive social process.
(*e*) developmental changes in physical, emotional, social and intellectual abilities.

3. A good guidance programme is an integral part of education. Both cannot be separated.

4. It helps the school staff to understand better the characteristics of all adolescents and the problems which emerge during adolescence.

5. It supplies information which may be useful in planning experiences for all.

6. It uses guidance data in promotional policy, and practice, in grouping within the classroom and in special placement of individuals.

7. It emphasizes and applies principles of learning.

8. It improves classroom relationship and emotional climate through emphasis upon democratic procedures.

9. It provides for adolescents with special needs.

10. It is a collective responsibility of many staff members and the administrator.

11. It stimulates the professional growth of all personnel.

12. It improves ways of working with parents and community.

13. It utilizes community service resources which can contribute to the welfare of adolescents.

14. It focusses attention upon the importance of evaluation, and uses appropriate techniques of evaluating the educational programme of the school.

Functions of a Secondary School Guidance Programme

The functions of guidance programme in a secondary school are as follows:

1. To assist the individual student to achieve an increasing degree of maturity in working toward the solution of his varied personal adjustment problems. A majority of students in a higher secondary and an intermediate college are between the ages of 12 and 18 years of age who face a number of problems in home, school and society due to developmental changes. The guidance programme should assist adolescents to understand their problems and to recognize resources which may be helpful in solving them. The guidance programme should be organized in such a way that the first goal is achieved by means of the following ways.

(*a*) helping the individual to develop a better understanding of himself.

(*b*) helping the individual and understanding of his opportunities.

(*c*) helping the individual to set up realistic goals to develop sound plans to achieve them.

(*d*) helping the individual to acquire the ability to handle problems of human relationship.

(*e*) helping the individual to bridge the gaps between different goals.

2. To assist the school staff in securing, interpreting, and using information concerning the characteristics, needs and opportunities of students.

The collection of useful data about individuals and groups of students requires the cooperation of the entire school staff. A guidance worker needs the help of teachers in gathering information from guidance personnel.

(*a*) Material useful in developing a curriculum that meets the needs.

(*b*) Information useful to modify classroom procedures which includes information on the following:

(*i*) Readings for learning.

(*ii*) Achievement in various subjects.

(*iii*) Special interests of students.

(*iv*) Health and personality problems.

(*v*) Personal goals and objectives.

(*vi*) Personal problems of students in schools.

(*vii*) Problems of drop-outs and those who have left the school.

3. To assist the school and its staff in understanding aind working closely with the community they serve.

There must be close cooperation between the school and the

community. A sound relationship can be established with the following activities:

(*a*) encouraging parent participation.

(*b*) visiting home.

(*c*) developing contacts with employers and representatives of the community.

(*d*) working closely with other community organizations.

4. *Counselling*. The school should assist the individual to understand his problems and help him in the planning of possible solutions to his problems.

5. *Placement*. Helping students to find out jobs according to their interests, aptitudes and mental abilities.

6. *Follow-up*. Maintaining contacts with all school leavers and checking individual achievement for the purpose of evaluating and improving guidance programme. Research should be conducted on different aspects of guidance services.

Some Basic Principles of Guidance Services

1. Guidance services are an integral part of the total education programme.
2. A sound guidance programme evolves out of cooperative planning and effort of the entire school staff. It grows in relationship to the needs of the school, community and individual characteristics.
3. The principal is the key figure who provides leadership.
4. The responsibility may be delegated to a senior member in big schools.
5. It provides services to all students.
6. Duties should be assigned to competent members.
7. In-service training of the staff is essential.
8. Counsellors and other guidance personnel should be assigned duties that will make use of their abilities. Routine clerical work should not be given to them.
9. The effectiveness of competent counsellors can be materially increased through the provision of time, materials and personnel necessary for the maintenance of records.
10. The guidance programme of a school can be greatly strengthened if it can call on the community for a number of services.

PROBLEMS IN ORGANIZING GUIDANCE SERVICES

(1) *Physical facilities for the guidance programme*: The first problem which guidance services face in the higher secondary schools where

they exist in this country are that they are housed very poorly. There is no separate accommodation provided for these services.

(2) *Counsellor's load of work*. The load of counsellor's work is so much that he cannot do justice to his job. Most of his time is wasted in clerical work.

(3) *Methods of assigning students to counsellors*. Students are assigned to counsellors at random.

(4) *Organization of counselling staff*. The counselling staff is not well organized and well qualified to meet the needs of students.

PATTERN OF ORGANIZATION

No single pattern or structure of organizing guidance can suit the needs of all schools — large and small, rural and urban, girls and boys. The organizational pattern should be planned in accordance with the needs of the schools and the facilities available in terms of building, finance and staff.

Two tentative patterns are given here — one, for a typical higher secondary school and the other for organizing guidance services at the state level. The reader should keep in his mind that they do not represent ideal plans. Rather they are practical adaptations of the ideal to local conditions. Modifications according to local conditions can be made in the plans.

The pattern of organizing guidance services for a higher secondary school can be as follows:

(1) *Principal*. The principal is the overall incharge of the administration and organization of guidance services in his school. He should provide space, finance and direction to the organization. The principal may delegate his responsibilities to one of the senior members of the staff interested in guidance services.

(2) *Teacher*. A member of faculty may be given the responsibilities of administering the programme. All teachers should be encouraged to participate in the guidance programme.

(3) *Counsellor*. A qualified and competent counsellor should be appointed.

(4) *Committee*. A committee should be formed to look after the total organization and functioning of the programme.

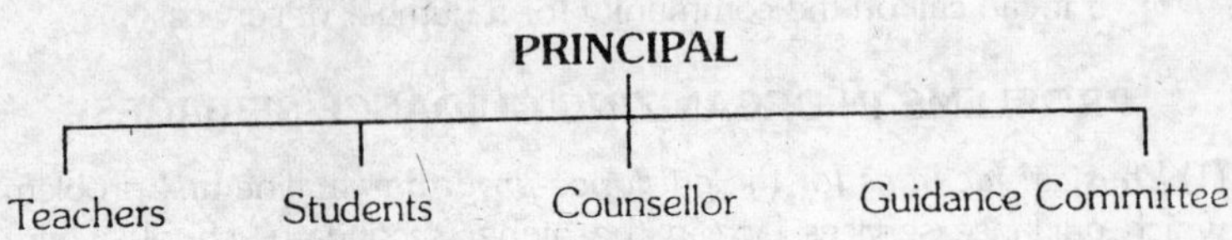

ORGANIZATION AT THE STATE LEVEL

1. Director of Education.
2. Deputy Director of Guidance Services.
3. District Guidance Officer.

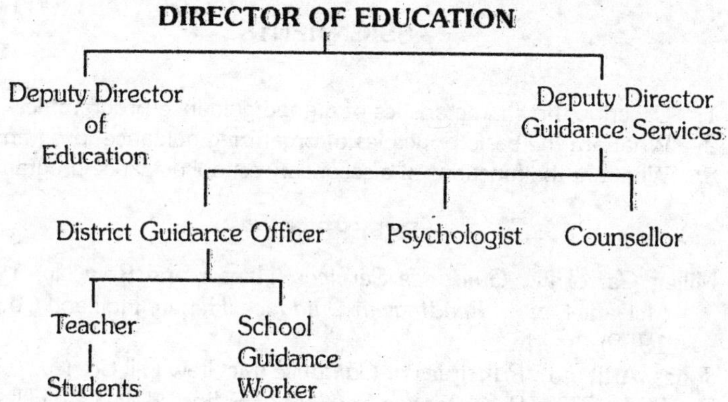

(1) *Director of education*. The director of education is the incharge of education in the state from pre-primary to university level. There are some big states where there are separate directors for primary, secondary and university education. The Director of Education should be the overall incharge of guidance services in the state.

(2) *Deputy director, guidance services*. In a big state more than one deputy directors may be appointed as incharge of guidance services. The deputy director should coordinate the guidance services provided in the district under his charge.

(3) *District guidance centre*. A guidance centre should be opened at the district headquarter in every district. The staff should consist of a psychologist, counsellor and a guidance officer incharge of the centre. The centre should coordinate the services of higher secondary schools in the district and should also provide guidance to the guidance workers.

(4) *School guidance workers*. Every higher secondary school must have a competent and qualified guidance worker. The number of guidance workers may be raised keeping in view the strength of the school. A school having strength upto 1000 (one thousand) should appoint at least one guidance worker who should be assisted by a senior staff member. Separate accommodation should be provided for guidance services.

(5) *School guidance committee*. A committee consisting of the principal, teachers, community leaders and parents should be appointed

in every higher secondary school to advise the guidance worker to facilitate his work. Parents and community leaders can play an important role in appraising the committee of the general problems and needs of the adolescents. The guidance committee should meet to review the cases of problem children.

ASSIGNMENTS

1. Describe the characteristics of a good guidance programme.
2. What are the basic principles of organizing guidance programme?
3. What are the functions of a secondary school guidance programme?

REFERENCES

Miller, Carrol H.: *Guidance Services* (Harper and Row Ny. 1965).
McDaniel, *et al*: *Readings in Guidance* (Henery Holt and Co., Ny. 1959).

Jones, Arthur J.: *Principles of Guidance* (McGraw Hill Co. Ny., 1951).

Frochilch, Cliffer P.: *Guidance Services in Schools* (McGraw Hill Book Co., Ny. 1958).

Chapter 18

Evaluation in Guidance

Evaluation is the process of finding the value of something. It consists of making systematic judgments of the relative effectiveness with which goals are attained in relation to specified standards. It is an important aspect of guidance programme to evaluate its effectiveness because it throws light on the strengths and weaknesses of the programme and consequently helps in improving the programmes in the light of the data.

Another important reason to evaluate the guidance services is that the community is interested to know whether guidance services have produced some specific desirable benefits — demonstrable behavioural change in students. Such evidence can be secured only through evaluation of, and research on, guidance programme.

Evaluation of guidance programme is mandatory if the effectiveness of its services is to be known and if its services are to be improved. Therefore, systematic evaluation of guidance programme enables the school personnel to judge how well they are doing and provides bases for deciding the nature of improvement in curriculum and classroom instructional methodology. If the systematic evaluation is not conducted, there is every possibility that the decisions that are made will often be shaped by prejudice, by traditions or by rationalization. Parents need to be informed of the present status of a programme if they are to participate intelligently in it and also assist in defining its directions and objectives. Therefore, it is very essential to evaluate periodically the effectiveness and efficiency of guidance programme.

In India, no evaluation at state or national level has so far been conducted to see the effectiveness of guidance services which are provided to students in schools and colleges. It is urgently needed to conduct a survey of existing guidance services to see their weaknesses and strengths so that in future remedial measures may be taken to improve them.

BASIC STEPS IN EVALUATION OF GUIDANCE PROGRAMME

Researchers in the field of guidance during the last two decades in the west have developed various approaches to evaluate the guidance services provided in schools. As regards our country, guidance services have not made much progress in the last 20 years. They are at the initial stage. A time may come when we would need the evaluation of guidance in future. There are certain basic elements which are inherent in any comprehensive evaluative process. These are as follows:

1. *Specification of objectives.* The first and foremost step is to clarify the objectives of the programme in observable behavioural terms. The anticipated outcomes of whatever is being done must be formulated in such a manner that they can be observed and verified objectively, with the help of some objective criteria.

2. *Methods.* Decide in advance the methods and techiniques that are to be used to attain the objectives.

3. *Examine data.* Examine the available data about students to determine if they include tests and measurements and other relevant information about students.

4. *Procedure.* A procedure must be developed to collect evidence as to whether the activities of methods will result in the attainment of objectives.

5. *Cooperation.* Consider the extent of cooperation with employers and school personnel, because without the active cooperation of school personnel, no systematic research may be conducted.

6. *Judgment.* The last step is to make judgments about the attainment of objectives of guidance and suggest remedial steps to improve upon the existing conditions.

METHODS OF EVALUATION

There are three methods which are generally used to evaluate guidance programmes. They are briefly described as follows:

1. Survey Method

Survey method is the most frequently used appraisal method in the school setting to evaluate the effectiveness of guidance services. This method usually focusses upon the intent and presence of certain services, the number of staff personnel, their qualifications, and use of time, physical facilities and other external factors.

Though survey method involves both objective and subjective judgments, it gives little evidence as to whether student behaviour is significantly affected by services.

The following steps are followed in survey method:

1. Selection of predetermined criteria for inventory.
2. Collection of evidence of the services being offered.
3. Making judgments regarding the degree to which these services are provided with reference to the predetermined criteria.

In survey method, the following techniques can be used to collect data to evaluate the guidance services.

(a) *Simple observation*. The effects of educational and vocational guidance programme can be surveyed by using observational technique of evaluation. The effectiveness may be judged to some extent by a reduction in the problems of students, reduction in reports of indiscipline to the principal, attendance improvement, reaction of parents to guidance programme as shown by the attendance in parent-teachers' association meetings.

(b) *Check list, questionnaire or rating sheet*. Check list, questionnaire and rating sheet can be prepared to evaluate the guidance services provided in different schools and industrial undertakings. A check list can provide information from teachers, parents, managers, and community agencies on different aspects of guidance services.

2. Experimental Method

Experimental method is the most systematic approach to conduct research study in any area of knowledge. It is carefully planned to study one or more groups of individuals in terms of one or more variables. Generally, the following steps are followed in an experimental study.

(a) Determination of objectives and methods of attaining these objectives.

(b) The development of ways to measure the attainment of these objectives.

(c) Selection of control and experimental groups.

(d) The process of carrying out necessary steps for the attainment of objectives.

(e) Measurement of the outcome of experimentation.

3. Case Study Method

The case study method is designed to assess the changes that take place in an individual as a result of introducing a variable such as counselling. Goals appropriate to the individual are formulated. Counselling takes place. Data are collected on progress towards the goal. These steps are followed, reviewed and assessment of changes in the individual that are attributable to the procedure employed is reported. This method has certain limitations. For exmaple, it depends on subjective evaluation and is also time-consuming.

Limitations of Evaluative Methods

All evaluative methods to assess the outcome of guidance programmes have certain limitations.

1. There is lack of clear acceptable objectives of guidance programmes.
2. Methods of evaluating guidance services fail to relate students objectives to all institutional educational objectives.
3. Use of immediate and easily available criteria and failure to validate such criteria against long-term goals.
4. Individual differences are ignored.
5. All methods make excessive use of subjective reactions.
6. All methods give little attention to satisfactory experimental designs.

THE CRITERIA FOR SUCCESSFUL GUIDANCE PROGRAMME

1. *Reduction in scholastic failure*. Guidance services may be effective if they enable the students to select courses of study commensurate with their abilities and consequently aid in reducing the scholastic failure in schools. They should enable the students to cope with their academic difficulties.
2. *Reduction in discipline problems*. A successful programme is expected to reduce the problems of students indiscipline in schools by providing them opportunities for the resolution of tensions and conflicts etc.
3. *Greater utilization of the counselling services*. A programme may be called successful if the people use the facilities' provided and are benefited by them.
4. *Reduction in programme changes*. Systematically planned guidance services should enable the students to have a sound plan for educational and vocational career.

The students should be made less prone to whimsical and frequent changes in their plans.

5. *Choice of suitable vocational goals.* Guidance services should make a student aware of vocational opportunities and should enable him to make vocational choice consistent with his ability and interest. Guidance should eliminate both a wastage of talent and choice of unrealistic goals.

STEPS TO SECURE CHANGE IN GUIDANCE SERVICES

Researchers have mentioned some steps which if properly followed will help in bringing changes in the presently available guidance services.

1. *Establish commitment to change.* The counsellor, administrator and the teachers should make a determined effort to bring changes for the improvement of guidance programme. No change can be secured by half-hearted efforts.

2. *Determine the needs.* Before starting to secure change, it is usually better to list the most pressing needs of change. For this purpose, a thorough and careful appraisal of the total programme should be conducted. The changes should be planned on the basis of money, time and personnel available.

3. *Study the school situation.* The guidance workers should use their diagnostic skills to determine which individuals are most complacent with regard to present practices.

4. *Clarify the present status.* Guidance personnel who wish to introduce change must perform three fuctions: (1) clarify present status (self-concept by evaluation), (2) describe the desired programme, and (3) point out discrepancies and introduce the aspect of needed innovation.

5. *Gain administrative support.* If some change is designed then it is necessary to gain the administrative support because without administrative support far-reaching improvements are unlikely to be made or if instituted, they will have no lasting or pervasive effect.

6. *Involve the staff.* To bring changes, the active participation of the staff is very essential. When teachers are unable to identify with modifications and accept responsibility to make use of them, there is little likelihood that improvement will last.

7. *Acquaint the community with the reasons and necessity of change.* Every community has certain expectations with respect to school programmes. So if some changes are to be effected the community should be aware of the necessity and urgency of the change. The cooperation of various agencies working in the community should be sought to bring changes in the programme of the school.

AN EVALUATION MODEL FOR GUIDANCE

Traditionally, decisions that affect guidance programme development and upgrading have not been based on systematic evaluation. Instead, decision-makers mostly have relied on insight, trial and error and other pseudo-scientific methods which have failed to evaluate objectively the guidance programme.

Edward Paul Dworkin and Garry R. Walz evolved recently an evaluation model for guidance which may be used to systematically evaluate guidance programmes. Their model is meant to evaluate career guidance services rather than for guidance broadly defined. The model for evaluation in guidance is briefly as follows.

Their model has the following features:

1. The model places guidance within the context of the nature of man, the nature of society and the nature of educative process.

2. It treats guidance as a result as well as focussing on each of its component parts and the inter-relation of its parts to one another and the whole.

3. It is relevant to important goals or outcomes.

4. It provides necessary information so that decisions can be made at appropriate times concerning any aspect of programme development.

5. It considers long-term as well as short-term evaluation.

CONCEPTUAL FRAMEWORK

The guidance evaluation model has been based on the following assumptions:

Assumption 1. Man engages in meaningful goal-directed activity. Individuals need more assistance with their career development and adjustment in home work.

Assumption 2. Society has a need to maintain itself and develop and this need can only be achieved if individuals engage in meaningful behaviour that both maintains and develops the society in which they live. Society must provide the necessary training for career development and adjustment to the individuals.

Assumption 3. Career development and adjustment is a continuous life-long process.

Assumption 4. An important goal of the educative process is to assist persons with their career development and adjustment so that they can satisfy their own unique needs and the needs of society.

Assumption 5. All educational endeavours are processes; they are not justified in themselves but only as they yield progress toward desired goals. The structural components of schools should function in an integrative manner to facilitate attainment of goals.

Assumption 6. The schools and other educative agencies should make continual adjustments in their structural make-up to accommodate the ever-changing needs of society. Failure to this may lead to irrelevancy and rebellion.

Assumption 7. The focus of the educative process is on the individual. If schools are to act as behavioural change agents, it is imperative that the persons to be changed are understood from many points of view. The needs of the individual should be identified at different points of time in the developmental continuum in order to develop learning experiences that will integrate these needs into the structural make-up of schools.

Assumption 8. It is essential that school and other educative agencies should work together toward the attainment of goals

EXPANDING THE CONCEPTUAL WORK

The conceptual framework described above suggests that guidance can serve a very central and functional role in the educative process. The following operations should be performed to translate the conceptual framework into practical terms.

1. Identify the need of the population with which your work.

2. Identify and describe the relevant characteristics and needs of the coummunity as well as the basic characteristics and needs of the country as a whole.

3. Develop the objectives of career guidance programmes on the bases of individual and environmental in-puts. Objectives of the programme should be clearly specified in behavioural terms so that they can be assessed and ranked in terms of priority.

4. The next step is to select the most feasible setting in which to implement the established objectives in whole or in part. It is important to identify and deal with constraints found in the selected settings with a view to make desirable changes.

5. A variety of methods for accomplishing the specified objectives must then be identified and developed. Innovative methods such as computer-based career guidance system should be used.

6. The degree to which each specified objective has been accomplished must be ascertained. This information can then serve as feedback to the planning and decision-making process that allows redesign and continuous improvement of the overall programme on a rational basis.

CAREER GUIDANCE EVALUATION MODEL

The six steps described above are cumulative in nature and should be performed in sequential order. They comprise the basic elements of a systems approach in the development of career guidance programmes. The following are the various parts of the system which should be periodically evaluated to modify the programme.

1. Individual Input Evaluation

The purposes of individual input evaluation are to identify the career needs of those individuals we wish to assist and to delineate problems underlying these needs.

Career needs of young children and adults should be identified. There is great need to identify the needs of women and retired persons and other disadvantaged groups in our society, because women have recently started entering all types of professions. And retired persons also seek some goal-directed activity to utilize their time in a purposeful way.

2. Environmental Input Evaluation

Environmental input evaluation allows the researcher to describe the environment, the unmet needs of the environment and problems underlying these needs. This means to describe the manpower needs and other related career aspects of the environment and describing the means by which the environment is meeting the career needs of citizens; and delineating problems associated with these. Decisions served by environmental input evaluation include the focussing of priority manpower needs of the community and country and strategies for utilizing existing community resources. Information generated from individual and environmental input evaluation will help build a stable foundation on which to develop objectives for career guidance programmes.

3. Objective Evaluation

The success of career guidance programme largely depends on the degree to which meaningful objectives have been specified. The formulation of objectives should be based on information generated from the two previous evaluation activities. The objectives should meet the following criteria.

(i) They should evolve from a sound conceptual framework.
(ii) They should derive from an integrating basic philosophy.

(iii) They should be stated in terms of behavioural changes.
(iv) They should be realistically achievable within a specified time period.
(v) They should be amenable to evaluation.
(vi) They should incorporate recognition of career needs.
(vii) Thev should be capable of being translated into practice.
(viii) They should be stated in sequence.
(ix) They should be independent.
(x) They should be flexible.

4. Setting Evaluation

Setting evaluation allows us to identify the most appropriate setting in which to implement career guidance objectives as a whole or in part, and to identify strategies for dealing with constraints associated with selected setting.

It is desirable to consider a variety of potential settings in which to implement career guidance objectives. The selection of appropriate setting should be based on careful analyses of potential strengths and weaknesses of a number of potential settings. Potential setting should be assessed in terms of time, money, resources, potential procedural barriers etc.

5. Process Evaluation

Process evaluation is an important step to identify and develop appropriate methods for accomplishing the career guidance objectives and to identify the potential sources of failure in the programme.

Developing and selecting methods include surveying the literature, consulting with authorities, visiting innovative career guidance programmes and using individual creativity.

6. Product Evaluation

Product evaluation provides information for making decisions to continue, modify, refocus or terminate as activity found in previous evaluation stages.

Guba and Stufflebeam (1968) have suggested the following guidelines for developing evaluation design.

A. Focussing the evaluation

(1) Define the decision situation to be served.
(2) Define the system to be evaluated.
(3) Define the evaluation specifications.

B. Collection of information

(1) Specify each item of information.
(2) Specify the populations, sources and sampling procedures.
(3) Specify the instruments and methods of collecting information.
(4) Specify the arrangements and schedule for information collection.

C. Organization of information

(1) Specify a format for organizing information.
(2) Specify the means for coding, organizing, storing and retrieving information.

D. Analysis of information

(1) Specify the procedure for analysing information.
(2) Specify means for performing the analysis of information.

E. Repointing of information

(1) Specify the audiences for evaluation reports.
(2) Specify the formats for the evaluation reports.
(3) Specify the means for providing the information.
(4) Specify a schedule for reporting.

F. Administration of the evaluation

(1) Summarize the evaluation schedule.
(2) Define staff and resource requirements and plans to meet these requirements.
(3) Specify means for meeting policy requirements for the conduct of the evaluation.
(4) Evaluate the potential of the evaluation design for providing valid, reliable and credible information.
(5) Specify means for periodic updating of the evaluation design.
(6) Provide a budget.

The guidance evaluation model presented above can be modified suiting to the local conditions and need of the individual and the community.

The implementation of the model may be difficult due to financial, personnel, time and other unforeseen constraints. However, each of the steps should be followed in sequential order so that programme development and upgrading can have maximum impact. Needless to mention that if the model is faithfully operationalized it will succeed in evaluating the guidance programmes more objectively.

ASSIGNMENTS

1. Why is evaluation important? Describe the methods of evaluation of guidance services.
2. Describe in brief the evaluation model for guidance.

REFERENCES

Cook David R., (ed): *Guidance for Education in Revolution.*

Shertzer, Brue and Stone Shelley C.: *Fundamentals of Guidance* (Houghton Mifflin Co., Boston, 1976)

Chapter 19

New Trends and Demands in Guidance

NEW TRENDS IN GUIDANCE

Guidance services in recent years have changed their emphasis from once-for-all activity to a continuous life-long process in the west where a number of programmes have been launched to make guidance services more comprehensive and effective. As regards our country, guidance is at its initial stage and it has not yet been properly organized at all levels. No experimental study has so far been conducted on a wide range of population to test its utility and feasibility.

The major trends in guidance may be categorized into three distinct categories — Guidance programmes and practice; Counsellor's preparation and Counsellor's role and certification. We can organize our guidance programmes keeping into consideration the following new trends and demands in guidance services.

A. NEW TRENDS IN GUIDANCE PROGRAMME AND PRACTICES

1. Career education will be stressed increasingly as an integral part of school's curriculum. It has been experienced that guidance programme was treated as an isolated programme at its initial stage but for the last few years educationists are convinced that it is urgently needed for primary and supportive services and leadership in education. It is further anticipated that teacher will actively participate in guidance programmes. Formerly only qualified persons were involved in guidance but now the trend is changing by seeking the participation of more and more teachers who can provide relevant information about the case. The new education policy introduced in the country stresses the need and importance of career education.

2. The second distinctive trend is that in future more schools will offer psychological education or a varient of it. It refers to the change against present education that in it intellectual development is emphasized to the detriment of personal development. Schools will

offer students curricular experiences that focus upon values, clarification of moral dilemmas, decision-making and principles of psychological well-being. The need and demand of such courses which will help in the psychological development will increase in future.

3. The organization and administration of guidance services will become more efficient than it is today. It is predicted that future administration of guidance services will be based on the coordinated uses of system-wise and geographically based regional resources, facilities and personnel. It may be that primary, secondary and tertiary guidance services will be organized into units specifically designed for these respective purposes so that the human needs of the students will be met in a prescribed geographic region. Delivery of guidance services of high quality will thus be distributed stepwise to all students from the primary to the university level. Increasingly, the responsibility for administration and coordination of the programme will be assigned to individuals who are personally inclined and professionally prepared to give it leadership. The ratio of students to counsellor will be reduced to provide better services to the community.

4. It is predicted that greater effort will be placed on the search for the causes and prevention of human emotional illness rather than continuously supporting the more costly treatment or repair of disorders once they occur.

5. Guidance personnel will be employed on full-time basis and their number will gradually increase.

6. School will enact policies governing the management, use and access to students' record.

7. An increasing number of other specialized people will be sought.

8. *Use of computers*. It is assumed that greater use will be made of automated equipment for the storage and retrieval of pupil appraisal data and other information about the community and school and career development programme. A brief description of the use of computer in guidance is given here.

The greatest contribution of the present-day technology is the development of computer and its successful use in all sectors of life. Computer-assisted guidance and counselling techniques have very recently been developed and have been used to facilitate the work of guidance personnel in the advanced countries of the world. Though in our country computers, at present, are being used in limited areas of data processing and decision-making but if the problems multiply with the present speed, there is every likelihood that we may also have to resort to the use of computers in the field of guidance and counselling to meet the challenges of a technologically-oriented society. Computers are being used in the following areas:

(a) Computers operate machines that design and draw largescale plans.

(b) Computers are used for the problems of scheduling, record keeping, grade reporting, school placement, student appraisal and educational planning etc. which are important aspects of guidance services and involve school counsellor in one or another.

(c) The most fascinating and revolutionary aspect of computer power lies in its capacity for natural language simulation. It is this promise that compels us to think that computer will become a substitute counsellor.

(d) Computers are used for marriage counselling.

(e) They are also being used to match worker characteristics with the job characteristics.

(f) Computer-assisted educational-vocational guidance systems have been recently developed where the client directly interacts with the computer for the solution of his problems.

9. *The concept of accountability*. Traditionally it was assumed that professionals had to be held accountable only for faithfulness to the teaching of their particular disciplines. So long as individuals were considered professionally competent and reliable, no one questioned their performance with clients.

Accountability has become a popular concept in the human professions in 1970s. Everybody agrees that accountability is an important concept in human investment.

The professionals working in the field of guidance and counselling, like in other professions, are being held responsible for their work by the providers of funds, legislative bodies, the general public and recipients of results of services. The opinion of all concerned with human welfare is gaining ground that unless professionals are held accountable, a programme cannot accomplish all that it is meant or purported to accomplish and indeed it may not be accomplishing the best possible results.

Meaning of Accountability

The concept of accountability in guidance and counselling is a recent one. There is no clear agreement as to what accountability means. Who is to be held accountable, for what and to whom? Let us first define the term. Stated simply, "a system of accountability involves evaluating the performance of an organization, and its staff in the accomplishment of clearly specified objectives and then applying appropriate consequences to define accountability as a system of providing feedback about the accomplishment of results without specifying consequences."

According to Robert Walker, accountability performance evaluation requires three steps (*a*) goal setting, (*b*) feedback on performance results to the providers of services, (c) consequences. Wynne says that accountability means "systems or arrangements that supply the general public as well as school men, without accurate information about school output performance — text scores and other data that show how well groups of children are learning in school."

Accountability System

In order to develop an efficient system of accountability based on performance evaluation, it is necessary to specifically define objectives related to both the effectiveness and efficiency, means of performance, performance expectation and definition of who was to be served and provisions for consequences based on actual performance. The accountability system in guidance and counselling involves the following operations:

(*a*) *Specification of objectives*. The most critical and most different part of the development of an accountability system for any organization is clarifying the goals and specifying the objectives to be achieved. The goals and objectives should be decided after discussion and considerable negotiations with different personnel involved in the system. Performance evaluation should be based on the accomplishment of clearly defined objectives.

(*b*) *Development of measures*. Measures are then developed for each of the objectives. This involves deciding who would be measured and who would do the measuring. The measures are the easiest part of the system to develop. The most difficult part is identifying the objectives and expressing them in a specific manner. It is also decided to apply the measures to individual counsellors as well as to the overall programme. The counsellors will have equivalent case loads and receive the same number of randomly assigned new clients. This makes it possible to apply the same measures to all counsellors to compare their results and hold them accountable for results.

(*c*) *Expectations*. Performance expectations are set for each measure. Expectations reflect the degree to which the organization believes an objective can reasonably be achieved in view of the nature of population and other factors operating in the system.

(*d*) *Weights*. The objectives are not generally considered to be equal in value, so relative weightage is given. The weightage makes it impossible for a counsellor to look good in the system without achieving on those measures given the most weights.

(e) *Who is served*. The characteristics of the clients served are monitored along with information on results.

They are described in terms of age, sex, education level, length of unemployment, minority status, number of dependants, presence of disability and history of legal involvement.

The characteristics of the clients, therefore, affect the performance expectations. One of the easiest ways to improve performance reports is to be more selective about who is served.

(f) *Feedback*. The accountability system provides the programme staff with its first objectives: feedback on performance. The staff members are given monthly reports on their performance and the performance of the total programme. Information is anonymously provided on the performance with those of the others.

The good performance as well as those whose performance had clearly been adequate are without objective results. Supervisors often judge counsellors on the basis of their style rather than their accomplishments. Performance reports are also regularly provided to the board and the agencies providing the funds for the programme in order that the director could, in effect, be held accountable for the results of the overall programme.

(g) *Consequences*. A performance system introduces accountability only when there are connsequences for both good and poor performance. Good performance must be rewarded in order to be maintained and action must be taken to correct poor performance.

Sometimes a programme provides financial incentives for outstanding performance.

What happens without accountability?

Without clearly defined programme objectives, performance expectations, and all the other elements of accountability, counsellors tend to do their own things. Each sets his own goals and the focus tends to be on process, style and activities rather than on results achieved by the clients. Without an accountability system and its clear definition of goal and performance feedback there is no way of determining which of these was the better performer on the system.

B. TRENDS IN PREPARATION OF GUIDANCE PERSONNEL

1. Major changes will continue to occur in counsellor preparation programme. Extensive research studies will be conducted to improve the criteria for the selection of guidance personnel.

2. The content of programme will increasingly affect an inter-disciplinary approach in the preparation of guidance personnel. More attention will be given to the essential psychological foundations of human behaviour and modification techniques.

3. The variety of external forces will increasingly influence counsellor preparation and staff certification.

4. Growing number of women will enter counsellor preparation programmes.

C. TRENDS IN COUNSELLOR'S ROLE AND FUNCTIONS

1. Practising school counsellors, as individuals and as a group, will increasingly assume initiative and leadership in determining counsellors' role and functions. The school counsellors will become more and more organized and sophisticated in shifting out and deciding for themselves what is relevant in defining the job of the school counsellor. They will become increasingly concerned that they, not others, are responsible for their role definition and job function.

2. The counsellor, at both elementary and secondary levels, is emerging as a counsellor to students and a consultant to teachers, parents and administrators. It is rapidly emerging as a broad role that includes the art of counselling pupils, individually and in small groups, and the functions of counselling with teachers, parents and administrators.

3. More and more counsellors will be attracted to part-time private practice. Several factors are expected to emerge in future, for example, improved public attitude toward the value and propriety of seeking assistance for personal concerns, behaviour reliance by business and industry on professional evaluation in the selection and promotion of employees and a broader preparation of counsellors that goes beyond the educational concerns and recognizes the importance of personal and situational dynamics.

4. School counselling is becoming a life-time career. It seems certain that school counselling now and in future will be a life-time profession with much to offer the person who brings something to it.

C. NEW DEMANDS IN GUIDANCE

It is needless to mention that revolutionary changes have taken place in all areas of life in the last three decades due to industrialization, socio-economic development, universalization of education, use of technology and automation. Traditional practices of guidance and counselling would not be able to meet the demands of the new problems emerging in human life.

Therefore, it becomes necessary to modify our guidance programmes and develop new strategies to cope with the future demands of the profession.

The following are the specific areas which demand urgent attention of guidance workers in India in 1980s.

1. Guidance for Drug Users

The use of drugs and narcotics is not a new phenomenon in our society. Their use can be traced back to the origin of man on earth. There are instances of drug use and alcoholism in ancient literature.

Asuras used drugs and narcotics for merry-making. The use of various drugs for intoxication had been made throughout the history of mankind in our country but the use of drugs and narcotics was prohibited for children and adolescents.

In the last two decades, due to westernization, frustration, conflicts and failure, our adolescents have started the use of dangerous drugs which has posed serious problems for parents, teachers and all persons concerned with the welfare of the society. It is becoming apparent that if the use of drugs continues with the present speed, ours will become a drug-oriented society and all types of crimes against persons and property will rise at an alarming rate.

Therefore, it becomes imperative to prevent the use of drugs among both school-going adolescents and general population by providing proper guidance.

The drug may be classified into two broad categories — soft and hard. Soft drugs are those usually referred to as non-addictive such as marijuana, ISD, cocaine and hard drugs refer to those that cause physiological addiction. The individual feels restlessness and physiological withdrawal if the drugs are not taken regularly. These drugs are opium, morphine, heroin etc. The use of drug passes through different stages till the user becomes an addict.

The guidance worker or the counsellor should familiarize himself with the language of the drugs and should take the addict into confidence for guidance.

Physical characteristics of the user, the language of the user and a knowledge of the effects of common drugs on the user are paramount requisites for the person working with the youth of today.

2. Guidance for Women

Since independence, the status of women has changed. They have been constitutionally granted equal rights in society and are entering all types of professions. The changed status and role of women is fraught with several problems such as conflict in home, tension and constant anxiety. The number of divorces, separations and suicides are increasing year after year. There is therefore a great demand for providing guidance and counselling services for women to adjust themselves properly in the new role in the society.

In addition to the above, the problem of finding suitable matches is also emerging as an important area which needs immediate attention in order to minimize the problems of future generation.

3. Guidance for Disadvantaged Children

Disadvantaged children in our country have so far been neglected and no provision exists for providing them guidance and counselling. They are left to their fate to survive or die in a society which is full of competition at every step. These handicapped children fail to adjust in the society and suffer from complexes.

If we believe, in socialism we must make provision for the guidance and counselling services for a large number of disadvantaged children, who could prove an asset to the society after proper training.

4. Group Guidance and Counselling for In-Service Teachers

Ours is a vast country. The in-service teachers may be trained in the methods of guidance and counselling. It will be useful if techniques of group counselling are employed because it will save time, money and human energy in the interests of the country. The trained in-service teachers would be able to cater to the guidance needs of a large percentage of student population.

5. Guidance for Retired Persons

There is an urgent need to make provision for the guidance and counselling for retired persons of different professions. Retired persons generally find themselves unable to adjust in home. They experience great difficulty in passing their time in some useful activity.

6. Guidance for Leadership

We have been a democracy for over three decades but till today we do not have any institution where training for leadership is provided. All agree that the success of democracy depends on the general awareness and consciousness of the population towards their rights and duties. The awareness among the masses can be created by honest, sincere and dedicated leaders who at present we do not have in sufficient number.

It would therefore be of great help if formalized guidance services are provided to the future leaders.

ASSIGNMENTS

1. Explain the concept of accountability in guidance.
2. What are the new trends in guidance services?

REFERENCES

Shertzer and Stone Shelley C.: *Fundamentals of Guidance*. (Houghton Mifflin Co. N.G. 1966):

Borrow, Henry (ed): *Career Guidance for a New Age*. (Houghton Mifflin Co. Boston, 1973).

Smith Glenn, E.: *Principles and Practices of the Guidance Programme*. (The Macmillan Co. NY 1957).

Cook, David R.: *Guidance for Education in Revolution* (Allyn and Bacon, Boston, 1971).

Chapter 20

Indian Adolescents: Their Characteristics and Problems

Adolescence is the most important period of human life. It has been described as the spring of life of human beings and an important era in the total lifespan. The word *adolescence* comes from a Greek word *adolescere* which means to grow to maturity. A number of definitions of the term *adolescence* have been given by psychologists from time to time. Some psychologists define it as the transitional period of life in which the child experiences a number of changes. This period runs between childhood and adhulthood and is sometimes called the period of teen age.

According to A.T. Jersiled, "Adolescence is that span of years during which boys and girls move from childhood to adulthood, mentally, emotionally, socially and physically." According to some psychologists, it is the period when an individual is capable of begetting offsprings which means that when the power of reproducing his own kind is attained by the individual then we can say that he has become an adolescent.

Chronologically, adolescence comes roughly between the years from 12 to the early 20's. The onset of adolescence varies from culture to culture, depending on the socio-economic conditions of the society. In this period, great changes occur in all developmental dimensions of the individual which create disequilibrium in the personality.

SIGNIFICANCE OF THE STUDY

To provide effective guidance, the guidance personnel must be well acquainted with the characteristics of adolescents and the problems they face. Adolescence is the most important period of human life. A major part of a country's population ranges between the ages 13 and 21 years. The country's success in various fields of life depends on the proper guidance of adolescents. The study is significanct for the following reasons:

1. *Understanding developmental characteristics and problems.* Every teacher, parent and guidance worker must know about the nature of the changes occurring in the transition period from childhood to adulthood. They must also know the various problems involved in developmental characteristics to be able to deal with them effectively. It is also necessary for them to be familiar with casual factors of the problems of adolescents so that proper individual, educational and vocational guidance may be provided to them for adequate adjustment in the home, school and society.

2. *Maintenance of mental health.* The progress of a country depends on the maximum exploitation of its human resources. A sound mental condition is one of the first requisites for proper development. Adolescence is marked with a number of problems which affect mental health. The study of adolescence is very important in order to preserve, cure and prevent incidence of maladjustment.

3. *Adjustment to responsibilities.* The study provides the knowledge of the needs and developmental tasks of adolescents. Parents, counsellors and teachers can help adolescents to adjust to their responsibilities. By understanding the needs of adolescents, the teacher and the administrator can frame curriculum, school policies and methodology of teaching for them.

We will now describe physical, mental, social and emotional characteristics of adolescents and the problems they face in this transitional period.

I. PHYSICAL DEVELOPMENT

The most important single feature of adolescent development consists in the changes that take place in the young person's body. These physical changes have significant behavioural implications. Following are the specific physical changes which take place during adolescence.

(i) *Changes in height and weight.* Almost all boys and girls show a spurt in growth during adolescence. There is a sudden shoot-up in height. The age at which it occurs varies from individual to individual. The growth in height is associated with pubertal growth period ranging from 13.10 to 17.50 years with an average of 15.33 years. There are sex differences in height and weight among boys and girls.

(ii) *Change in body proportion.* In addition to increase in height and weight, there is general change in the proportions of the various bodily parts. The different parts of the body grow at different rates and attain their maximum development at different times. The pelvic bones of girl become broadened and their wrist becomes circular. The arms and legs grow in length and become finer. Boys develop round shoulders. Early maturing boys tend to be more feminine and the late maturing girl more masculine.

(iii) *Voice*. The change of voice in boys is a commonly recognized feature of adolescent development. This change does not occur at a fixed age or even at any fixed time in relation to other pubertal changes. The voice of boys becomes hoarse and that of girls becomes sweet during this period. The change of voice, sometimes, has notable effects on the behaviour of adolescents.

(iv) *Secondary sex characteristics*. The secondary sex characteristics develop during adolescence. Genital organs in boys increase in size. In girls sex organs acquire maturity. The growth of breasts and the widening of the pelvis in girls are among the physical development that have significant influence on the adolescent girl's perception of her physical self. These changes in external physical organs make the adolescent girl self-conscious. There is a marked change in her gait. She becomes conscious of changes in her physique.

(v) *Hair growth*. Changes in hair growth is associated with puberty. In case of boys hair appears on upper limbs, the chin and the public region. Hair in arm-pits appear in both boys and girls.

(vi) *Physiological changes*. There is change in the internal systems of the body. All systems, respiratory, circulatory, digestive heart and pulse rate acquire their full growth. Brain is fully developed by the age of 18 years of age. The date on menarche has been collected in all parts of the world. It is generally believed that girls in tropical and subtropical countries mature earlier than in cold countries. The average age of menstruation varies from 13.5 years to 16 years.

There is positive correlation between certain physical measurements and mental ability. Abernethy conducted a survey of adolescents' physical development and mental development and reported that there is low positive correlation between mental and physical status. The degree of this relationship decreases after the age of 14 years. It has been shown that the interests and behaviour patterns of children are closely allied to the pattern of their physical and physciological development. Physical development has a psychological effect on their attitudes towards themselves and on their attitudes to others. The physical development is an important factor in social development and approval. If the girl is ugly, underdeveloped, she tries to avoid social situations. If the boy is physically handicapped or has some physical defects then his intellectual and social development is definitely affected.

(vii) *Change in strength speed*. There is a great increase in muscular strength in adolescents as reported by psychologists who conducted muscular strength tests and physical power as shown by heavier grip strength. The adolescents become more active in their work. Girls seem to mature earlier than boys in physical development.

(viii) *Growth trend in motor performance.* Eopenscheda (1940) conducted a study on the same boys and girls for a number of years on tests of running, throwing a ball and jumping. There was great difference in the performance of boys and girls. Boys were better. They are superior, particularly in activities which involve speed, and muscular strength. The boys continue their interest in physical activities while there is a sharp decrease in the interest of girls. There is a sharp increase in throwing events from 13 to 15.5 years. Many of sex differences in motor and mechanical activities are not due so much to a genuine sex difference as to a difference in amount on interest, experience and practice. The difference becomes greater at each age level. There is a close relationship between motor performance and other traits. Popularity in adolescence is more closely related to physical strength and skills in athletics than to intelligence and school achievement. The cluster of physical traits as physical skills, bravery and strength shows a high relationship in social situation and heterosexual relations. These findings emphasize the importance of physical education and recreational activities for adolescents. The importance of physical strength is much greater in an aggressive military culture than in a culture that is intellectually more sophisticated.

NEEDS OF ADOLESCENTS

1. Physiological needs: hunger, thirst, oxygen, and sex.

2. Social or status needs: need for status, need for independence, need for security, and need for affection.

3. Ego or integrative needs: need for a satisfying philosophy of life, and need for personal achievement.

The Concept of Developmental Task

The term *need* has become so much confused in psychological literature that educationists and psychologists have developed another concept, that of *developmental* task. This concept was developed by Havighurst. It stands midway between a child-centered and a teacher-centered education. It stands between basic needs and theory of determination of needs by the society.

It is a recognized fact that in every culture of the world, it is possible to learn certain skills and behaviour at some stages which make the adjustment in society more adequate. Every culture of the world sets a number of tasks for the successful adjustment of the individual in the society.

Needs and Developmental Tasks of Adolescents

The term *need* occupies a central position in the educational system of a country. Educational policy, planning, curriculum construction for various age levels, and formulation of the objectives of education — all depend on the concept of needs. The term *need* has been defined in various ways. According to some psychologists needs are theoretical explanation of observed behaviour of the organism and cannot be directly observed but are inferred from the behaviour of the individual, B.C. Tolman defines a need as, "A readiness or tendency to persist toward and perform a consumatory response." He classified human needs into three broad categories (*a*) primary needs as hunger, sex and thirst, (*b*) secondary needs as affiliation and dominance, (*c*) tertiary needs as wealth and academic achievement.

Murray defines a need as a hypothetical construct. It is resultant of forces. One need succeeds another. Needs have been interpreted in two different ways: the first interpretation is that needs are child-centred and must be fuilfilled if the child is to develop harmoniously. When we translate this approach of needs, then our education becomes child-centered. We must formulate our curriculum in accordance with the needs of children.

The second interpretation of the term *need* is in terms of social deficiency. The society feels that deficiency of children should be corrected for social progress. When we interpret needs in relation to the society, then the whole concept changes and our education becomes teacher-centered.

Havighurst proposed a system of developmental tasks for American adolescents. He described in detail the developmental process and its relation to educational objectives. According to Havighurst, "A developmental task is a task which arises at or about a certain period in life of the individual, successful achievement of which leads to his happiness and success with later tasks while failure leads to unhappiness in the individual, disapproved by the society and difficulty with later tasks."

Havighurst points out that any particular developmental task becomes appropriate for an individual when one or more of the following characteristics have developed.

(a) Physical maturation: There are certain tasks which arise out of physical growth of the child, as walking.
(b) The society expects certain behaviour from the individual and the individual under cultural pressures learns these tasks, as vocational preparation.
(c) The personal values, aspirations and psychological competence.

Importance of Developmental Tasks

The reader should keep in mind that developmental tasks are not a once-for-all business. They change with the socio-economic development of the country and can be replaced by new developmental tasks suited to the needs of the individual and the society. The developmental tasks are important for the following reasons:

1. The concept of developmental task is very helpful in specifying the course content and its objectives in definite terms. They serve as guidelines to the individual. He can know in advance what the society expects from him at a given age level. Parents can be guided in teaching their children skills and other social competencies which the society expects from them.

2. It also serves to show the individual what lies ahead and what will be expected of him when he reaches the next stage of development. This develops purposefulness in the effort of the individual by providing a definite goal. It creates motivation in the individual.

3. The concept of developmental task is also very helpful to the teacher to be prepared to avail himself of the opportunity and of preparing an appropriate atmosphere to achieve a developmental task. Educational efforts can be tuned with the developmental characteristics of the individual. The educational efforts will not go waste because now they may be organized at the appropriate moment.

The Developmental Tasks for Adolescent

Though the developmental tasks given below ere developed in the American social set-up where the cultural and socio-economic conditions are quite different from our conditions but even then they provide us a general pattern of developmental activities which may be adapted to our conditions with certain modifications. The following is the list of ten developmental tasks for adolescents:

(i) Achieving new and more mature relations with age mates of both sexes.
(ii) Achieving a masculine or feminine role.
(iii) Accepting one's physique and using the body effectively.
(iv) Achieving assurance of economic independence.
(v) Achieving emotional independence of parents and other adults.
(vi) Selecting or preparing for an occupation.
(vii) Preparing for marriage and family life.
(viii) Developing intellectual skills and concepts for necessary civic competency.

(ix) Desiring and achieving socially responsible behaviour.
(x) Acquiring a set of values as a guide to behaviour.

The physical development during adolescence has far-reaching effects on the personality development of adolescent boys and girls. Any abnormality or handicap in the pattern of development which deviates from the normal pattern may cause concern in the mind of the adolescent which may affect his/her nomral functioning at home, in school or in society. The guidance worker and the counsellor while counselling should keep the physical abnormalities of adolescents in mind.

II. MENTAL DEVELOPMENT

All studies on the mental growth have reported that mental abilities increase with age. Mental development in adolescence accelerates on many intellectual fronts. The following are the characteristics of mental development in adolescence.

(i) *Increased ability to generalize*. One noticeable characteristic of mental operations in adolescence is increased ability to generalize the facts. Children usually generalize in relation to concrete objects because their intellectual development operates on a perceptual level but in adolescence the ability to generalize on a conceptual level develops. The adolescents can generalize in an abstract way.

(ii) *Depth of understanding*. There is an increase in the ability to see relationship and to solve problems of increasing complexity and difficulty. His depth of understanding develops and he can solve more difficult problems.

(iii) *Increased ability to deal with abstraction*. An adolescent can think not only in general but also in abstract terms to a greater degree than children. He can think in terms of symbols rather than concrete objects. Ability to carry on abstract thinking is not something that suddently develops in adolescence; rather it is relative. This ability to comprehend and to communicate meanings in abstract qualitative concepts is an important aspect of intellectual maturity in adolescents.

(iv) *Development of memory and imagination*. The memory in adolescence develops tremendously with the growth in vocabulary. The adolescent can imagine a situation which is not physically present before him. His long-term memory also increases. He can retain facts for a longer period. He can anticipate future needs and can plan for it. The idea of the historical past can also be grasped by adolescent. Time concepts become clear to him. He can now integrate past and present facts and can anticipate the future.

(v) *Problems solving ability*. The ability to solve problems increases in adolescence. The adolescent can solve problems with the help of symbols. He is now able to deal with ideas that do not represent something in which he is directly involved. He is able mentally to deal with events in a world that extends far beyond his own immediate sphere of activity.

(vi) *Increased ability to communicate with other persons*. The adolescents on roads and in coffee house and tea stalls can be seen arguing for hours on topics of their interest which indicate their increased ability to communicate with others.

(vii) *Identification with conditions and characters in the larger world*. Another important change in intellectual orientation that takes place near the beginning of adolescence appears in the child's ability to identify himself with the circumstances and people outside his own immediate environment.

(viii) *Ability to make decisions*. The individual has to make many decisions in his daily life. Decision-making ability is necessary for successful adjustment in life. During adolescence we expect the growing child to gain increasing confidence in his own opinions. There is a certain amount of independence in thinking, certain freedom in exploring and in weighing alternatives that is involved in the kind of maturity that enables him to make decisions of his own. The adolescent has the ability to think about his future. He can differentiate between ideas and actuality.

(ix) *Understanding of moral concepts*. The children without questioning the validity of moral training obey the moral code framed by parents, but as he enters adolescence he critically examines the moral code and asks a number of searching questions. The adolescent is able to differentiate what is good from what is bad for him.

Cognitive Development: The Piagetian System

Jean Piaget and co-workers have been conducting research on congintive development from birth to adolescence since 1920 and enormous literature has been produced on cognitive development and aspects of development. He has studied developmental process of understanding and working of the child's mind. Though his system did not express definite opinion on educational practices but it can be of great value to assess teaching, the structure and sequencing of subject matter in the curriculum, and organisation of various activities in the classroom and outside the classroom.

Developmental Stages

Jean Piaget advanced a quite new theory of development of cognitive abilities. He proposes that cognitive development proceeds through an orderly sequence of stages. The important concept in his theory is not the age at which the child moves from preferred mode of response to another but the fixed progression from one stage to another. The child cannot adopt the strategies of a later stage at an early stage of development without having first acquired and exercised the strategies of earlier stage. Ausubal commenting upon the developmental stages of Piaget writes: "Piagets' stages are identifiable, sequential phases in an orderly progression of development that are qualitatively discriminable from adjacent phase and generally characteristic of most members of a broadly defined age range."

The stages of cognitive development are inter-related in that they represent forms of adaptation but these froms are qualitatively different; that is, the adaptive functions are transformed as the child moves from one stage to the next. This theory of development is quite different from the traditional theory of associationists which emphasizes the gradual accumulation of responses. The following are the developmental stages.

1. *The period of sensorimotor adaptation*. The period from birth to two years is marked by an extraordinary development of mind. The infant starts from reflex domination and reaches the state of senorimotor schemes in a means-to-end relationship. The development of this period is very important for future life.

2. The intellectual development at this age is marked by four fundamental characteristics:

(a) Object concept formation.
(b) Coordinated space.
(c) Objectified causality.
(d) Objectification of time.

The objects exist in the psychological world of an adult irrespective of their physical presence but in the world of the child they only exist when they are physically present and the child looks at them, grasps them and acts with them. As soon as they move out of his range of acting, grasping and listening, they do not exist for the child. In the first year of life, the child develops the concept of permanance of objects. He, then, attempts to retrieve an object that disappears from his range of action. When the child acquires the scheme of object permanence, he is likely to exercise it at every opportunity. He drops objects of his play and then tries to find them out.

The second characteristic is that of coordinated space which is integrated with the formation of the object concept. The spatial world at first is fatally uncoordinated. Each sensory modality has its own space and is centered on the child's current activities. By the end of two years, the child develops the concept of space which is characterized by relationship among objects and between objects and his own body.

The concept of causality depends on the activity of the child. Any action of the child which brings about an effect is taken as the cause of that event. The child by a number of activities develops the concept of causality by the end of two years of age. The fourth and the last concept of objectification of time indicates that the child develops the sense of time.

2. *The development of preconceptual thought*. At the end of sensorimotor period, the child starts dealing with the world by means of ideational representations. By imitation and other forms of behaviour, he demonstrates that he is capable of extending his world beyond here and now. These actions of the child indicate the use of symbols. By the age of 4 years the child develops ways of representing the environment in the absence of perceptual cues and will build a set of symbolic schemes.

3. *The period of intuitive thought*. At this stage, the child is able to use concepts as stable generalizations of his past and present experiences. His reasoning is not logical and is based on intuition rather than on systematic logic. The intuitive thought of the child is mainly concerned with stages or static configurations and reflects tranformations. The child talks about this or that momentary static conditions but cannot adequately link a whole set of successive conditions into an integrated totality by taking into account the transformations which unify them and render them logically coherent.

4. *The period of concrete operations*. Concrete operation means that stage of cognitive development when the child is able to direct his attention away from the static conditions and can focus on the whole set of successive changes that occur in the process of transformation. At this stage the child can reason well. Transformation could return to its starting point. Piaget has given a long list of operations which make possible the handling of numbers in various relations to each other, the arrangement of objects into classes and sub-classes and the ordering of objects according to one or more attributes. He has coined a term "grouping" to describe a set of operations. We shall describe how the first basic grouping of the concrete operational period operates.

The starting point of concrete operations is always the real rather than potential. The child of 7-11 years acts as though the primary task were to organize and order what is immediately present. During the period of concrete operations, there are some logical inconsistencies in that child's thinking. Piaget calls this deficiency "Syncretism".

5. *The period of formal operation*. At this stage the child's thought process becomes quite systematic and reasonably well integrated. These qualities of the child's thought process are evident when events are present. Reality guides his contemplation of possibility. He starts a form of hypothetical deductive reasoning. The use of formal operations is what is called the controlling aspects of comprehending.

The child, at this stage, in his formal thinking can free himself of the here and now in a lawful and systematic way. His wisdom lies in the masterful administration of the unforeseen. When an adolescent is faced with a problem, he uses formal operations to identify the variables that seem relevant to the solutions and then considers all the possible combinations of these variables.

The formal thought of an adolescent is of propositional nature. The adolescent using formal operations views the concrete date as inducing a set of propositions and he, then, applies operations to these propositions which are themselves primary operations. Formal thinking is thus interpropositional and interoperational and entails working out propositions after propositions or applying second order operations to primary ones. The development of formal operations enables the adolescent to transfer understanding from one situation to another. The adolescent shows a particular orientation to problem solving. He analyses, and organizes his approach before he attempts a specific empirical test.

III. EMOTIONAL DEVELOPMENT

C.T. Morgan emphasizing the importance of emotions writes that emotions are basic, primeval forces of great power and influence, designed by nature to enable the organism to cope with circumstances which demand the utmost effort for survival or success, or to "add colour and spice to living. If there had been no emotion in the life of the organism, the life would have been without any aspiration. In the absence of emotions, social life and family life would have ceased and progress would have been checked. The word emotion has been derived from the Latin word *emovere*, to move out. Emotion may be defined as "the stirred up condition of the organism involving internal and external changes in the body." Young says that "an emotion is disturbed state of organism: an emotion includes visceral changes due to increased activity of autonomic nervous system and an emotion originates within the psychological situation. It is expressed in love, anger, laughter and fears etc."

It involves feelings of jubilation or depression and impulse to action-awareness of perception. Basically human beings are creatures of feelings or emotion. Our emotions control our behaviour. Emotion in the organism is a dynamic internal adjustment that operates for the protection and welfare of the individual. Adolescence is marked by heightened emotionality. The history of the world is full of the heroic deeds when many adolescents sacrificed their lives at the alter of freedom of the country. Heightened emotionality is evident from nail biting, tension, conflicts, quarrels with parents, sibling and classmates etc.

Causes of Heightened Emotionality

(a) *Adjustment in home, school and society*. As soon as the child enters the period of adolescence, his social roles and responsibility change. Change of roles requires adjustment to new situations in a different way. The adolescent has to change his old habits of childhood at home and in school and society. The change-over to a new pattern of habits creates emotional tensions in them. The process of weaning from total dependence to an independent role with greater responsibility disturbs the adolescents.

(b) *Unfavourable relations in home*. Parents in most cases are responsible for heightened emotionality in adolescents because they do not prepare their sons and daughters to meet the problems of adolescence. They do not change their own attitudes towards them. They still treat them as children which creates rebelliousness in adolescents against their parents. There are quarrels with parents and siblings on small matters.

An adolescent needs money to meet his recreational and other demands like other boys of his class. He becomes emotionally disturbed when he fails to meet these demands.

The adolescent has to meet new social situations which disturb him, as talking with the member of opposite sex and meeting officers or elders.

(c) *Social expectations*. When the child becomes an adolescent, society and parents expect him to think and act like an adult, for which he is not yet physically and intellectually mature enough. The adolescent fails to decide his status in social setting and failure to meet social expectations results in emotional disturbances. The adolescent because of the shifts of roles has to make new adjustments in different social situations. He has to leave his accustomed patterns of childhood. He has to learn new adjustments in short period.

(d) *Adjustment to the member of opposite sex*. We observe that in later childhood, there is little interaction between boys and girls. In adolescence, there is attraction towards the members of the opposite sex but the adolescent is not able to understand the correct social behaviour — how to make friends with members of the opposite sex. These problems create emotional tensions.

(e) *Religious conflicts*. Every child is trained in a special setting of religious beliefs and values. The child without questioning the authenticity of teachings of his parents, obeys them but as he grows up, he critically examines the beliefs and values and starts questioning the teachings of his parents. This leads to conflicts in his mind.

(f) *Partiality*. The Indian society is divided into several sub-groups, each following its own religious beliefs. One caste hates the other. The adolescent is very sensitive to the feelings of hatred, partiality and nepotism in the society.

There is a great gulf between the values and teachings preached by the school and their actual practice in the society. The adolescent is disturbed by all these actions — school failures and frustration of needs cause heightened emotionality so much so that many adolescents commit suicide, leave home and, sometimes, give up education.

(g) *Vocational problems*. The most pressing problem for Indian adolescents is the future vocation after schooling. When he finds lakhs of adults roaming on the road without any means of livelihood, he is disturbed and grows anxious. Particularly those adolescents who come from poor families and are the only support of their families are more disturbed.

Symptoms of Emotional Disturbance

There are certain symptoms which are evidence of emotional disturbances in adolescents. The teacher and the guidance worker can locate these adolescents in school and provide individual guidance to them.

Oral symptoms. Excessive nail biting, thumb sucking, biting the lips, excessive abusing, smoking and addiction.

Nasal. Scratching the nose.

Hirsutal. Pulling or twisting the hair, scratching the head.

Facial. Picking the face, touching the face with the hand, and leaning the face on the hands etc.

Use of other mechanisms. Aggression, rocking legs, inattention, shyness, withdrawal and hyperactivity.

Characteristics of Emotions in Adolescence

(1) *Complexity.* By the age a child reaches adolescence he experiences a number of emotional upheavals and storms. His emotional development becomes complex because of these experiences. We cannot understand an adolescent by the overt emotional expression, but we have to fathom deep to understand him. The adolescent learns to conceal his true emotional experiences.

(2) *Development of abstract emotion.* Generally, children show emotional expression in relation to concrete objects but an adolescent can express his emotional feelings in relation to objects which are not present in a concrete form.

(3) *Emotional feelings are widened.* As the child grows he starts taking account of his past and imagines about his future and thus we can expect him to become more patient and able to tolerate delay. He gets pleasure from what he expects in future.

There is a great shift in his social sphere. Now he starts making friends with his classmates. The sphere of his social relation widens. He starts appreciating elder and younger people. Sometimes he is emotionally attached to a hero of his choice who may be a historical figure, a politician or a hero or some other leader according to whose principles he wants to shape his own life.

(4) *Bearing of tension.* Adolescents develop the competencies to bear tensions in different social situations. The emphasis is on self-control. The adolescents feel a kind of inner freedom, freedom to feel and experience in an intimate, personal way.

(5) *Capacity to share emotions.* The adolescents develop the capacity for concern about the feelings of others and an increased capacity for sharing emotional experiences with others. In childhood, children are not able to control their emotions. Sharing of emotional experience reaches its fullest development when an adolescent is able to relate himself to anothor person in such a way that the satisfaction of that person is just as important to him as his own. It means he begins to love his neighbours and others as much as himself.

(6) *Loyalties expand.* Emotional development begins from the home environment of the infant and during adolescence it is expanded beyond home and neighbourhood. These loyalties are identified with leaders of various fields.

(7) *Realism in emotional experiences.* Now the child enters the period of reality. An adolescent can perceive and appreciate people around him. He recognizes the weaknesses and strengths of the character of those around him.

(8) *Reviewing of hopes and aspirations.* Adolescence is a period of life when one has high hopes and aspirations for his future life. Some adolescents work realistically to achieve their expectations and others do little to realize their hopes. They remain in illusion, and in the world of daydreams and flights of fancy which make them unrealistic.

(9) *Toleration of aloneness.* The adolescents develop a tendency to be alone. Sometimes they like to be alone in their home. The adolescent learns to externalize his feelings in the various situations of external environment he moves in. He can project his feelings on others..

(10) *Increased compassion.* Compassion is the single quality which enables a man to achieve the highest peak and the deepest reach in his search for self-fulfilment. Compassion means feeling of fellowship. It denotes an ability to enter into kinship with the feelings and impulses involved in any sort of emotional experience, whether it be joy or sorrow. To be compassionate means that a person is able to share and appreciate the feelings of others.

Effects of Emotions

Emotions have a profound effect on the life of an individual. They can make or mar one's life. There are two kinds of effects of emotions.

(A) *Good effects*: (*i*) Emotions are the source of motivation and they work as motives which drive the organism for an action. Love, fear, anger and curiosity help us to achieve our goal. Classical stories show that young men sacrificed their lives for their beloved. Fear of failure motivates one to study hard for the examination. Emotions prove a motivating agent to further our efforts towards our goal.

(ii) *Source of enjoyments.* Routine activities create monotony in the individual. Emotions add enjoyment in our life. They give excitement. Adolescents read novels, see movies, theatres and T.V. etc. which overcome the deficiency of emotional excitement in daily life.

(iii) *They give strength and endurance to body.* Emotions give strength to our body. An individual can do unusual work under emotional excitement which under normal conditions appears difficult. A person chased by a dog can jump a 5 ft. high wall which he cannot jump under normal circumstances. Emotions give strength and endurance to our body. Fatigue does not set in during the emotional state. If a child loves his subject, he can work for hours together without signs of fatigue.

(B) *Bad effects of emotions.* Emotions also have damaging effects on the behaviour of the individual. The most damaging effect of emotions is on the physique of the individual. Constant emotional tension may cause lack of sleep, restlessness, headache, chronic fatigue, insomnia and lack of appetite.

Kuhlen conducted a research on the effects of continuous emotional tensions. He reported that emotional tension affects the efficiency of the individual and causes instability, shifts of moods and inconsistency in behaviour. It also affects the memory. Forgetfulness increases in emotional state. The individual cannot reason, think or concentrate on a problem. Constant emotional pressures disturb reasoning and ability. Fear, anger etc. cause the most damaging effect on thought process in the form of moodiness, irritability etc. They bring changes in our attitudes towards life.

IV. SOCIAL DEVELOPMENT

Man is basically a social animal. His existence without a social set-up can hardly be imagined. He is born in society, develops, works and progresses in society. Social development is very essential for proper adjustment in society. The social adjustment of the child starts from early infancy. The foundation of social development is laid by parents in the family. The success in future social adjustment depends on parents and other members of the family who lay the foundation of social development. In adolescence, the child enters quite a new field of social responsibilities. The society and parents place upon him new demands which sometimes bewilder him and he fails to adjust successfully in the new roles.

The adolescent has to make the following new adjustments in the society.

The most characteristic social development is the increased influence of peer group. As the child grows, he remains most of the time with his friends. The friends and type of peer group the adolescent joins shape his behaviour to a great extent; his interests, attitudes and values are influenced by his peers. Studies show that adolescents in urban areas are more guided by their peer group and adolescents in rural areas are more guided by their parents and elder family members.

The adolescent becomes self-conscious of his place in the society. He desires that his peers should accept him and he should be respected. Therefore, the adolescent conforms to the norms of peer group and he can do anything for the sake of pleasing his peers.

Changes in Social Behaviour

The most marked change in adolescence is in the place of the adolescent in family. In India, a special ceremony is held to celebrate the entry of child into a new social role. The parental attitude changes and they now assign him social responsibilities. He is taken into confidence on important matters of the family.

The circle of the adolescent narrows down to a small group. His interests become specialized. He now starts identifying himself with adults and tries to take on the role of an adult.

The most marked and important development appears in his relation with members of the opposite sex. In childhood boys play with boys and girls with girls and vice versa. There is hetero-sexual trend in companionship in adolescence. The adolescent boys and girls form their groups based on their common interests and goals. The social group of boys is larger than that of girls because boys in our society have more freedom than girls. But a new trend toward giving more freedom to girls has lately been emerging in big cities. The adolescent boys and girls have a variety of grouping.

Friendship

Adolescents make friendship with those wbo conform to their standard and possess the personality traits they like. The number of friends decreases but the affiliation becomes more permanent. There is keen interest to make friendship with the members of opposite sex. The adolescent does not tolerate the interference of parents and other members in the matter of selecting friends. Sometimes because of his immature decision, he is bluffed in the selection of friends. The friendships of this period tend to be permanent.

Social Interests

1. *Parties and celebration*. There is an increasing interest in adolescent boys and girls to attend parties, celebrations and fairs where members of both sexes meet.

2. *Conversation*. An adolescent takes interest in talking of various types of problems. He shows interest in social problems of wide variety. Talking plays a cathartic role for adolescents.

School and Social Development

Adolescents need guidance in the development of healthy social relations and for this purpose school is the most appropriate place where a variety of activities can be organized to foster social development. These activities could be to:

(a) *Organize social functions*. The teacher should organize informal social functions in which students may come closer to each other and have an opportunity to understand the interests and aspirations of each other. The students may be divided into smaller groups to discuss their problems informally. Social functions should be organised in such a way that they must cater to the needs of all types of students.

(b) *Arrange excursions and trips*. Excursions and outings provide more opportunity for informal conversations and close contact with each other.

(c) *Organize games, debates and seminars*. The teacher should organize group games, debates and seminars to train adolescents to participate in social activities.

(d) The teacher should make an appraisal of each student's social interests, his socio-economic conditions and organize activities to foster socialization.

Characteristics of Adolescents' Interests

1. *Stability*. In early adolescence the adolescent boys and girls have a variety of interests. Everything which is new draws their attention. But by the end of adolescence their interests stablize. They concentrate on selected interests.

2. *Expansion*. No doubt, many of the childhood interests are carried on and some are new ones. The field of interests expands with the development of intellectual and social development. The adolescent shows interest in national and international affairs. By the end of adolescence, the interests become stable and specialized.

Another characteristic of adolescents' interests is the shift in the value of different interests. The major interests of childhood may become minor and some new interests may become major interests.

Factors Affecting Interests

1. *Physical development*. Physical development is very important in deciding the development of interests. If the adolescent is physically sound and strong, he can participate in those sports and games which require strength. But if the adolescent is physically handicapped then his interests will be confined to different kinds of activities, mostly indoor.

2. *Sex differences*. There is a great difference between the interests of adolescent boys and girls. The differences may be attributed to the physiological differences and cultural influences. Girls participate in those games and sports which need less vigour; boys like competitive games of muscular dexterity. The differences among the play interests of boys and girls are not only caused by sex difference but by the cultural conditions, educational level of the boys and girls and also environmental conditions.

3. *Environment*. Environment plays an important role in deciding the interests of adolescents. It influences the availability of opportunities

to come in contact with various interests. The geographical and climatic conditions influence the interests of boys and girls from rural and urban areas. Culture also influences the interests of adolescents.

4. *Socio-economic status.* Socio-economic condition of the family also plays an important role in deciding the interests of adolescents. Adolescents belonging to lower socio-economic condition remain busy in the work. They do not have money to purchase articles of games or books, magazine etc.

5. *Intelligence and play Interest.* Lehman and Witty conducted a survey of interest in play activities as shown by gifted and dull adolescents. They reported that gifted adolescents participate in solitary types of play. They prefer games which involve rules and a well-organized system. They do not like those activities which require muscular strength but on the other hand they like problem-solving activities. Dull boys participate in social games requiring muscular strength.

Types of interests

1. *Social interests.* The social sphere of adolescents extends beyond the home and neighbourhood. He now comes into contact with more people. He develops an urge to communicate with others. Most of the time he remains in the company of his friends outside the home. He identifies himself with a group, with whom he discusses different types of problems. His talks generally centre round the following themes.

Discussion. Adolescents discuss many problems facing the society from every possible angle. Discussions are serious in nature and cover a wide range of subjects and topics. Discussion is more satisfying because it gives an opportunity for freedom of expression.

Arguments. Arguments grow out of discussion. A discussion starts out to be a friendly exchange of views in which each adolescent contributes his knowledge of the subject. When the points of view in a discussion differs, it becomes an argument.

Studies have been conducted by psychologists to survey the topics of conversation of adolescents. It has been invariably reported by all the investigators that these conversations centre round sex, clothes, shady stories, vocations, criticism of home, school, adults and teachers etc.

2. *Recreations.* Recreation contributes to the mental health of adolescents by providing them opportunity to express their pent-up emotions and release their tension which develops in classroom teaching. In addition to all this, recreation develops creativity and engages adolescents in constructive activities.

There are unfortunately many Indian adolescents who are deprived of recreational activities. Rural adolescents coming from a low socio-economic status have less opportunities for constructive recreational activities. Girls in rural areas have even lesser opportunities than girls in urban areas. In the last two decades, recreational activities have tremendously increased with the socio-economic development and technological development in the country.

Changes in recreational interests. When children enter adolescence, there is an abrupt change in their recreational interests.

Girls who used to play hide-seek, doll play, tag, jumping rope, now engage in such increational activities as reading, movies, dance, and group games.

Boys take interest in kabaddi, basketball, hockey, movies, cricket, reading, spectacles of athletic contests, and, football etc.

Types of recreations. From 12 years to 17 years, all types of games and sports are played by boys and girls but sports, requiring physical strength, are more popular with boys. Boys who are physically stronger engage in games requiring muscular strength and competition. Weak boys engage in games of individualistic sort with little competition. Girls with strong physique also engage in competitive games.

Hobbies. A hobby is an activity in which something is created or constructed for the purpose of fun. In our country, adolescents in rural areas hardly get time to engage in any hobby. Their 'hobby' is to help their parents in their occupation but in urban areas, adolescents develop some hobby to utilize their time and enjoy themselves. Adolescents in cities engage in hobbies like free drawing, gardening, writing, collection and photographing etc.

Adolescence is a period of life which is full of physical vigour. Adolescents take interest in adventurous activities as climbing mountain peaks, exploring unfamiliar places and fishing etc. These activities give pleasure to adolescents because they are undertaken free from the supervision of adults, and full freedom is given to meet the challenge.

Reading. Reading in adolescence is very important for various reasons. One reason is that reading gives an opportunity for identification with the characters of the reading material. It gives knowledge and entertains the individual. Reading interest reaches its climax in adolescence, Adolescents read novels of their choice secretly. They develop a mania for reading novels, short stories, adventure stories and light poetry. Reading interest in adolescence is influenced by a number of factors such as intelligence, socio-economic condition, availability of the reading material, urban-rural factors and sex. Adolescents read books, magazines, novels, comics, news-papers. Radio listening is very popular among adolescents. They listen to the radio hours together without caring for their food. They pretend that they can study better while the radio is on. It satisfies their desire for companionship. Radio listening is very much preferred to movies and books. Adolescents like light music, sports news, serial plays, detective, mysterious and crime stories, humorous sketches and plays etc. Preferences in radio programme listening is influenced by sex, age and intelligence of the adolescents. T.V. is a very recent innovation. In India, it has covered not only all major cities but also a good percentage of rural population. It has changed the interest of adolescents. It has also reduced the popularity of radio and cinema among adolescents. Foreign channels and private channels are becoming more popular among adolescents. Recent discovery of computer has made internet more popular than T.V. among adolescents.

Movies, in recent years, have greatly influenced the life of adolescents. They are the best means for relaxation and an opportunity to identify with the characters of the story. Movies satisfy the basic desires which most often are inhibited in social environment and work as escape mechanism. Adolescents go to movies for entertainment, pleasure, and to pass the time. They like action, suspense, romance, mystery. There is also an increasing interest in historical pictures as the adolescents grow in age. It has been reported by research workers in USA that there is the same pattern of interest in adolescents on the three media of communication i.e. T.V., radio and movies. Sex differences are also found in the preference of movies. Boys like romance, adventure, delinquency, newsreel, etc. while girls like romance, tragedy and social movies. Movies have affected the behaviour of adolescent boys and girls in both positive and negative directions. New styles of dress, hair, mannerism, love-making and techniques of delinquency have been learnt by adolescents from movies.

3. *Personal interests.* Adolescents are more interested in showing off than in any other thing. They want to attract the attention of others by their muscular body and facial beauty, coloured clothes, style of hair, and their gait. Social success in adolescence depends on physical appearance. The areas of personal appearance are the body size, hair style, face and nail in girls. The adolescents take interest in developing their body size according to the standard of the culture he lives in. He dresses his hair in new styles and makes use of cosmetic to beautify his face.

Interest in clothes also becomes prominent in the life of adolescents. He wears multicoloured dresses and dresses of new styles. The adolescent girl who wears extremes in style draws more attention of the people and arouses feeling of admiration and envy on the part of other girls. Adolescent learns from his experience in society that clothes are a major factor to make or mar one's future.

In recent years, we bave been observing a strange trend in clothes of boys and girls. Boys try more and more to look like a girl and girls try more to look masculine. At times one can hardly differentiate between an adolescent boy and girl wearing modern dress. In clothes bright colours are generally liked by adolescents but choice of bright colours decreases with the advancing age. New style and ornamentation of dress as flowers, trimming laces, embroidery etc. are used to attract the attention of onlookers.

Adolescents are also interested in, and conscious of, physical health and its importance in society. They know the value and influence of good health on their general well-being in society. They want to know as how to avoid diseases and how to develop good health.

GENERALIZATIONS ABOUT ADOLESCENTS

From the specific developmental characteristics in physical, mental, emotional and social dimensions of development which we have described, following generalizations have been drawn. These generalizations will be of great help to guidance personnel to organize guidance services effectively.

1. Adolescence is a transition period from childhood to adulthood marked by a number of physiological and psychological characteristics.

2. Physical and sexual maturation in both boys and girls results in shifts in attitude toward the proper masculine and feminine roles.

3. Adolescence is a period when an individual searches for emotional, social and economic independence. It is a time for individuals to utilize at a more mature and complex level the ability to give as well as the get, to communicate with others and to trust them and to learn what is harmful and what is good for themselves and others.

According to Erickson, "the hazard of adolescence is identity diffusion or role conclusion. He believes that many adolescents temporarily experience a degree of role confusion. He cites such experiences as falling in love, and inability to commit oneself to an occupational endeavour or to a set of ideological beliefs as examples of role confusion or identity diffusion. Most adolescents, however, emerge from these experiences with a sense of identity and are able to commit themselves to intimacy with another person."

4. Adults have described adolescents and have emphasized such factors as resistance to family authority, critical attitude toward parents and other adults; over-sensitivity to adult suggestions regarding friends, hours and appropriate use of time.

5. Adolescents are concerned about their adjustment to body changes. Physical abnormalities cause constant anxiety in adolescents.

6. Adolescents strive to attain independence. This may be seen in an emerging interest in vocational pursuits, in a desire for work experience, and financial independence.

7. Adolescents critically re-examine the personal values blindly accepted as a child.

PROBLEMS OF ADOLESCENTS

Any period of change is likely to be accompanied by many potential difficulties. Adolescence is also a period of transition from childhood which implies many developmental changes. G.S. Hall has called this period, a period of strain and stress fraught with many problems but other psychologists have laid emphasis on cultural conditions as the cause of problems in adolescence. Problems of adolescents have been studied by psychologists since a long time.

S.R. Laycock grouped the problems of adolescents under the following major areas:

1. Adjustment at home and in School and society and to opposite sex.
2. Freedom from home.
3. Adjustment in suitable vocation.
4. Developing a sound philosophy of life.

Charlotte Pope made an extensive study of the problems of adolescent boys and girls and reported the following areas of problems:

1. Teaching-learning relationship in school.
2. Occupational adjustment.
3. Personal adjustment.
4. Home life relationship.
5. Social and health adjustment.

1. *Teaching-learning relationship in school.* Most of the adolescents face a great problem in adjustment with teachers. Teachers are at times rigid, conservative and do not change their attitude.

Some adolescents reported the problem of favouritism by the teacher to some students. Students also resent the amount of home work.

It is unfortunate that our curriculum is purely theoretical and there is hardly any activity on the part of the students. Sitting passive in the class creates annoyance among adolescent boys and girls.

2. *Occupational adjustment*. The greatest single problem which bothers the mind of adolescent boys in India is uncertainty about their future vocation. The problem of what they will do after study haunts the mind of adolescents. When he sees that thousands of adolescents are unemployed, the mind of the adolescent agitates against the social order, and he becomes rebellious. It is further unfortunate that most of our adolescents study without future planning. When they finish their study, they find themselves incapable of taking an independent means of livelihood.

3. *Financial problem (money)*. If we recollect the problems of the adolescents of pre-independence period in India, we find that problems at that time were limited. The problems of adolescents have multiplied with the socio-economic development of the country. The problem of money is one such problem. There are many activities of an adolescent which involve money. The adolescent needs money. He feels ashamed of asking for it from parents. Parents too are conservative in providing money for extra activities of their sons and daughters.

4. *Home life relationship*. An adolescent wants more freedom to attend to social functions but parents do not permit them to move outside the home. This is particularly true in case of girls in rural areas.

A second important problem relates to the high aspiration of parents regarding the achievement of their sons and daughters and when they do not come upto their expectations, there is constant quarrelling between parents and the adolescent. Sometimes these quarrels lead to very bad consequences. Adolescents run away from their home or even commit suicide.

There is a lack of understanding between parents and adolescents, regarding limitation of freedom and money. The parents treat the adolescent like a child. They never discuss his problems.

5. *Social and health adjustment*. Physical health is a very important factor for adequate social adjustment. Both boys and girls are very particular regarding their physical appearance. Those adolescents who are either under-developed or overdeveloped have great problems in adjustment. The important problems in this area are weak eyes, poor teeth, too short a status or too tall, poor complexion, headaches, frequent colds etc.

SEX EDUCATION AND ADOLESCENTS

Adolescents have to live in the society. Their development depends on proper types of social interactions. We cannot isolate our adolescents from the social set-up. The social environment offers many occasions when adolescents come to know about sex and its problems. The child comes to know about sex from the early age of six. Surveys made by Ramsey and Hamilton prove that children cannot be kept ignorant of sex knowledge. The following are the important sources which provide sex knowledge to children:

1. Friends, 2. Literature, 3. Old people, 4. Movies, 5. Drawings, 6. Reproduction, 7. Physiological development.

These and a number of other sources are responsible for providing a knowledge of sex. The knowledge which is received from these sources is injurious to the mental and physical health of adolescents. Many boys and girls suffer from venereal diseases (V.D.) because of their wrong information about sex and lack of proper guidance. All teachers, social workers and psychologists agree that sex education should be provided to children.

The provision of sex education should be made from the early life of the child. It is the responsibility of parents to inculcate good habits in their children and develop positive attitudes toward sex problems. In our country, most of the parents are illiterate. They do not have the knowledge of sex problems. They are conservative in their outlook regarding sex and its problems. These illiterate parents cannot be held responsible for providing knowledge of sex problems and their solution. A very negligible percentage of parents can be called really knowledgeable who can provide sex education. But our adolescent boys and girls hesitate to discuss their sex problems with their parents. Our social values are quite different from those of western countries where adolescents discuss sex problems with their parents.

In the present circumstances, parents cannot be given the responsibility of providing sex education. This duty can be given to the teacher, the doctor and the social worker. The doctor can impart the physiological aspect of sex education. He cannot impart knowledge about the social aspect of sex. The social worker can give instruction regarding the importance of sex in social life. The teacher is the only person who can competently provide sex education with occasional help from the doctor and the social worker. But all teachers cannot be held responsible for sex education. Only those teachers who are emotionally stable, cooperative and have genuine interest in adolescents and their problems should be entrusted with sex education. Sex education should not be imparted in separate classes because then it will become the subject of mockery. It should be given a non-emotional title like personal relations of life adjustment or health hygiene. Sex education should form an integral part of the regular curriculum. Various topics of sex education should be incorporated in subjects like science, home science, psychology, sociology, etc. schools should provide effective guidance in this area of the adolescent's life.

Studies conducted in the USA show that 80 per cent of teachers, parents and students want that school should provide solid sex education to boys and girls for their adequate adjustment in social life. In our country sex education has been completely neglected in the past. We should change our attitude toward sex and its problems. We should make provision for sex education right from the elementary school with the support of parents and community as a whole. There is no doubt that if sex education is introduced in right earnest from the elementary level, most of the sex problems of adolescents will be checked.

The Adolescent of Twenty First Century

The speedy industrialization and westernization society is creating a number of problems. The adolescent of twenty first century different types of problems. The guidance worker and the counsellor should prepare themselves in advance to solve the future problems of adolescents. Our society is passing through a transitional phase in the areas of socio-economic and political developments with far-reaching consequences for the adolescents.

The specific problems in the twenty first century may be increasing unemployment among the educated adults, challenge to traditional values, problems of women, increasing rate of crimes, and use of drugs among adolescents.

The sexual behaviour of adolescent boys and girls is entering a new phase of permissiveness in our closed society.

ASSIGNMENTS

1. State the characteristics of social development during adolescence and point out their educational implications.
2. What are the needs of guidance in higher secondary schools?
3. "The adolescence in the most critical and difficult adjustment period in the life of an individual."

REFERENCES

Elizabeth B. Hurlock: *Adolescent Development* (McGraw Hill Book Company NY. 1959).

Arthur T. Jersild: *The Psychology of Adolescence* (Macmillan Co. NY. 1957).

Thomas F. Station: *Dynamics of Adolescent Adjustment* (Macmillan Co. NY. 1953).

Grinder Robert E: *Adolescence* (Wiley and Sons. NY. 1973).

Appendices

Appendix A

Intelligence Tests

1. Hindustani Binet by C.H. Rice.
2. Group test of intelligence by C. Satyanand.
3. C.I.E. Verbal test of intelligence for 11 plus to 12 plus.
4. General group test of general knowledge and general intelligence developed by Psychological Bureau, Allahabad. The test is meant for adults.
5. Verbal group test of intelligence for 10 plus in Hindi (Psychological Bureau, Allahabad). Psychological Bureau, Allahabad had developed several other tests of intelligence.
6. Group intelligence test by Prayag Mehta. The test is meant for 12-14 years of age. It is in Hindi.
7. Test of social intelligence by M.B. Buch of Baroda.
8. Test of general intelligence by S.M. Mohsin.
9. General mental ability test by Deptt. of Education, Gorakhpur University, Gorakhpur.
10. Group test of intelligence for classes V to VII by C.L. Bhatt.
11. Group test of general intelligence by S. Jalota. The test is meant for 11 to 16 years of age.
12. A battery of performance tests of intelligence/individual. This battery is meant for children below 11 years of age.
13. Battery of performance tests of intelligence by C.M. Bhatia. It is meant for 11 to 15 years of age.
14. Adaptation of Draw-a-man test by Goodenough. This test has been adopted in Indian conditions and norms have been developed. The test is meant for 4 years to 12 years of age. P.D. Patel and P.L. Shrimali have done work on this test.
15. Adaptation of Raven's progressive Motives test. The test has been adopted by Psychological Bureau, Allahabad.

Students are advised to consult the first 'Measurement Handbook for India' published by the NCERT.

PERSONALITY TESTS

Several inventories have been adopted and developed in Indian conditions. It is not possible to give the names of all the instruments. The names of some of the instruments are given below:

1. *Insecurity questionnaire*: It was developed by G.C. Pati. The questionnaire can be used for all levels of education.

2. *Extroversion: Introversion inventory*. This inventory was developed by V.S. Shanthamani and A. Hafeez. It consists of 20 items of which 10 items each relate to extroversion-introversion traits of the personality. It can be used for college students. The scale is available in English and Hindi.

3. *Dependence proneness scale*. It was developed by Jai B.P. Sinha. It is used for college students. The scale is available in English and Hindi.

4. *Personality inventory*. It was developed by E.L. George and associates at the University of Trivandrum to measure five important factors of personality i.e., social activity, tolerance, maladjustment, extroversion and masculinity.

5. *Work association test*. It was developed by Psychological Bureau, Allahabad. The test material consists of 55 Hindi words. It can be used for all levels.

6. *Personality inventory*. It was developed by Psychological Bureau, Allahabad to measure the four important areas of personality, home, school, health and interpersonal relationship. The inventory is in Hindi and can be used from 14 years to 20 years of age.

7. *Personality type questionnaire*. It was developed by B. Krishnan at the University of Mysore. The questionnaire is in English.

8. *Allports A.S. reaction test for adolescents*. It was adopted by E.G. Parameshwaran and co-worker to Indian conditions. The language is English and Telugu.

9. *Berneuters personality inventory*. It was adopted by S.K. Pal and P.C. Saxena for Indian conditions. The language is Hindi.

10. *Cattells' 16 P-F. Test*. It has been adopted by S.D. Kapoor for Indian conditions. Norms are available.

11. *Children's apperception test (Bellacks')*. This projective technique test has been adopted for Indian conditions. The pictures and settings of the original test have been modified according to our own culture. Psychological Bureau, Allahabad and Uma Chowdhury of Calcutta have adopted this test.

12. *Eysenks' neuroticism scale*. It has been adopted by A.K. Sinha. The reliability of the scale by test-retest and split-half methods has been reported 86 and 84 respectively.

13. *Murrays' thematic apperception test.*· This test has been adopted at Psychological Bureau, Allahabad. Pictures and setting have been modified according to Indian conditions. Scoring system has also been developed. Uma Chowdhury of Calcutta has also adopted this test. The test is available in its adopted form.

14. *Rorschach ink blot test.* Psychological Bureau, Allahabad has adopted this test. Instructions in Hindi have been developed. The detailed material is available.

15. *Adjustment inventory.* It has been developed by Dr H.S. Ashthana of Saugar University. The inventory contains 42 'Yes', 'No' type items in Hindi. It is useful for counselling purposes of Hindi knowing school or college students.

16. *Adjustment inventory for college students.* The inventory has been developed by A.K.P. Sinha and R.P. Singh. The inventory consists of 102 items of five major areas of adjustment.

17. *Bells' adjustment inventory.* This inventory has been adopted by several psychologists in India. Bureau of Educational and Vocational Guidance, Bihar adopted this inventory for the state of Bihar. The language is Hindi. Second adoption was done by P.A. Abrahamand E.I. George at Kerala University, Trivandrum. The third adoption was done by Tewari and Tewari at the Muslim University, Aligrah. The fourth adoption was done by B.G. Karkare and B.C. Keskar of Bombay.

INTERESTS

1. *Vocations interest inventory.* It has been developed by H.D. Badami at the University of Ahmedabad. It can be used for college and senior high school students. It is available in Gujarati. It gives the profile showing relative interests in various occupational areas.

2. *Vyasaya ruchi ki janch.* It has been developed by Central Bureau of Educational and Vocational Guidance, New Delhi. It is meant for 11 to 16 years boys and girls.

3. *Interest test.* It has been developed by A. Hafeez for guidance and counselling purposes of high school boys.

4. *Vocational preference record.* It has been developed by Bureau of Psychology, Allahabad, for guidance and counselling purposes of 10th and 11th class students.

5. *Kuder's preference record.* It has been adapted by Bureau of Educational and Vocational Guidance, Bihar. It is available in Hindi.

6. *Strong's interest test.* It has been adapted by A. Hafeez and K. K. Kuttappa. It is available in English.

1. *Teacher attitude.* It has been adapted by S. P. Ahluwalia. It is meant for students, teachers and practising teachers. It is available in English and Hindi both.

2. *Attitude towards teaching profession.* It has been developed by H. Visvasaran and co-worker to find out the attitude of teacher-trainees towards teaching as a profession.

3. *Minnessota teacher attitude inventory.* It has been adapted by T.N. Raina of Regional College of Education, Ajmer.

Appendix B

Specimen of a Cumulative Record Card

Name............................. School ....

Class............................. Section ....

1. General Information:

Sex..................... Date of Birth ....

Religion..................... Birth Place ....

Parent's or

Guardian's Address ....

2. Environmental Information:

Name of father....................... Education ....

Occupation ....

Name of mother....................... Education ....

Occupation............................. Number of ....

Children ....

Position of child ....

Type of community in which the

pupil has lived before joining

the school (village, town or city)

Occupation of the parents ....

3. Educational institutions Attended:

S. No	Name	Place joined	Left	Head

4. Psychological Data:

Intelligence I.Q.

Interest

Specific Ability

5. Achievement Data:

S. No	Subject	Max. Marks	Marks Obtained
1.	English		
2.	Hindi		
3.	Maths		
4.	S. Studies		
5.	Gen. Science		
6.	Sanskrit		

Pass.................Fail................Promoted................Detained............
Position in the class/section.....................
Fee concession ....
Scholarship..
Attendance..

Class Teacher's Remarks, if any.

6. Emotional Data:
   Persistence A B C D E
   Confidence
   Initiative
   Industry
   Sociability
   Resourcefulness
   LEADERSHIP
   Interest in — Humanities Science
   Commerce
   Arts
   Agriculture
   Technical

7. Health Condition:
   Height.................... Weight...................................
   Physical handicap (if any) ....
   Any serious disease suffered from.....................................

8. Co-curricular Activities:
   1. Athletics...................... 2. Games.....................
   3. Dramatics.................... 4. Music........................
   5. Dance.......................... 6. Drawing & Painting..................
   Library Activities Excursion
   Hobbies................ ....

Signature of the Counsellor

Principal

Appendix C

List of University Employment and Information & Guidance Bureau

BUREAUX

1. Andhra University, Waltair
2. Osmania University, Hyderabad
3. Shri Venkateshwar University, Tirupati
4. Gauhati University, Guwahati
5. Dibrugarh University, Dibrugarh
6. Assam Agricultural University, Jorhat
7. Bihar University, Muzaffarpur
8. Patna University, Patna
9. Ranchi University, Ranchi
10. Bhagalpur University, Bhagalpur
11. Punjab University, Chandigarh
12. Delhi University, Delhi
13. Jamia Millia Islamia, New Delhi
14. M. S. University, Baroda
15. Gujarat University, Ahmedabad
16. Vallabh Vidyanagar Anand
17. Saurashtra University
18. South Gujarat University, Surat
19. Kurukshetra University, Kurukshetra
20. Haryana Agricultural University, Hissar
21. Mysore University, Mysore
22. Karnatak University, Dharwar
23. Kerala University, Trivendrum
24. Cochin University, Cochin
25. Calicut University, Calicut
26. University of Jabalpur, Jabalpur
27. Vikram University Ujjain
28. University of Saugar, Sagar
29. Ravi Shanker University, Raipur
30. M.D. University, Rohtak
31. Himachal Pradesh University, Simla

The Employment Officer,
University Employment
Information & Guidance Bureau,
Bangalore.

The Employment Officer,
University Employment
Information & Guidance Bureau,
Dibrugarh.

The Employment Officer,
University Employment
Information & Guidance Bureau,
Kameshwar Singh Darbhanga
Sanskrit Vishvavidyalaya
Darbhanga.

The Employment Officer,
University Employment
Information & Guidance Bureau,
Kohlapur.

The Employment Officer,
University Employment
Information & Guidance Bureau,
Jodhpur.

The Employment Officer,
University Employment
Information & Guidance Bureau,
Burdwan.

The Employment Officer,
University Employment
Information & Guidance Bureau,
Amritsar.

The Employment Officer,
University Employment
Information & Guidance Bureau,
Ranchi.

The Employment Officer,
University Employment Information & Guidance Bureau,
Bhagalpur.

The Employment Officer,
University Employment Information & Guidance Bureau,
Muzaffarpur.

The Employment Officer,
University Employment
Information & Guidance
Bureau, Chennai.

The Employment Officer,
University Employment
Information & Guidance
Bureau, Vallabh Vidyanagar.

The Employment Officer,
University Employment
Information & Guidance
Bureau, Allahabad.

The Deputy Chief,
University Employment
Information & Guidance
Bureau, Agra.

The Employment Officer,
University Employment
Information & Guidance Bureau,
Sri Venkateshwar Univ., Tirupati.

The Employment Officer,
University Employment
Information & Guidance Bureau,
Andhra University, Waltair.

The Employment Officer,
University Employment
Information & Guidance
Bureau, Meerut.

The Employment Officer
University Employment
Information & Guidance Bureau,
Jammu & Kashmir University,
Srinagar.

The Employment Officer,
University Employment
Information & Guidance
Bureau, Annamalainagar.

The Employment Officer,
University Employment
Information & Guidance
Bureau, Bhubaneshwar.

The Employment Officer,
University Employment
Information & Guidance Bureau,
Patna.

The Employment Officer,
Jawaharlal Nehru University,
Delhi.

The Employment Officer,
University Employment
Information & Guidance Bureau,
U.P. Agri. Univ., Pant Nagar.

The Employment Officer,
University Employment
Information & Guidance Bureau,
Kalyani Univ., Kalyani.

The Employment Officer,
University Employment
Information & Guidance Bureau,
Siliguri (West Bengal).

The Employment Officer,
Vocational Guidance Unit,
Directorate General of Employment & Trg., Shram Shakti
Bhavan, Rati Marg, New Delhi.

The Employment Officer,
University Employment
Information & Guidance Bureau,
Shri Ravi Shanker University,
Raipur.

The Employment Officer,
University Employment
Information & Guidance Bureau,
Jiwaji University, Gwalior (MP).

The Employment Officer,
University Employment
Information & Guidance Bureau
Hyderabad.

The Employment Oflicer,
University Employment
Information & Guidance Bureau,
Waltair.

The Employment Officer,
University Employment
Information & Guidance Bureau,
Madurai.

The Employment Officer,
University Employment
Information & Guidance Bureau,
Ahmedabad.

The Employment Officer,
University Employment
Information & Guidance Bureau,
Baroda.

The Employment Officer,
University Employment
Information & Guidance Bureau,
Trivandrum.

The Employment Officer,
University Employment
Information & Guidance Bureau,
Jabalpur.

The Employment Officer,
University Employment
Information Bureau, Sagar.

The Employment Officer,
University Employment
Information & Guidance Bureau,
Ujjain.

The Employment Officer,
University Employment
Information & Guidance Bureau,
Mumbai.

The Employment Officer,
University Employment
Information & Guidance Bureau,
Nagpur.

The Employment Officer,
University Employment
Information & Guidance Bureau,
Mysore

The Employment Officer,
University Employment
Information & Guidance Bureau,
Guwhati.

The Employment Officer,
University Employment
Information & Guidance Bureau,
Delhi-7.

The Employment Officer,
University Employment
Information & Guidance Bureau,
Cochin, Kerala.

The Employment Officer,
University Employment
Information & Guidance Bureau,
Jaipur.

The Employment Officer,
University Employment
Information & Guidance Bureau,
Aligarh.

The Employment Officer,
University Employment
Information & Guidance Bureau
Gorakhpur.

The Employment Officer,
University Employment
Information & Guidance Bureau,
Lucknow.

The Employment Officer,
University Employment
Information & Guidance Bureau,
Roorkee.

The Employment Officer,
University Employment
Information & Guidance Bureau,
Varanasi.

The Employment Officer,
University Employment
Information & Guidance Bureau,
Cuttack.

The Employment Officer,.
University Employment
Information & Guidance Bureau.
Ludhiana.

The Employment Officer,
University Employment
Information & Guidance Bureau,
Calcutta-32.

The Employment Officer,
University Employment
Information & Guidance Bureau,
Tirupati.

The Employment Officer,
University Employment
Information & Guidance Bureau,
Kurukshetra.

The Employment Officer
University Employment
Information & Guidance Bureau,
Patiala.

The Employment Officer,
University Employment
Information & Guidance Bureau,
Jadavpur.

The Employment Officer,
University Employment
Information & Guidance Bureau
Pune-7.

Index